Teachers, parents and classroom behaviour

Teachers, parents and classroom behaviour

A psychosocial approach

Andy Miller

Open University Press

Open University Press
McGraw-Hill Education
McGraw-Hill House
Shoppenhangers Road
Maidenhead
Berkshire
England
SL6 2QL

email: enquiries@openup.co.uk
world wide web: www.openup.co.uk

First published 2003

A catalogue record of this book is available from the British Library

ISBN 0 335 21156 9 (pb)   0 335 21157 7 (hb)

Library of Congress Cataloging-in-Publication Data
CIP data has been applied for

Typeset by RefineCatch Limited, Bungay, Suffolk
Printed in the UK by Bell & Bain Ltd, Glasgow

Contents

Introduction

Concerns about the behaviour of students in schools have featured high on the agenda of everybody involved with education for many years now. In 1996, I published a book called *Pupil Behaviour and Teacher Culture* in order to set down in one volume a series of research investigations carried out over the preceding decade. During the same period I was also involved in a range of work in schools with teachers, students and parents, attempting to cement the often insubstantial links between research and practice in this area. Since that time, there has been no diminution in the attention paid to behaviour in schools. Public pronouncements from many quarters, legislation, media coverage and 'test cases' have flooded into the public consciousness at an increasing pace. Also in this intervening period, policy and practice developments and an increasing range of research studies have been accruing in a steady, if less dramatic, fashion.

As a consequence of the previous book, I have been fortunate to be invited to present some of its major findings in lectures and seminars to many hundreds of educational psychologists, behaviour support teachers and mainstream school staff. These occasions, and especially the lively discussions during periods for comment and questions, have helped to confirm that a number of the findings hold currency for many professionals closely involved in the daily task of helping teachers, students, parents and others in the most difficult and demanding of circumstances.

These continuing debates and discussions, the expanding range of publications describing techniques for improving school and classroom behaviour management practices and the slowly accumulating body of academic research have all acted as a stimulus for the current book. Since carrying out the research in *Pupil Behaviour and Teacher Culture*, I have been involved with a continuing set of studies to extend a number of its themes. Most of this research has been carried out with colleagues and teachers studying to become educational psychologists in the School of Psychology at the University of Nottingham. The ideas expressed in this current book also owe much to the energy and imagination they have brought to these endeavours. Consequently, the present book consists of revised and updated versions of the most prominent chapters from its predecessor, combined in roughly equal measure with new sections covering subsequent developments.

Any book attempting to tackle such a potentially large and untidy subject as the behaviour of students in schools will have to opt to lay emphasis in certain areas at the expense of others. Readers of a certain theoretical and philosophical bent will no doubt already be reacting to what might be seen as an uncritical and implicit assumption behind the use of the term 'difficult behaviour of pupils in schools'. These readers will argue that 'difficult behaviour' is to some extent a perception, a 'construction', and should not be treated as something that exists completely independent from the person who is experiencing and reporting the phenomenon. At the other end of the spectrum we might find readers with a distinctively pragmatic agenda, especially teachers experiencing daily the pressures at the 'chalk face', for whom workable and effective strategies are the overriding requirement.

This book aims to be sensitive to these, and many other, disparate perspectives. It intends to stay close to the concerns of practitioners: school-based teachers, related external agencies such as educational psychologists and behaviour support teachers, and others with an explicit brief for policy making in this area. However, this is not another book devoted solely to strategies, to tips and techniques. Within the chapters there are many examples of effective interventions carried out in schools, but an explicit and major aim of the book is to show, in a coherent fashion, *how* and *why* these approaches achieve their aims.

Consequently, discussion will not shy from theory. Educational 'theory' has acquired a bad reputation in and beyond many school contexts, perhaps, in some instances, deservedly so. If esoteric theory, or the just plain unintelligible, has created scepticism about all theory relating to education, this is unfortunate. Systems of explanation that attempt to give a coherent account of why things do or do not happen, how change may or may not come about and the extent to which we can predict future events from information about the past and present – all hallmarks of good theory – have proved to be of major assistance to many of the endeavours of advanced and civilized societies.

If all we lacked to put right the problems surrounding difficult behaviour in schools were more strategies, surely the swelling ranks of books containing these to be found in publishers' catalogues and on booksellers' shelves could, by now, provide the answer. We are no longer short on suggestions. What we may, however, lack is the rationale by which to judge what is really of worth among all this and what will endure beyond the latest raft of legislation, the next fashion in terminology and the continuing evolution and hard sell of commercial enterprise in this field.

The particular theoretical focus of this book, as its subtitle proclaims, is on the *psychosocial*, defined by the *Oxford English Dictionary* as 'the interrelation of social factors and individual thought and behaviour'. In among all that seems to change around the issue of behaviour in schools (and some will argue that this is continual change in the form of deterioration), certain other things remain relatively constant. Students are still educated in social groups, teachers often work in their classrooms as the only adult or have to negotiate shared or differing responsibilities with another adult present. Staffrooms are a forum with their own distinctive dynamic in which views and opinions are forged, challenged or discouraged. Young people move between the social systems of home and school, radically different in psychologically significant ways, even in those households where the value of schooling is enthusiastically promoted. Teachers and parents negotiate the boundaries of their respective responsibilities, sometimes through overt and explicit means, sometimes with subtle nuances of language and interpersonal behaviour. These are some of the *social* factors to be found within the book's psychosocial approach.

At the *psychological* level, the links between the behaviour and thought of teachers, parents and pupils are explored in some detail. Beliefs and judgements, and the way these are formed, may be seen as 'internal' processes taking place, in a sense, inside the head of each individual. But these may also, clearly, be viewed as part of a 'dance' in which the moves of each party stand to influence and shape those of the others. These psychological processes will again owe something to the social systems, especially school and home, in which these individuals spend their time. Lest this appears too cognitive and arid, however, anybody remotely connected with issues of behaviour in schools will need no reminding that practice in this area is often a case of walking on eggshells, with intense emotions seldom more than the slightest slip away.

And it is to the sensitivity surrounding this topic that I now wish to return. In talking about the ideas in this book to teachers undertaking further academic study, to educational psychologists and to behaviour support teachers over many occasions, I have had a variety of responses. There have been, for example, further examples and extensions to the ideas presented, challenges to some of the conclusions drawn, with differing interpretations offered, and questions about research methodology. These have been most rewarding discussions.

From teachers in mainstream schools, however, reactions have been noticeably more mixed: not spread across a spectrum, but polarized into two opposing camps. The research has received considerable positive reaction from headteachers, special educational needs coordinators and classroom teachers, with some indicating that reviews of practice within their schools will follow as a result. But it is only fair to acknowledge that another, smaller group has been disquieted by some of these same messages, and these discussions have also stimulated some of the ideas contained within the following pages. The purpose of the sequence of research studies remains the study of real and effective ways to improve the school experiences of all, teachers and students alike, especially in those tough and demanding circumstances in which behaviour is judged to be unacceptable or unmanageable.

The social and psychological features above apply to both primary and secondary levels of schooling. Despite clear differences in the nature of the curriculum, the numbers of teachers involved with each pupil (and vice versa) and the sheer size and complexity of large secondary schools compared to small village primary schools, student behaviour in both sectors is still frequently characterized by strained relationships between home and school. Beliefs and judgements made by teachers, students and parents about each other, and group processes for both staff and students alike, also come into play, whatever the age of the student and whatever the level of organizational complexity.

Consequently, this book applies to both primary and secondary schooling and is intended for teachers and other school staff in both settings, as well as for the increasing range of professions and other bodies involved from an external base with student behaviour in schools. So, the examples of research into effective management of relatively young pupils quoted in this book may be seen to have some application with older age groupings. Conversely, the examples of interventions with student peer groups and the methods for addressing with teachers staff culture and policy in tandem are drawn from work in secondary schools but may be replicated directly in primary schools. And straddling both phases of schooling, to emphasize the central relevance to both, the discussions of teacher, student and parent attributions draw upon work carried out at the higher age range of primary and the lower age range of secondary schools. This deliberately wide range of research and practice examples is intended to show that whatever else changes between the primary and secondary sectors, psychosocial factors remain intimately implicated in student behaviour and must be both appreciated and addressed in either context before any positive outcomes can be attained.

Given that behaviour in schools shows no sign of slipping from the educational agenda, the coherent psychosocial framework adopted here, and the research studies that draw on the accounts of classroom teachers and others, may have an important contribution to make to debates and discussions about the way forward. In this sensitive and pressing area, there are clearly no glib and easy answers. Careful and rigorous research, theory that genuinely aids understanding and a willingness to 'get stuck in' alongside those closest to the issues must all have a contribution to make. The old adage warns that we cannot make an omelette without breaking a few eggs, and these may be the very eggshells we have to walk upon as we seek to fashion more effective and satisfying forms of practice for all.

The research carried out at the University of Nottingham and reported in this book has been based upon the active participation of a large number of teachers, school students and parents. Although they remain anonymous in the studies, this book could not have been written had not they all volunteered to help to move understanding forward in this potentially complex and contentious area. I am deeply grateful to them all.

I have also been supported and encouraged by a large number of professional colleagues. In addition to everyone who has contributed to lecture and seminar discussions, I particularly wish to acknowledge the various important contributions made by the following people: Joe Elliot, Adrian Faupel, Eamonn Ferguson, Norah Frederickson, Peter Galvin, Simon Gibbs, Peter Gray, Anthea Gulliford, Joan Hingley, Trevor Holme, Jane Leadbetter, Geoff Lindsay, Liz Malcolm, Sue Morris, Jayne Nash, Jim Noakes, Mick Pitchford, Rea Reason, Bill Rogers, Kevin Rowland, Sonia Sharp, Jonathan Solity, Phil Stringer, John Thacker, David Thompson and Hugh Williams.

I have also enjoyed and benefited greatly from debate and argument with all the teachers who have undertaken postgraduate studies to train with us as educational psychologists at Nottingham, and I wish to acknowledge especially the contribution to my thinking made by those who have pursued related research themes within the ongoing Behaviour Project: Anastasia Andre-Warren, Rob Beadel, Laura Black, Melanie Bobb-Semple, Irene Byrne, Geraldine Colston, Sarah Euinton, Halit Halusi, Victoria Hobley, Alistair James, Nathan Lambert and Elie Moore. Thanks are also due to my colleagues Sarah Dean, Alan Reynolds and Neil Ryrie for their patience and support and to Luke Miller for his skilled assistance with IT and graphics.

Finally, this book is dedicated to my long time colleague, collaborator and friend, Gerv Leyden – a compassionate, wise, witty and creative man, and one with whom it has been such a privilege to share voyages of discovery.

PART 1
The Context of Difficult Behaviour in Classrooms

1 Emerging perspectives on behaviour in classrooms

Introduction

This chapter examines the various ways in which teachers, researchers, legislators and other interested bodies have attempted to make sense of and respond to what is seen as the pressing and probably escalating problem of difficult student behaviour in schools. It attempts to show how policy developments and legislation have evolved as a response to public and professional concern on the one hand and as a result of academic and governmental investigations on the other. Parallels are drawn between trends in the UK and the USA in order to illuminate the discussion by illustrating common and contrasting themes. Finally, a number of 'sticking points' – issues that continually seem to evade resolution despite the determined efforts of all involved – are highlighted as major challenges for the arguments set out in the remainder of this book.

Where to begin?

For the past quarter of a century at least, the idea that the behaviour of pupils in schools is becoming more unruly and uncontrolled has never been absent for long from newspaper reports and political discussion. As Gillham (1981) observed, 'There was a point in the early seventies when it seemed as if many secondary schools in the major urban areas were heading for breakdown.' Teachers, parents, pupils, communities, employers and politicians all have a perspective and these become picked up, intertwined and widely dispersed by the forceful gusts of public opinion. And within all this concern, there is a danger that the rhetoric will further inflame anxieties and undermine a belief in the potential of professional problem-solving, collaborative action and sensitively targeted research.

There are, however, many legitimate questions embodied within this public concern. Are children becoming more out of control? Are parents abdicating their responsibilities? Have schools been deprived of adequate funding and teachers been undervalued by governments and society at large? Are there too many experts or too many armchair philosophers? Is the pressure on schools to raise attainments and avoid being shamed in league tables somehow linked to levels of difficult behaviour? Is the move towards greater social inclusion resulting in more disruptive pupils being placed in mainstream schools?

All of these questions, and others, deserve answers. For some of them research studies have provided definite, and for others tentative, clarification. However, no amount of empirical evidence can seem to displace some passionately held convictions. But where do such beliefs come from: a professional lifetime of open-minded learning, personal reflection or regular contact with the lurid tabloid newspaper headlines that this topic so easily provides?

Instead of taking questions such as these one by one and attempting to provide answers, this book begins with a set of personal anecdotes.

Until he died at the age of 84, there was a white scar of about half a centimetre across my father's left-hand little finger. It was the result of his being caned across the hand at seven years of age on his first day at junior school. A senior member of the staff had entered the classroom all those years ago and asked him an arithmetical question. Because his answer was inaudible, he was summoned to the front and instructed to extend his left hand, as a warning to all. When I first heard this story as a child and inspected that permanently whitened line of skin, I seethed with anger. He, on the other hand, bore no noticeable malice or sense of injustice.

In the mid-1960s, I lived for a while in a hall of residence attached to a teacher training college. Meetings in this all-male establishment frequently decried the lack of 'standards' that were perceived to characterize the wider student body within the college. One night one of my fellow students had an intense and sudden religious conversion and subsequently proclaimed widely and publicly about his spiritual upheaval. In a small kitchen area on one of the floors, a few evenings later, a group of about fifteen trainee teachers blocked the doorway and goaded on one of their number as he beat up the new convert.

On the first day in my second teaching post I asked a 10-year-old boy to sit down and he gripped the sides of his table, fixed me directly in the eyes and grinned, with all the unrestrained mischief of a puppy ready to play. In my first post I had been seen as a successful teacher and discipline had never been a consideration. This stood me to no advantage and a growing sense of excited anticipation rippled around the class. Drawn to contemplating chasing the boy around his desk, and the débâcle that would ensue, I felt very alone.

In recent years I worked with a primary school staff and the parents of a boy who by the age of six had been excluded from one previous school and removed from a second before the same thing could happen. In his 'last-chance' third school, this little boy's difficult behaviour became slowly replaced by a positive and enthusiastic response. Nearby, in a secondary school, a team of teachers maintained in mainstream schooling a boy who had experienced tragic early life circumstances. His bizarre and unsettling behaviour reduced considerably as a result of the conscientious, individualized planning carried out by staff. Not only did this improve his prospects with a range of public examinations, it also prevented his removal to a special school where his opportunity for contact with the full range of adolescent social behaviour would have been denied. Stories of very young children being excluded from, or refused entry to, schools and of teenagers seemingly out of control make for dramatic headlines in the press. Success stories such as these, however, usually remain as silent and unspoken achievements.

The point of these personal anecdotes, which are, I hope, more than an indulgence, is to suggest that the behaviour of pupils in schools is a subject that is not easily reduced to a few pragmatic questions. Instead, these diverse examples hint at a large and untidy set of issues: authority and control, justice and fairness, rationality and emotion, the conditions for optimism, the effects of peers, the professional socialization of teachers, their potential isolation, the persisting influence of our own personal experiences and recollection. In order to advance discussion, this chapter introduces a structure. But author and readers alike should bear in mind that beneath the order and progression lies a set of complex ethical, philosophical, psychological and social themes, often ill-disciplined in themselves, ready always to chase around the table the proponents of both the easy answer and the logical and detailed analysis.

One way of beginning to structure the discussion is to recognize that historically at least two very different approaches to difficult pupil behaviour have been taken. One has concerned itself with what might be called school processes and the craft of the teacher in terms of classroom management or control. Another very different strand of thinking has grown up around the study of the 'problem child' (Miller and Todd 2002). Interestingly, these perspectives have traditionally had very little to do with each other, the former until fairly recently existing at the level of staff room folklore and the latter deriving from varying theoretical positions.

This chapter briefly describes each of these perspectives and illustrates their influences upon legislation and government advice to schools concerning the management of difficult pupil behaviour. The contents of the remainder of the book are then briefly introduced.

School processes: classroom management and school effectiveness

The Elton Committee, in its report *Discipline in Schools* (DES 1989), found a fairly common belief among teachers that group management skills were a 'gift' and that teachers were either 'born with them or not'. After pursuing this line of enquiry through teacher training institutions, local education authorities and surveys of teachers, the committee concluded:

> First, that teachers' group management skills are probably the single most important factor in achieving good standards of classroom behaviour. Second, that those skills can be taught and learned. Third, that practical training provision in this area is inadequate.
>
> (DES 1989: 70)

Traditionally, research into this area has taken the form of empirical studies in classrooms using various structured observation methods. Galvin and Costa (1994: 146) have reviewed some of the most significant of these studies and concluded that

> The classroom management research movement has identified a wide range (almost too wide) of factors that can reasonably be considered as the basis of good classroom management practice. Room layout, classroom routines, managing transitions, maintaining momentum, curriculum issues, managing groups and getting the year off to a good start are just a few of the key areas of preventing misbehaviour from occurring in the classroom.

Supplementing the studies of classroom management has been the body of investigation usually collected under the title of 'school effectiveness' research. This has shown that the standard of pupil behaviour as well as academic attainment can vary between schools, irrespective of a school's catchment area, and can be partly influenced by factors within a school's control.

Although Reynolds (1992) has pointed out that the research on 'social outcomes', such as the behaviour of pupils, is not as advanced as the work linking school processes to pupils' academic progress, none the less studies have certainly indicated likely influences. Some of these factors were identified by Rutter *et al.* (1979) in their influential study *Fifteen Thousand Hours*. By examining 12 London secondary schools in detail, this research suggested that, among other things, 'effective' schools had common policies on behaviour, made consistent use of rewards, created a pleasant working environment and paid careful attention to issues of classroom management. Another major British study by Mortimore *et al.* (1988) focused upon 50 London primary schools and identified 12 school factors that were related to school effectiveness, mainly again in the form of pupils' academic achievements. One set of these factors, such as purposeful leadership by the headteacher, represented school-level processes, whereas the other, which included record-keeping, might be characterized at both a school and a classroom level.

Although school effectiveness research is becoming more and more widely promulgated, Reynolds (1992) provides a salutary reminder that this work has been highly contentious and that, after very early work that found delinquency rates varying considerably between schools (Power *et al.* 1967, 1972), the researcher in question was refused access to schools for further investigations.

The 'problem child'

Whereas the Elton Report reflected the growing practical implications of the school effectiveness and classroom management research literature, and encouraged schools to adopt or extend their practice as organizations, a continuing paradox continues to surround the notion of the 'problem' or 'impossible' child (Lane 1990). Obviously, the pupil whose behaviour is so challenging, pervasive and unresponsive to all that teachers appear to have to offer will make a major impact on those responsible for his or her education. Yet the more extreme the problem, the more likely it is that professional groups outside mainstream education – those in psychiatry, psychology, social work or a separate special education system – will be seen as the appropriate bodies to provide an explanation for this behaviour and/or effect a solution.

Lane (1994) has reviewed the range of theoretical perspectives that have been employed in an attempt to account for difficult pupil behaviour, and has shown how these have influenced different types of professional responses. He considers the roots of the child guidance clinic movement within psychoanlytic traditions and the later attempts, mainly by psychologists enthused with the promise of the early research studies into behavioural approaches, to use these approaches more directly in their work with schools. In a wide-ranging review, Lane also considers the extent to which explanations involving congenital, family, neighbourhood, subcultural and cultural factors have been utilized and the extent to which they have contributed to practical intervention measures. He also examines social processes such as discrimination and labelling.

No one could argue that unsupported teachers should be solely responsible for managing the most extreme behaviour of a very small minority of pupils. But a case can be made that, by separating off expertise into agencies outside schools, teachers are less likely to acquire knowledge, skills and confidence that might be of help to them in their work with slightly less challenging pupils who none the less stretch their professional capabilities. And, in some ways, with expertise not being acquired for those levels of problems, the pattern is then able to repeat itself, with a less practised professional response being available for the next gradation of lesser seriousness, and so on.

Clearly, the issue is one of drawing lines: between the reasonable and the unreasonable, the feasible and the impractical, the unsupported initiative and the complete transfer of responsibility. Put more specifically, how far can school processes be expected to extend down to meet the most extreme challenges presented by pupils in mainstream schools and how far into the total body of pupils should non-educational 'problem child' explanations and professional responsibilities extend?

Legislation, categories and the drawing of lines

In 1994, the British government issued a series of circulars to schools (DfE 1994a, b, c) offering advice on just these issues. These documents posit a spectrum of children who might display difficult behaviour:

- children who are 'disruptive or naughty', or experiencing some emotional stress within normal and expected bounds;
- children whose symptoms are those of a serious mental illness, the occurrence of which is rare;
- children with emotional and behavioural difficulties, who lie on a spectrum between these other two groups and should be construed as having some form of learning difficulty.

'disruptive or naughty', some emotional stress, normal and expected bounds	emotional and behavioural difficulties	a rare serious mental illness

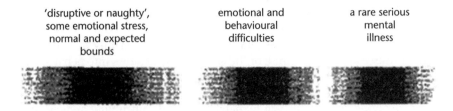

Figure 1.1   The spectrum of 'difficult behaviour' proposed in DfEE Circulars in 1994

The circulars avoid over-simplistic categorizations and attempt to offer advice based upon research studies and professional opinion of the type discussed above. For instance, the first category of pupil is seen as the responsibility of the school and class teacher, and associated recommendations draw on the research into school processes. Circular 8/94 (DfE 1994a) states that 'individual instances of disruptive behaviour are bound to occur at times' and that, in response, 'interventions have to be carefully judged by teachers, using their knowledge of individual pupils or class groups'. These teachers should do 'no more than is needed to secure the desired change in the pupil's behaviour'.

At the other end of the spectrum, the grouping of pupils with a 'serious mental illness' is described as being very small but consisting of 'young people [who] develop severe emotional and behavioural disorders which require care and treatment beyond that which can be found in school, including special school' (DfE 1994c). Children characterized in this way 'may be referred to a unit, often on a residential basis, because they have exhausted the resources or the ability to cope of their community, family and school and require an environment which can facilitate cognitive and emotional growth' (DfE 1994c).

The third grouping, the children with emotional and behavioural difficulties, are likely to have a persisting problem which constitutes a learning difficulty. Such a view conceives of difficult pupil behaviour as arising primarily either from an inadequate repertoire of socially desirable behaviour or from the learning of unacceptable methods of responding to certain social demands, especially those encountered within school settings. As a form of learning difficulty, emotional and behavioural difficulties should be met via the stages of assessment and intervention set down in the *Code of Practice on the Identification and Assessment of Children with Special Educational Needs* (DfES 2001).

Much of the tenor of the descriptions of these categories suggests that the qualities of the children are relatively fixed and likely to be manifested across a range of contexts. Perhaps this is less so for the first group, the pupils who are 'disruptive or naughty within normal and expected bounds', where there is an implication both that this state of affairs may well be transitory and that mainstream teachers can exert a significant influence over its future direction. Construing emotional and behavioural difficulties as a *learning difficulty*, however, carries a more definite message that the problem exists with and 'within' the pupil. But even here, Circular 9/94 (DfE 1994b) acknowledges that external factors can be implicated not only in the definition of such difficulties but in their possible maintenance, amplification or amelioration:

> Perceptions of whether a child's behaviour constitutes an emotional and behavioural difficulty are likely to differ according to the context

in which it occurs as well as the individual teacher's management skills, tolerance levels, temperament and expectations.

(DfE 1994b)

The category of children with a rare 'serious mental illness' certainly seems a less ambiguous entity, at least at first sight. For children in this category, the 'problem child' paradigm immediately transfers the responsibility for making sense of the difficulties outside education and into the realm of medical diagnoses and explanatory mechanisms. While this is clearly and entirely appropriate in the cases of children and young people where a definite physiological, neurological or hormonal mechanism is at work, it can be more questionable for other types of diagnosis originating from a psychiatric perspective. The problem is not that these perspectives are 'wrong', but that they give an unequivocal message, not necessarily intentionally, that the difficulties are lodged deeply and totally with the pupil.

Controversies still exist about the extent to which a number of psychiatric 'illnesses' do have an environmental component. Clearly, a common-sense view would be to ensure that, with any children who might appear to merit this type of description, multiprofessional liaison and cooperation must be of the highest order. Gray and Noakes (1992) have detailed the complex of reasons why very different professional perspectives such as medicine and education can be so hard to reconcile in the case of difficult pupil behaviour. It is obvious that teachers do not have a medical training but it can be less obvious to those outside education (and less easy for some within to admit) that individual teachers' 'management skills, tolerance levels, temperament and expectations' can vary and have some effect upon pupils' behaviour in schools.

At this stage in such a discussion, some may begin to despair. Reducing the apparent argument to a stark example, they may ask whether it is being implied that the most vicious or anti-social acts by children, perhaps committed well outside the school premises, are going to be swept away by a gesture such as the pupil being allowed to wash out the paint pots – the fairy's kiss school of ivory-towered expert opinion. This is not what is being suggested.

There are empirical as well as anecdotal grounds for suggesting that schools and teachers can, with or without the support of others, move pupils some distance along the DfE's spectrum – in either direction! How far? Sometimes only a small distance, at other times a whole category or even more. There is not necessarily anything completely fixed or immovable about pupils' behaviour and the major disadvantage of thinking too much in categories is the resulting strong implication that there is.

Later in this book we examine in detail case studies of successful collaborative work between teachers and educational psychologists. What shall we say of the infant school deputy headteacher who was wound to such a pitch by a small boy's behaviour that her family life began to deteriorate and she questioned whether she could continue to work as a teacher? How far down the spectrum of seriousness must that little boy's behaviour have been? And how far along the spectrum must he have travelled if, after a period of sensitive collaborative work, this rejuvenated teacher could say, 'I can honestly say that he's not like the same child'?

The Special Educational Needs Code of Practice

Another major government initiative, as mentioned above, has been the Special Educational Needs Code of Practice, first published in 1993 and subsequently revised in 2001. Within this, schools are required, via class teachers, to identify children with special educational needs and make an appropriate school-based response in liaison with their special educational needs coordinator (SENCO). Essentially, if these and other efforts prove unsuccessful in meeting the pupil's learning needs, schools should supplement their own skills with those of support services outside the school. In the case of children with emotional and behavioural difficulties, these outside agencies are most likely to be behaviour support teachers and educational psychologists. Subsequent stages, if the pupil's difficulties are still resistant to intervention, allow for 'statutory assessments', which may then lead on to local education authorities (LEAs) issuing Statements of Special Educational Needs. These may then recommend the provision of additional resources or an alternative placement for the pupil.

The procedures laid down in the Code follow a clear pattern and LEAs have devised a range of criteria to indicate how and when movement through these stages should take place. The Code also suggests methods for record-keeping and early-stage interventions. Although these can form a structure for professional action, the Code can do little to influence many of the untidy and powerful processes referred to earlier in the anecdotal illustrations. For example, a teacher who feels defeated, less competent than colleagues or exhausted is unlikely to embrace enthusiastically suggested strategies, simple or complex, from close colleagues or relative strangers. And if teachers have reached a point where they have little or no sympathy for a pupil who has made their life a misery, then the *sine qua non* for any intervention – not the whole intervention but one essential ingredient, a positive and valuing approach – will be unavailable. Going through the motions, with any of these typical emotional reactions present, will only lead to rapid progress through the stages, supplemented by a dossier of failed interventions reinforcing a picture of the pupil's position as irredeemable. While the Code and sensitive professionals are anxious to avoid feelings getting to this pitch, the power of difficult pupil behaviour to get deeply under the skin of teachers in a relatively short time should not be underestimated.

As indicated above, the present book gives detailed examples of successful interventions at various stages of the Code, but one of the major findings from the research reported here is that teachers do not pass these interventions on to colleagues experiencing similar difficulties with pupils. They are, in fact, extremely reluctant to discuss them in the majority of cases, despite often experiencing a major turnabout in a problem they had judged to be the most difficult they had encountered in their whole careers! Many of the teachers also describe feelings of debilitating isolation in respect of the difficult pupil, despite the existence in many cases of school-wide behaviour policies and colleagues on the staff who are generally perceived as a supportive group of people. In the light of such evidence, things do not augur too well for the Code of Practice being easily able to promote successful and professionally satisfying work with difficult pupils, at least in the early stages. There seems to be more to the successful management of difficult pupil behaviour than even the most comprehensive and well structured set of guidelines can fully hope to address.

Social inclusion

Parsons (1999) reports that exclusion of students from schools, almost always for behaviour judged to be unacceptable, rose dramatically in the UK through the 1990s. This escalation led the government to describe these figures as 'unacceptably high' and, in 1998, to set a target for a reduction in this number by one-third by 2002. This requirement was set within a much wider political ambition to reduce social exclusion, which was seen as an umbrella cause of a range of social and economic ills.

The drive to promote greater social inclusion involved much more than educational initiatives, though, with the Blair government in its first term championing the case for 'joined-up thinking' and 'joined-up professional working'. Within such an approach, problems of social exclusion were seen to impact across wide areas of society and were to be addressed by a range of multi-agency approaches. These would involve professional bodies such as teachers, health and social services workers, the police, housing department officials and a range of voluntary agencies, overseen and encouraged by less fragmented and less isolated government departments. Circular 10/99 (DfEE 1999) also required schools to accept a certain degree of responsibility by noting 'a significant degree of variation in rates of truancy and exclusion, even between schools in similar areas and with similar challenges'.

This trend towards greater inclusion has also been paralleled in the USA:

> Based largely on the extension of racial minorities' demands for equal treatment to students with disabilities, the mainstreaming movement resulted in efforts to make certain that those with emotional or

behavioural disorders spent as much of their school experience as possible in contact with students without disabilities – in mainstream classes and activities.

(Kauffman and Smucker 1995)

This drive was embodied in the Individuals with Disabilities Act (IDEA) in 1990, and promoted educational placement in what became termed the most normalized or the 'least restrictive' environment.

In the UK, the target figure for a reduction in exclusions from school by one-third by the year 2002 became the focus of serious resentment by teacher associations and this government requirement was abandoned before a reckoning could take place in 2002. Exclusion rates, none the less, appeared to turn a corner and begin to drop at the end of the millennium.

Child and adolescent mental health initiatives

A broader approach to social inclusion originated within a health context in relation to mental health, which was seen to have been relatively neglected previously given its very high incidence and also strongly linked to wider problems of social exclusion. In the late 1990s, the Department of Health launched a programme of National Service Frameworks to lay down models of treatment and care that people would be entitled to expect in every part of the country, giving an equally high prominence to both coronary heart disease and mental health problems.

With a younger population specifically in mind, an influential report by the Mental Health Foundation (1999) proposed a series of initiatives for promoting the mental health of children and young people. An ambitious series of projects was also funded, in which Child and Adolescent Mental Health Services (CAMHS) teams, consisting of members from a range of professional backgrounds, were to develop and evaluate a range of projects aimed at prevention and reduction.

The DfES (2003) pointed out that schools had a major role to play, in conjunction with other professionals:

Schools can play a vital part in ensuring that mental health problems are quickly recognised and treated. If mental health problems are not recognised early they can lead to school or home breakdown, or both, with significant costs for education or social services. On the other hand, unrecognised learning difficulties can themselves lead to emotional and conduct problems. There is often a poor long-term outcome for children who have disruptive behaviour problems if their difficulties go untreated, with a greater likelihood of these children becoming involved in crime, alcohol and drug-related problems and having severe relationship difficulties in adulthood.

Once again, similar developments may be detected in the USA, where, for example, federal block grants have supported comprehensive school-based or school-linked health services. Deriving from recognition that 'behavioural patterns established in youth are the leading cause of the most serious and costly health and social problems that affect our nation' (Riccio and Hughes 2001), these block grants have encouraged or required states to grant considerable discretion to local communities. Projects financed in this way have often been organized and run by advisory groups comprising such people as parents, school administrators, local health care providers, religious leaders, business leaders and representatives from youth and family service agencies.

Legislation to delineate home and school responsibilities

A theme running through UK government advice and legislation for some time now has been that of 'responsibility'. The SEN Code of Practice and the subsequent legislation into which this became incorporated spelt out the procedures that school staff were to follow in respect of a pupil they deemed to have special educational needs, including students with emotional and behavioural difficulties. The statutory duties of other personnel, particularly educational psychologists and school doctors, were also stated. Continuing with school staff, a government Circular in 1994 also required schools to develop and clarify their internal policies and procedures regarding student behaviour (DfE 1994a). This was followed by the further expectation that LEAs confirm and make clear their coordinating role by means of published LEA Behaviour Plans (DfEE 1998b).

While these various publications also referred to pupils and parents, their central thrust was in terms of the obligations placed upon organizations such as schools and LEAs. The extension of prescription towards parents, in particular, can be seen in a subsequent Circular requiring all schools to draw up and adopt 'home–school agreements' (DfEE 2000a). These documents require respective responsibilities to be listed, and then signed by both school staff and parents to indicate their intention to adhere to the contents. In addition, the governing bodies of schools are also encouraged to take 'all reasonable steps' to ensure that the parental declaration is signed, indicating that parents understand and accept the agreement. Of particular relevance to the theme of this book is the requirement that these agreements include a statement of the school's and parents' respective responsibilities concerning pupil attendance and behaviour, and government advice is that agreements will work best where they are 'a product of genuine discussion between all parties concerned' (DfEE 1998b).

The strong emphasis on the rights and responsibilities of parents is also emphasized in Circular 10/99 (DfEE 1999), which states that schools should set up a pastoral support programme for students experienced as particularly difficult to manage and seen as in danger of being excluded from school. In this multi-agency programme, parents should contribute to strategy planning and 'be regularly informed about their child's progress'. Again, this government recommendation is founded on the belief that by making expectations between school and home agreed and explicit, a subsequent exclusion may be averted.

Behind all these developments is a strong and understandable desire to make clear and unambiguous to all – particularly students, parents and teachers – who should be responsible for what. In addition to policies and practices to develop cooperative, preventive and proactive strategies, especially between school and home, there are, however, often strong statements of mutual recrimination and blame to be heard. Earlier, the present author characterized the continuing public concern over difficult pupil behaviour as creating a situation in which

> blame tends to shift from pupils to teachers and on to parents before coming around again to teachers, as if proceeding around the points of a triangle. Legislative initiatives which are introduced in an attempt to delineate the relative responsibilities of each party have a habit of floundering when the public attention shifts to another point on the triangle. Teachers can feel they have little chance if their efforts are not supported at home. Parents will complain that they are unable to exert control over how their child behaves during a particular lesson at school. And young people themselves lack the power and psychological sophistication to act as mediators between clashing home and school perspectives.
>
> (Miller 1999)

Multi-agency professional approaches

Sensitivities over who should take responsibility, and be accountable, for what extend beyond schools and parents, however. Because the issue of difficult student behaviour creates such strong emotions in all concerned, initiatives that attempt, for all the best motives, to encourage wide, multi-agency responses also run the risk of becoming bogged down in disputes over roles, rights and responsibilities. Mention has already been made of the discussion by Gray and Noakes (1992) of the differing nature of medical and educational perspectives on this topic, and the ways in which the school processes/ problem child balance may be variously construed.

More latterly, Hammill and Boyd (2001) conducted an interview study of over one hundred professionals working on a multi-agency youth strategy initiative, which was an attempt to pool skills and expertise to help young people with social, emotional and behavioural difficulties 'holistically' across one Scottish local authority. Involved in the study were education welfare officers, juvenile liaison police officers, community education workers, social workers, teachers, educational psychologists and others. This intensive study found some evidence of 'sporadic inter-agency cooperation, often at grass roots level', but listed a number of barriers to effective inter-agency work.

Among the factors militating against the more successful pooling of expertise were those that Gray and Noakes (1992) had suggested almost a decade earlier. Differing perspectives on what are salient features of problems, how they may be caused and maintained, the contexts in which others work, the texture of life in schools and in some families' homes and professional 'cultures' all seem to interfere with the aspirations that lie behind the repeated calls for multiprofessional, or 'joined-up', working in these sensitive areas.

Clearly, the ideal of pooled skills and expertise is not as easily realized as might be wished. Just as the differing responsibilities of home and school can so easily become the subject of inflamed debate, so too, although usually to a less intense extent, may multiprofessional working become dogged with confusions over relative roles and responsibilities.

The aims of this book

This brief overview of key legislation and ensuing policy developments sets the scene for the themes to be developed within this book. The struggles to define and categorize, to delineate responsibilities and to identify and draw effectively upon the most skilled expertise continue to defy easy resolution. Pressure to demonstrate a return on the investment of expensive resources, to achieve outcomes equally satisfactory to a range of differing and sometimes conflicting expectations, continue to tax and stress almost everyone involved.

In order to address some of these major challenges, this book adopts a perspective that is predominantly psychological in orientation. It concerns itself with the thoughts, beliefs and feelings of major interested parties, not only, or even predominantly, students but also teachers, parents and other professionals. However, this is not a wholly individualistic psychology. The second major theme running through the book is the social context in which these parties find themselves, the complex organizations and affiliations that are schools and families, the informal as well as formal groupings to which individuals belong, the public and the private. The interplay between the social and the individual is manifest throughout, especially the distinctive forms this takes when an individual student's behaviour is deemed to challenge the effectiveness and well-being of a much larger group. In short, the book takes a psychosocial approach.

In taking such an approach, the book has a broad set of aims:

1   It attempts to advance the social inclusion of probably the most challenging group of pupils by paying particular attention to practice in mainstream schools.

2   An emphasis is placed on evidence as the basis for action. Although detailed discussion of research methodology is avoided, some critical consideration is given to the notion of evidence-based practice to ensure that discussion moves beyond mere sloganeering.

3   A coherent approach is taken to what is usually a broad and disparate set of perspectives and concerns. Theoretical models are employed, explained and justified in order to provide a rationale for 'joined-up thinking' in this area.

4   With the rise in multi-agency approaches, a detailed account of school processes is necessary so that their full complexity may be acknowledged, and engaged to maximum effect.

5   Examples of successful practice are provided. These are related back to the coherent framework as an aid to deeper understanding rather than presented as shining, all purpose solutions to be 'cut and pasted' directly into any organization. An overall intention of the book is to illuminate the psychological conditions for, and barriers to, effective practice, and to counter the view that any simplistic set of 'tips and techniques' will ever bring a satisfactory resolution.

6   The continuingly vexed area of teacher–parent relations is explored and addressed at some length, and within the overall psychosocial framework.

7   Finally, the human and the social are emphasized and demonstrated to be essential perspectives in this area of work, as a counter to growing reductionist and/or determinist views promoting drug treatments or future spin-offs from human genome research as the arenas holding most promise for the future.

Chapter 2 turns directly to the psychosocial framework that forms one of the unifying structures to the book. After illustration of some key psychological themes, the framework is outlined and set to serve as a spine around which the remaining chapters are organized.

2 Difficult behaviour in classrooms: the psychosocial perspective

In order to present a coherent account of difficult behaviour in schools, a number of concepts from systems theory are introduced in this chapter. In particular, the chapter employs an extended example involving a teacher, parent and student to consider the phenomenon of 'causation' within a complex social system such as a school, and illustrate the contrast between notions of linear and circular, or recursive, causation. A distinction is also drawn between factors that might be seen as original causes of difficult behaviour and factors that might incline it to be maintained in a school setting. Other concepts from systems theory, in particular that of 'the boundary', are introduced here, and developed further in later chapters as an aid to understanding teachers' relationships with parents and with their colleagues. Finally, a psychosocial model of a school is presented as the comprehensive structure around which the chapters within this book are organized.

Introduction

Chapter 1 has demonstrated that much legislation and policy-making, in both the UK and USA, has made certain assumptions about the nature of difficult behaviour in schools and classrooms. Implicit in many of the developments and discussions outlined has been a focus upon making sense of 'causation', either in terms of the characteristics of individual pupils (with their emotional and behavioural difficulties) or in terms of school processes such as effective behaviour policies or teachers' classroom organization and management skills.

This search for 'causation' has, in general, served us well as a civilization. If there is an outbreak of disease we look for the original contaminating source in order to isolate or eliminate its potential to cause further infection. If there is a civil engineering disaster, a collapsed road bridge or whatever, we attempt to determine the precise nature of the structural or material fault in order to effect a full repair and to learn cautionary lessons for similar future projects. Problem-solving in this fashion is the hallmark of much successful adaptation, both for resourceful individuals in their everyday lives and for whole societies in such areas as significant medical and technological accomplishments. When faced with the ongoing challenge of difficult student behaviour in classrooms, it is small wonder then that, while acknowledging the complex interaction of causes, we none the less seek to track back from the current problem in an attempt to identify the major contributory cause or causes for the origin of the current situation.

This chapter discusses the reasons why this seemingly obvious and sensible approach to the causes of student behaviour in classrooms, sometimes referred to as *linear causation,* may fail to provide an understanding that leads on to real and effective progress. A set of examples is used to illustrate the alternative concept of *circular causation,* leading in turn to a more general consideration of the behaviour of complex human systems such as schools. Finally, a model of the school as a *psychosocial system* is outlined and justified as a theoretically coherent and practically useful framework from which real and effective interventions can be, and have been, devised. In addition, as this framework is introduced, the opportunity is taken to illustrate the ways in which this provides a structure for the remaining sections of the book.

Cause and effect in a complex school system

Take the example (from Miller 1994) of a primary school teacher who feels that a mother is not supporting her efforts to manage her son's difficult classroom behaviour, because the mother does not appear to accept that there is a problem to be addressed. The teacher may decide that it is necessary to keep the mother informed of all misdemeanours, so that the classroom behaviour can gradually be more fully appreciated at home. However, suppose the mother initially interprets this as making an unnecessary fuss over relatively minor matters and concludes that the teacher is 'picking on' her son. She may decide that the best way to stick up for him – to be a good mother to him – is to challenge the teacher's judgement about the seriousness of much of this reported behaviour. The teacher may then perceive this as further confirmation of her view that the mother is refusing to accept that her own concern is valid and may redouble her efforts to convince. A 'vicious circle' may then result, wherein each move can be seen to act as the trigger for the next (see Figure 2.1), a phenomenon referred to by some family therapists (Dowling and Osborne 1994) as 'circular causation'.

In such circumstances, instead of there being one party who is the obvious cause, with the other the passive recipient, once the pattern is in motion each can be clearly seen as the stimulus to the beliefs and behaviour of the other. If the teacher is giving her account of the situation to a colleague, or the mother hers to a relative, then each will present a perspective that is 'legitimate and

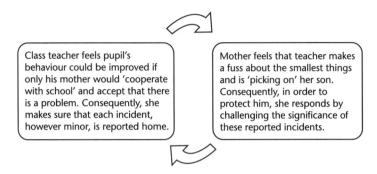

Figure 2.1 An example of circular causation between a teacher and mother

understandable' in their own eyes. Where we stand within a pattern of circular causation, and the time at which we are presenting our account, referred to by some family therapists as the *punctuation point*, will inevitably influence our account.

In such a cycle, either party's behaviour can appear to be the more prominent, reasonable, inflammatory or whatever, depending not only on whose account is actually being presented but also on *the time at which the circular causation is being punctuated*. From this angle, talk of a single or original cause, to be identified before it is possible to consider any remedy, can be seen as a misplaced quest and one likely to exacerbate further the cycle of blaming and recrimination. Instead, the challenge becomes one of finding a mutually acceptable punctuation point, at which the influence of each party on the other can be seen to make sense in that party's own terms.

Of course, finding such a starting point, a difficult enough endeavour in itself, is made many times more problematic by the fact that each party will almost inevitably have become enmeshed within a whole network of 'wheels within wheels'. For example, the teacher may have invited some disapproval from less sympathetic colleagues who believe, in keeping with a general staff culture, that more drastic action should be taken by the headteacher because the pupil's behaviour is irredeemable. The class teacher, in response, may become more determined to show that the pupil can improve and may try harder to engage the mother's cooperation by redoubling her reporting home of incidents at school. Similarly, we might imagine a situation in which the boy's father feels his wife is being too sensitive about reports from school and that by responding to each of these she is getting a bad name for herself and in turn causing their son to be further criticized in school (see Figure 2.2). His wife may then feel that she has to try harder still to succeed with her strategy in order to demonstrate that she has in fact acted in the best interests of their son.

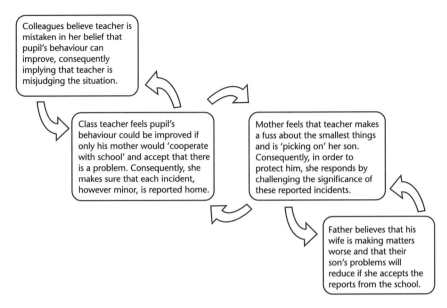

Figure 2.2 A more extended example of circular causation within a school and family

It is relatively easy to imagine other interacting circles emanating out from those shown in Figure 2.2, a headteacher perhaps intervening in an attempt to stave off a perceived conflict between various staff over the best way forward with the particular student, or other family members being influenced by and reacting to the expressed differences of opinion between husband and wife.

This growing complex of 'wheels within wheels' or 'circles upon circles' can be seen to be based upon one particular interaction between a student's teacher and mother. However, it is also possible to begin with another basic interaction and envisage similarly complex and recursive patterns built upon this.

Remaining with the scenario above, we might imagine that some aspects of the student's behaviour would lead to a reaction from others in the class. Depending upon the general pupil culture, this may be one of either rejection or glorification, or some mixture of the two. This general reaction from classmates will then in turn be liable to provoke further responses from the student, responses with the potential to send more reverberations around the myriad of interlocking circles that may be assumed to exist. Seen in this way, even actions that can be construed as helpful contributions towards a solution can have a range of unintended effects. For example, the headteacher may decide that some of the time of a non-teaching assistant – a precious school resource – should be allocated to working in this classroom with the specific brief of assisting this specific student and containing any further difficulties.

In creating this particular form of staff organizational grouping – the addition of a non-teaching assistant to the classroom – the potential for further recursive interactions is created. For example, the student may resent or welcome being the recipient of this extra individual attention, triggering consequent patterns of behaviour that impinge upon teacher, assistant and other pupils, in turn eliciting their own responses. The teacher and assistant may struggle to come to a clear understanding of where each other's responsibilities begin and end, or may form such a positive working relationship that other staff fear that their 'share' of the assistant's time may become reduced. Others in the class may see the provision of extra adult help as an indication of the target student's lack of abilities and communicate this in some way, perhaps by taunts or teasing or acting superior, or they may resent it and turn this feeling towards the teacher or assistant. And so on, the possible repercussions being very many and various.

This extended example has deliberately left vague and unelaborated the nature of the 'difficult behaviour'. The purpose has been to demonstrate some of the social and psychological aspects of the school context in which the behaviour is located. Of course, difficult behaviour is usually discussed in terms of specific actions on the part of students: defiance, rudeness, aggression or whatever. The suggestion being made here, which is not to belittle or dismiss the effects of behaviour such as this when it occurs, is that the search for causes as the precursor to taking action may not be a straightforward procedure. The assumption of a linear cause and effect relationship, which has demonstrated such explanatory power in so many areas of human endeavour, may serve less well here.

In the example under consideration, there may be any number of circular or recursive interactions, rather than just one set between two people, and these will be linked to many others throughout the social edifices of the school and family. Although intimately linked, some of these will be far removed from the original teacher, parent and child, perhaps involving deeply ingrained beliefs and important organizational procedures within the school or family. When a particular student's behaviour becomes a topic of concerned discussion, the punctuation point usually follows closely after some dramatic incident such as an abusive remark or aggressive act. When the focus is on that specific behaviour, for obvious and understandable reasons, the contribution of many less immediately apparent recursive processes may well be overlooked. Yet, if real and effective outcomes for all concerned are to be achieved, it may be imperative that these other cycles be subjected to scrutiny, or at the very least their contribution be appreciated, in order to understand fully the complex of factors causing *or maintaining* the difficulties.

This line of argument may be more clearly appreciated after a brief consideration of some basic principles embedded within the larger field of study generically referred to as *systems theory*.

Some key characteristics of systems theory

Systems theory has its origins within biology in the early parts of the twentieth century and has since contributed to the development of a wide range of disciplines, from economics to psychiatry. We have already referred above to concepts such as the punctuation point and circular causation, ideas developed by family therapists working from a systems theory perspective. Later chapters examine in more detail the ideas of theorists, researchers and practitioners that are especially pertinent to student behaviour in schools. At this introductory stage, though, it will suffice to mention a number of key characteristics of systems theory.

A system is often defined as an assembly of parts that are connected together in an organized way. The emphasis is upon the word 'organized', even if our current state of knowledge does not allow us to describe the exact nature of all these interconnections (as in the example above). Clarke (1985) illustrates the point graphically: 'the stones on the beach do not form a system, the cells in the brain do'. In the school example above, there is an implication that a student's behaviour may be seen as located in, and hence more fully understood as, part of a system that incorporates a teacher, pupil, mother, other staff, family members and pupils. In some academic disciplines, such as economics, complex forms of mathematical analysis and statistical modelling have been devised to enhance their explanatory and predictive power. In the example of student behaviour, however, it is necessary to accept that knowledge about the extent and influence of the various interconnected parts comes nowhere near to having this degree of precision.

Another major assertion of systems theory is that the parts of the system are affected by being within the system and that attempting to study parts in isolation will yield an inaccurate or incomplete picture:

> You cannot find out what somebody's heart does by taking it out. In the first place, whatever it does, it stops doing it when you remove it. Secondly, what is left of the body does not go on obligingly displaying all its normal properties and capacities . . . What does happen, needless to say, is that an intact functioning system gets split into two parts, neither of which works without the other. All very obvious and rather silly, you may think, but what of a harder case? What if you study the members of a family as separate individuals, hoping to understand the family as a whole? Admittedly they do not cease to function completely, like a heart removed from the body, but they may not function

> *in the same way* outside the family, and the family may not be the same without them. If not, the study of each person in turn will not finally 'add up' again to the totality which was to be investigated.
>
> (Clarke 1985: 17)

A final major aspect of systems theory that needs to be introduced at this stage concerns the *boundary* of the system: which events, people, groupings etc. are to be considered within the system and which as part of the system's environment:

> What makes a particular collection of things a particular system is not an unchanging fact of nature, but a purposive decision by the people who study it. For one purpose, all the blood vessels of the body and their contents make up 'the circulatory system'. For a different purpose *the system* might be the respiratory apparatus, consisting of the lungs and their associated airways and blood vessels . . . What is part of the system and what is not depends on what we are studying on that occasion and why.
>
> (Clarke 1985: 17)

What we are studying on this occasion, in this book, is the behaviour of school students in a system with a boundary drawn around, and hence including, significant school and home personnel and processes. The reason for doing so springs from some of the recent legislative advances discussed in Chapter 1 and from a range of developments within educational and psychological research, theory and practice – a set of themes that will provide the content for the remainder of this book.

Such an approach has been described in varying ways. In the USA, Aponte (1976) coined the term 'eco-structural', whereas in the UK, Dowling and Osborne (1994) described work carried out at the Tavistock Clinic as a 'joint systems' approach. Further, both Molnar and Lindquist (1989) in the USA and Cooper and Upton (1990) in the UK have illustrated an 'ecosystemic' approach. While there are some differences to be detected between these authors in terms of theoretical slant, practical approaches and contexts, great overriding similarities reside in their recognition of the importance of such issues as the interconnectedness within social systems, the complexity of causation and the nature of the boundary between school and home.

The psychosocial system of student behaviour in schools

In the example of student behaviour used above, it was suggested that a set of recursive interactions between a number of individuals – primarily student, teacher and parent – could be thought of as 'surrounding' the student behaviour. Other 'processes', such as the grouping of staff, the culture among pupils and the relationships in the student's home, it was suggested, might also be implicated in some way. Figure 2.3 is an attempt to represent these processes, which are psychological and social in nature, as the parts of this larger system involving home and school.

This book is structured around the framework in Figure 2.3, drawing on theory and research findings to demonstrate why this way of conceptualizing the context of student behaviour in schools is a valid and useful one. In addition, the model is used as the springboard from which coherent approaches to tackling school-based problems may be launched. Practical examples of interventions are therefore described and located within various parts of the system.

Most readers will recognize the terms used in the boxes in Figure 2.3. However, in an attempt to prevent any ambiguity at this stage, brief

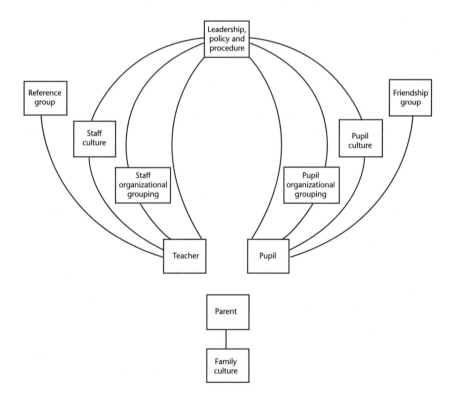

Figure 2.3   The school as a psychosocial system (from Miller and Leyden 1999)

descriptions are offered for some of the key concepts, most of which receive much more substantial examination in subsequent chapters of the book.

Leadership, policy and procedure

Policy and procedures within schools (and in other organizations) are usually formal and public, are almost always available for scrutiny in some written form and constitute the documentation against which many accountability and evaluation exercises are carried out. Leadership refers, again fairly obviously, to the actions of those charged with developing and implementing these aspects and with ensuring the smooth running and future development of the organization. In terms of student behaviour, we have already noted in Chapter 1 that schools have a responsibility to provide leadership in devising appropriate ways of ensuring the prosocial behaviour of students and reacting to difficulties when these arise. As the psychosocial model of a school is subjected to more critical examination through this book, the real and powerful organizational processes that challenge and facilitate effective leadership, policy and procedure concerning student behaviour will become increasingly apparent.

Staff culture

The culture of a school has been described by Dalin (1993) as

> what we experience as the 'way things are' in an organisation, the written and unwritten rules that regulate behaviour, the stories and the 'myths' of what an organisation has achieved, the standards and the values set for its members.

Deal and Kennedy (1982) have put it more simply as the 'system of informal rules that spells out how people are to behave most of the time'. This may obviously be compared and possibly contrasted with the various public pronouncements or policies that purport to describe how an organization is structured and functions.

Argyris and Schon (1978) have referred to these two phenomena as 'theory in use' and 'espoused theory' respectively, and have claimed that one of the most important steps in understanding an organization is the detection of the possible gaps between its espoused theory and its theory-in-use. Argyris and Schon point out that organizations are extremely well practised and effective in 'defensive routines' when there is any possibility of a gap between their espoused theory and their theory-in-use being revealed. This is a potentially sensitive and highly contentious assertion and it should be emphasized that Argyris and Schon were organizational psychologists commenting generally.

(Their claims may, for instance, be applied equally to university departments, educational psychology services and academic publishers!)

A major research theme that develops in this book, however, concerns the particular forms that the gap between espoused theory and theory-in-use can take around issues of student behaviour – a phenomenon that may paradoxically not act in the best interests of any of the parties involved.

Pupil culture

In contrast to the staff culture in a school, there will also be a parallel set of rules, stories and myths that define 'the way things are' among pupils.

One area of recent research and practice that has engaged prominently with this concerns bullying in schools. Although bullying can be seen as, among other things, a manifestation of abusive elements within the peer culture, it is also among the peer group that some of the most effective remedies may be found. Sharp (1996), for example, has described a variety of peer-centred intervention strategies that have been shown to lead to large reductions in levels of bullying behaviour and increases in the number of pupils willing to tell teachers if they are being bullied.

Another intervention strategy that operates by harnessing the peer culture, and by helping to build friendship groups, is the Circle of Friends technique (Forrest *et al.* 1996). Both formal evaluation (Frederickson and Turner 2003) and casework reports demonstrate impressive results. In Britain, Newton *et al.* (1996) have described the setting up of 20 Circles of Friends for pupils aged between four and 14, primarily pupils with severe emotional and behavioural difficulties. Where other approaches had been tried and failed, Newton *et al.* managed to prevent permanent exclusions from school and to avoid segregation into special education. The process is beginning to reveal the powerful role of peer cultures to support and include socially isolated students, including those with the most serious forms of anti-social behaviour.

Staff organizational grouping

This part of the system refers to the way in which staff are organized into groups in order to manage certain educational objectives. These are formal and public processes initiated by senior management, with obvious examples being of staff organized into year or academic subject groupings or in terms of seniority. In professional work with pupils displaying difficult behaviour, the allocation of additional teaching or non-teaching personnel to specific pupils can be a major issue and, as Chapter 1 has already revealed, SEN legislation has implicated LEA educational psychologists heavily in the assessment of the 'resource-worthiness' of certain individual students.

Although staff organizational grouping is neither an explicit nor central theme of this book, its prominence as a concern among many in schools makes it worth pointing to a small but important evidence base in what have become known as 'room management' studies, which will be briefly described here.

This line of research originated with McBrien and Weightman (1980), who observed that, in a special school for pupils with severe learning difficulties, the injection of extra assistants into a class did not increase the measured engagement of pupils on an educational task. This engagement remained at around 30 per cent whether the number of staff in the class was one, two, three, four, five or six! The training of staff in room management, however, to carry out one from a set of three clear roles, led to an almost doubled rate of pupil engagement.

Thomas (1992) replicated this study with a more sophisticated methodology in a mainstream primary classroom and was able to show highly significant differences in pupil 'on-task behaviour' resulting from training of the classroom team of teacher and parents in room management. Thomas also found that various interpersonal processes, often maintained by school procedures and staff cultures, could militate against an effective evolution of these types of role differentiation.

Room management studies hence demonstrate that this form of training in explicit staff organizational grouping can improve the quality of teacher–pupil interactions; a research finding with potentially very important implications when two or more adults are trying to manage student behaviour in a classroom.

Pupil organizational grouping

This part of the psychosocial system refers to the various ways in which the school may decide to group its students, the most obvious and pervasive example being 'the class'. Straightaway, longstanding and contentious debates about streaming, setting and mixed ability grouping come to mind. But in addition to these, special arrangements, perhaps part-time groupings involving small group work, are often made within schools.

Reference group

The importance of a *reference group* for teachers was identified by Nias (1985), who examined in an interview study the experiences of 99 teachers from various parts of England who had been teaching for between two and nine years. Among her findings, Nias concluded that these teachers needed a group of 'like-minded' people, whose norms and values they identified with and used in order to evaluate themselves. Many of the teachers appeared to need this referential support from only one other – a colleague, headteacher or visiting professional. Nias comments that the amount of support provided by such a group was out of all proportion to either the size of the group or the time spent in communication.

The majority of teachers interviewed found themselves at some stage working in schools where they had no adult reference group and then they often sought it in outside courses, previous colleagues or people with whom they had originally trained as teachers. The particular outlook of this reference group, Nias suggested, becomes 'internalized' and then acts as 'a "frame of reference" that is brought to bear on all new situations'.

Given the subject matter of this book, it may be extremely important that teachers can find a reference group from which to draw support for particularly demanding work, but also one whose norms and values do actually lead to activities and approaches that are likely to be most effective when working with challenging student behaviour.

Friendship group

In certain ways, friendship groups for pupils may be seen to act in a similar way to the reference group for teachers, in many ways resembling its 'mirror image'. Either internal or external to the school, friendships are universally seen as of immense importance, providing students (and all of us) with models and support in almost all aspects of our lives. Perhaps of particular interest here is to note again the Circles of Friends approach, which, when explicitly organized within a school, may be seen as an intentional attempt to create the powerful effects of a friendship group for the benefit of a student experiencing serious difficulties with some form of social acceptance.

Key features of the psychosocial model

The psychosocial system presented in Figure 2.3 may be subdivided in a number of ways in order to reveal aspects of its structure. For instance, and rather obviously, the peripheral parts – reference groups, friendship group and families – may have their physical existence external to the school's physical boundaries, whereas the top and central parts all reside within the bricks and mortar (or temporary, prefabricated outbuildings). Another view might see that the left-hand side clearly refers to staff, the right-hand side to pupils and the bottom to families. As a *psychosocial* framework, however, a more significant structure might be that highlighted in Figure 2.4, in which the unshaded boxes represent formal, public and 'espoused' aspects of the organization, with the shaded areas representing those parts that are more informal, hidden and only discernible 'in use'.

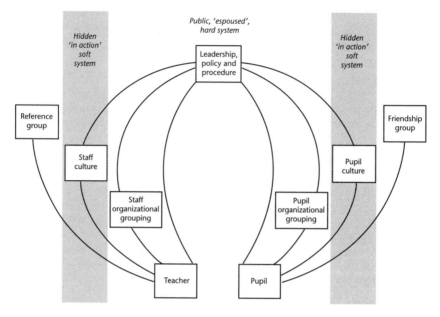

Figure 2.4   The public and hidden subsystems of the school

The structure of this book

The psychosocial model is used as an approximate structure around which to organize the following chapters, with the research studies, theoretical formulations and examples of effective practice in turn providing further support for the model as a coherent and meaningful framework. So, Chapter 3, for instance, focuses upon the 'pupil' box and examines the research evidence base for interventions with individual students whose behaviour in classrooms is deemed by their teachers to be difficult to manage. Chapter 4, on the other hand, examines the issues involved in working with teachers (and parents) in order to help them to extend their skills and abilities in this demanding area of their work. In both cases, quoted research is embedded in its theoretical context and practical examples that arise from this are illustrated.

Chapter 6 turns its attention towards research into the more hidden aspects of support and social interaction between teacher colleagues within a school. After considering possibly controversial research into the ways in which these staff cultures may discourage a belief in the possibility of successful strategies, Chapter 9 goes on to examine examples of the ways in which creative, problem-solving staff cultures may be, and have been, built.

Mirroring this, Chapter 7 turns its attention towards what is known about the effects of pupil cultures, the aspects of social behaviour between students that are often hidden from staff, the extent to which this culture may act to support prosocial or anti-social behaviour and the interventions that schools may make in this respect

Chapter 9 is also concerned with larger-scale organizational change within a school, giving examples of interventions with school staff to move forward the development of policy and practice in respect of difficult behaviour. An approach that is illustrated in some depth – soft systems methodology – is particularly sensitive to the need for less accessible, but potentially very powerful, aspects of staff culture to be harnessed and engaged if strategic change of this type is to be effective within schools. Chapter 10 builds on much of what has been already been discussed, returns to the vexed question of partnership between teachers, parents and pupils and draws together the research evidence base and the practice initiatives explored within this book.

PART 2
Working with Individual Students, Teachers and Parents: The Evidence Base

3 Strategies with individual students: the evidence base

This chapter examines early, classic research studies and shows how these have continued to influence the developments in practice and legislation outlined in Chapter 1. A detailed description and discussion of one particular pioneering American study is provided, as a number of its principles and assumptions can be seen to have provided the foundation for a massive development of further research initiatives, training approaches and legislation. Criticisms of some of these research directions are discussed as are the ever-present challenge of marrying a research evidence base with classroom practice, to the mutual benefit of each. Finally, the enduring legacy of behavioural approaches is discussed.

Introduction

Plans, strategies, targets, rewards, sanctions, clear explicit rules: such is the lexicon of much of the current legislation and practice outlined in Chapter 1. These terms are to be found in abundance within, for instance, the SEN Code of Practice, pastoral support programmes and the guidance for writing home–school agreements. Such terms, and the mindset from which they originate, can be shown to have grown in large measure from early research into 'behavioural approaches', discussion of which constitutes the major part of this chapter. SMART targets (specific, measurable, achievable/attainable, realistic and time-related), for example, as promoted strongly within the Code of Practice, are shown to be a clear echo down the years from research first carried out in the late 1960s.

Similarly, these early developments were to provide a basis, to a greater or lesser extent, for a host of popular training packages, such as *Behavioural Approach to Teaching Package* (Wheldall and Merrett 1985), *Preventative Approaches to Disruption* (Chisholm *et al.* 1986), *Building a Better Behaved School* (Galvin *et al.* 1990), *You Know the Fair Rule* (Rogers 1990) and *Assertive Discipline* (Canter and Canter 1992). Publications that are variations on and extensions to such themes continue to flood the educational book lists and form the basis of much of the training offered to teachers and others.

Behavioural approaches in classrooms: public relations disaster or Trojan horse?

The term 'behavioural approaches' is redolent with connotations. For some it may be rats in mazes and psychologists in white coats. For others, it is bribery, coercion or an unjustly tolerant attitude towards disobedience and disorder. For others again, it is the one tune of the remote and unworldly visiting 'expert' with star charts and smiley faces spilling from his or her arms. In the light of these common perceptions, and the assertions above about the undoubted influence of behavioural approaches within education – for good or bad – perhaps the subtitle for this section should read 'public relations disaster *and* Trojan horse'.

Teachers have always retained a considerable scepticism towards behavioural approaches and it is probably true that these methods no longer claim a strong allegiance among psychologists working in educational settings. There are philosophical, practical and methodological objections to their credibility, but their influence persists.

This chapter takes a dispassionate and critical look at behavioural approaches to difficult classroom behaviour, first by examining in some detail a pioneering research study that laid the foundation for much subsequent work, and then by examining some of the major ensuing debates and developments. The book itself demonstrates that behavioural psychology is a vastly incomplete psychology as a framework for helping schools to become more satisfying and productive environments for all concerned, and promotes a far fuller psychosocial framework. However, this particular chapter suggests that, behind some of the stereotypes and worst excesses, research and practice in behavioural approaches have produced some challenging research findings and nuggets of insight that merit consideration if we are serious in our quest for a comprehensive evidence base.

The pioneering study by Madsen and colleagues

The first published study by Madsen *et al.* (1968) was carried out in American schools and consisted of accounts of helping three pupils to improve their classroom behaviour. Two of these children were in the same middle-primary classroom and the other was in a kindergarten class. His teacher characterized the behaviour of this last little boy when he entered the class as 'wild'. He would 'push and hit and grab at objects and at children. He had no respect for authority and apparently didn't even hear directions. He knew how to swear profusely. He would wander round the classroom and it was difficult to get him to engage in constructive work. He would frequently destroy any work he did rather than take it home.' It is salutary, when we become concerned that difficult student behaviour is an escalating, contemporary problem, to be reminded that his description – and there are many others from the same era – issues from a period that some might wish to commemorate as a golden age.

In this original study, the researchers were concerned to illustrate the major tenet of behavioural psychology: that behaviour is learned and that pupils can thus learn acceptable and productive classroom behaviour. The experiments show a concern with clearly defined and observable behaviour rather than assumed personality characteristics or motivations of pupils. The careful collection and recording of data, often in graphical or tabular form, is another key feature that is conspicuously present in the study. This attention to the clear presentation of data serves the very important function of allowing those concerned with interventions, especially the young people themselves, to have unambiguous information about how the strategy is progressing. Finally, behavioural approaches are structured around the principle that behaviour is governed by the settings in which it occurs (setting events) and by what follows it (consequences). Setting events, or antecedents, can comprise a whole range of educational, social and physical factors and in this study are prominent in the form of the clear exposition of classroom rules. Consequences, on the other hand, are present in the study as contingent praise and the ignoring of specific behaviour.

Because this was a research study, it not only attempted to bring about positive changes in these pupils' behaviour, but also employed a strict methodology in order to demonstrate the nature and extent of these changes. Consequently, two observers were trained over a two-week period to make precise records of the pupils' behaviour in the classroom. A set of categories of inappropriate behaviour was devised and confirmed with the class teachers concerned. Nine different categories of inappropriate and one of appropriate behaviour were described. The former consisted of gross motor, object noise, disturbance of others' property, contact, verbalization, turning around, other inappropriate behaviour, mouthing objects and isolate play. This last category was included because observations were to take place during structured group activities, and playing alone would then be seen by the teacher as inappropriate.

Each of these categories was then split into a number of precisely worded and observable behaviours. For example, the category 'verbalization' was elaborated to include: carrying on conversations with other children when this is not permitted, answering the teacher without raising a hand or without being called on, making comments or calling out remarks when no questions have been asked, calling the teacher's name to get her attention, crying, screaming, singing, whistling, laughing, coughing or blowing loudly. These responses could be directed to the teacher or the children.

The appropriate behaviour category was defined as 'answers questions, raises hand, works on assignment. Must include whole 10-second interval except for Turning Around responses of less than 4-second duration.'

It is important to stress here that the aim of the experiment was not to reduce or eliminate every aspect of inappropriate behaviour, with these massive lists being put before a five-year-old child like the labours of Hercules. These definitions were *for the observers only*, the purpose being to allow a very precise and detailed record of pupils' behaviour to be kept over the experimental period. For this reason, some definitions were made with such a high degree of specificity as to appear ludicrous on first sight if their purpose is not appreciated. For example, 'turning around' was described more explicitly as 'turning head or head and body to look at another person, showing objects to another child, attending to another child. Must be of 4-second duration, or more than 90 degrees using desk as a reference.' And so on.

The emphasis on such a detailed list of inappropriate behaviour also gives a misleading impression of the major aim of the project, which was to see whether pupils' *appropriate* behaviour could be increased during specific classroom activities. The more detailed list served an important function, however, in that it provided a greater number of items and thus increased the sensitivity of the observations. Because of the fairly exhaustive nature of these categories, if inappropriate behaviour was shown to decrease then this could reasonably be assumed to be as a result of an increase in appropriate behaviour.

The aim of the study was to investigate experimentally the effects on pupils' classroom behaviour of teachers varying their use of praise, ignoring and the explaining of rules. For the purposes of the experiment, the teachers were asked to adopt certain procedures for formulating and explaining classroom rules to the children in their classes. These were to be no more than five or six in number, short and to the point, and framed in a positive rather than a negative form (for example, 'sit quietly while working' rather than 'don't talk to your neighbours'). The teachers were asked to keep a tally sheet on their desks and record the number of times they reviewed the rules, aiming for at least four to six repetitions each day at times other than when someone had misbehaved.

The second phase of the experiment involved ignoring inappropriate behaviour unless this was leading to a pupil being hurt. The reason for this phase of the experiment was to test the possibility that inappropriate behaviour was being strengthened in some cases ('reinforced') by the attention paid to it by the teachers, even though this attention was intended to act as a punishment. Perhaps not surprisingly, the teachers in the study found this a particularly difficult strategy to implement and sustain as an intervention on its own.

The third phase, the praise condition, was framed as 'catching the child being good'. The teachers were asked to give praise, attention or smiles when the pupil was doing what was expected during the particular class in question. The teachers were also encouraged to 'shape by successive approximation', starting by giving praise and attention to the first signs of appropriate behaviour and building towards greater goals. Emphasis was to be placed on positive and helpful social behaviour and following group rules. The general principles were to give praise for behaviours that facilitated learning, to tell the children what they were being praised for and to try to encourage behaviours incompatible with those to be decreased.

Figure 3.1 shows the proportion of inappropriate behaviour displayed by the kindergarten pupil during different phases of the experiment. The baseline period consisted of a record of the pupil's behaviour before the introduction of any of the three experimental conditions – rules, ignore and praise. The observers kept a record of five 10-second intervals in every minute over a 20-minute period on three occasions each week. The percentage of intervals in which *any* inappropriate behaviour occurred was then graphed over the various sessions. Thus, the higher the scores on the graph in Figure 3.1, the greater the amount of inappropriate behaviour, and almost certainly the lower the amount of appropriate behaviour.

When the experiment began, the teachers were trained in the use of each phase before recording took place and were asked to apply the phases to the whole class, not just the target pupils, and for the whole time rather than just the observation periods. In the primary school observations took place during seat work or group instruction, and in the kindergarten class during structured

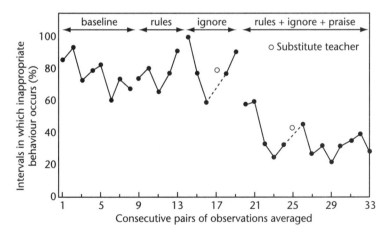

Figure 3.1 Inappropriate behaviour of one problem child in Classroom B as a function of experimental conditions (from Madsen *et al.* 1968)

activities rather than 'free play'. Two observers were present in each classroom in order to check the accuracy of each other's recordings ('inter-observer reliability'). The teachers and the pupils were reported to learn quickly not to respond to the observers (although one of them was attacked by a kindergarten child!) and the experimental recording did not commence until the two observers had settled into a pattern of consistent agreement in their recordings.

The results for the two pupils in the primary class were similar to those from the kindergarten setting shown in Figure 3.1. As this illustrates, the rules and the ignoring phases on their own produced little change from the baseline condition but the combination of rules, praise and ignoring proved highly effective in reducing inappropriate behaviour.

From this relatively detailed account of the first published study of behavioural approaches, it has been possible to illustrate many of the major characteristics of the behavioural approach. The effect that altering antecedents and consequences can have upon the ability of pupils to learn new ways of behaving in classrooms has been demonstrated. Likewise, the precise descriptions of behaviour have allowed careful records to be kept in graphical form, thus giving the pupils, teachers and researchers clear feedback that the strategy had achieved its aims.

Key issues in the development of behavioural approaches

The study by Madsen and his colleagues created considerable interest among professionals with a direct responsibility for helping teachers to manage the difficult behaviour of some pupils. In 1971, Ward repeated the experiment in a Manchester school with similar results and published the first British replication of this work. A major reason for the early growth of interest in behavioural approaches derived from the concern within the approach about the careful collection and recording of data. Results such as those in Figure 3.1 provided clear evidence that teachers could affect the behaviour of some of the most difficult pupils in mainstream primary schools.

This optimistic prospect was in strong contrast to the then dominant trend of 'pathologizing' difficult students, either as fixed deviant personality types or as members of families or subcultures immutably hostile to the efforts of the educational establishment. Behavioural approaches, on the other hand, because they emphasized the role of learning, enabled pupil behaviour to be seen as situation-specific. So, although schools were not necessarily in a position to compensate for a range of social factors, the approach did encourage the belief that teachers could have an effect upon the behaviour of pupils while they were within their charge.

However, although behavioural approaches soon attracted a group of professionals keen to extend the research base and to proselytize among the wider educational community, they also managed to generate a considerable degree of controversy, opposition and hostility. Some of this resistance may have stemmed from the rather restricted rationale for the approaches put forward by some early proponents, while other misgivings might be seen more as a reaction to a partial appreciation of the nature of the methods themselves. The remainder of this chapter deals in a little more detail with some of the major developments that have taken place in an attempt to overcome early weaknesses in practice and meet the misgivings and apprehensions from professional quarters.

The overreliance on consequences

In the minds of many who came upon behavioural approaches, an overriding emphasis seemed be placed upon the rewards and punishments that followed pupils' behaviour. Although antecedents, in the form of clear explanations of rules, were prominently contained within the Madsen *et al.* (1968) study, the focus of immediately subsequent work was very much upon the consequences of behaviour. Antecedents were generally not considered to be sufficient on their own to have a significant impact on some behaviour, whereas consequences were seen as much more likely to determine whether or not a behaviour was strengthened and maintained. It was this emphasis on consequences – rewards and punishments – that became most firmly associated with the term 'behaviour modification', a term that attracted many negative connotations.

Two of the earliest British proponents, Harrop and McNamara (1979), took stock of their practice after a five-year period of gathering casework and group workshop experience with teachers using behavioural methods. They commented on their move towards giving greater emphasis to classroom rules, as well as praise and ignoring. They made the point that behavioural interventions had to ask whether the curriculum within the classroom where the difficult behaviour was being manifested should be altered to meet the pupil's interests and aptitudes before embarking upon a fuller behavioural intervention. Similarly, Wheldall (1981) pointed to the dangers of what he termed 'behavioural overkill', the use of very powerful reinforcers in an attempt to change behaviour where a less powerful and more 'natural' reinforcer would suffice. He was also another who stressed that behavioural approaches needed to take the focus away from the consequences of behaviour and place it more upon the antecedents.

Pursuing this line, Wheldall and Austin (1981) carried out an experiment with two classes of 10- and 11-year-olds in a junior school. The amount of 'on-task' behaviour was recorded over a two-week period while the children were seated around tables, the measurements then being repeated for a further two weeks while the children were seated in rows. The mean on-task behaviour was higher for the rows condition, and when the children were subsequently returned to tables for a further two weeks, their mean on-task behaviour declined. Examination of the data revealed that the rows condition had the greatest effect on the children with low initial on-task behaviour, the very pupils for whom behavioural interventions were usually devised.

Although this study might be seen as contributing to discussions about classroom layout, its relevance here is as an early experimental demonstration that contingencies – consequences delivered following the occurrence of specified target behaviours – are not the only factors that can bring about changes in classroom behaviour. And although experiments in such areas as classroom layout need not necessarily originate with proponents of behavioural approaches, it could certainly be argued that the methodology developed within the behavioural paradigm, especially the recording of pupil behaviour, enabled or at least encouraged this early study to be conducted.

This change of emphasis to include the possible triggers to pupils' behaviour and the setting conditions in which they occur has become incorporated into the standard texts on the subject, but has probably not altered the 'carrot-and-stick' caricature of behavioural approaches that lodged firmly in some sections of the public mind, as well as in the understanding of some education-based professionals.

The focus upon 'on-task' pupil behaviour

Following on from the study by Madsen and his colleagues, many subsequent publications about work in primary schools and some special school settings consisted of case studies concerned with increasing the 'on-task' behaviour of pupils. With the steady accumulation of accounts of practice, some psychologists began to voice misgivings about the general direction of such work. Surveying the American scene, Winnet and Winkler (1972), for instance, cautioned that the current thrust of behavioural approaches in classrooms at that time could be summed up in the injunction to pupils to 'be still, be quiet, be docile'.

In a similar vein, McNamara and Harrop (1981) commented on what they saw as the 'waves of development' of behavioural approaches in Britain, and concluded that until the early 1980s much practice had been 'somewhat naive' in focusing so much attention upon 'on-task' behaviour, as opposed to 'academic work output' and other skills and socially acceptable behaviour. They argued that if behavioural approaches were to move beyond encouraging what might be only a superficial pupil compliance, a lot more attention would also have to be paid to manipulating such aspects of the setting events as lesson preparation.

As a result, a far greater number of subsequent studies switched their focus to include a greater emphasis on academic work output and on encouraging the development among pupils of a range of new skills. Developments such as these were driven by the recognition that pupils who were more able to succeed at conventionally valued school work were more likely, as a result, to identify more closely with the aims of the school and receive more naturally occurring praise and encouragement for their efforts.

Central features of the behavioural approach, such as stating clearly defined target behaviours, task analysis (splitting tasks and targets into smaller steps) and recording schedules, have also been adapted for a far wider set of educational and social purposes. Burland (1979), for example, described work in a school for pupils with emotional and behavioural difficulties in which behavioural principles were rigorously but creatively employed to teach pupils a range of social and leisure skills – everything from juggling to riding unicycles. In addition to introducing an element of fun and getting away from the image of behavioural approaches as being always aligned to control and conformity, this work had a serious intention. Not only did it display the versatility of the approaches, but for a group of children with underdeveloped social skills and restricted friendship groupings these new talents became a source of satisfaction in themselves and a probable entry into wider social acceptability.

Applications beyond the individual pupil

Extensions of the techniques also moved beyond work with individual pupils displaying difficulties to inform the practice of teachers in managing whole classes of pupils. The first British experimental validation of the behavioural approach's positive contribution to management of a whole class was provided by Tsoi and Yule (1976), who used extra break time as a reinforcer. Two types of strategy were shown to be effective, one where the behaviour of a single child formed the basis for reinforcement for all the class and one in which changes in the behaviour of the whole class were required. The study was well designed and thus able to demonstrate objectively the experimental effects.

Merrett and Wheldall (1978) employed a similarly rigorous methodology in a study that was again concerned with management of the whole class, in this instance combining a 'rules, ignore and praise' approach with a 'timer game'. In essence, this involved a teacher using a cassette tape prepared so that it gave a random signal on average once a minute. On the signal, target children were observed and house points were awarded to all the children on the target child's table if he or she was following the set rules. Merrett and Wheldall (1987: 28) commented that 'no teacher would want to use such a device often, or for long periods, but it remains a very useful strategy for gaining, or regaining, control of a group of children who display difficult and/or disruptive behaviour'. Rennie (1980) subsequently employed other game strategies with whole classes, again with success.

Whereas much of the discussion in this chapter concerns interventions that aim to help pupils who present management difficulties to their teachers, there were also developments of a more proactive and preventive nature. In an influential set of resource materials, *Building a Better Behaved School*, Galvin *et al.* (1990) pulled together the research on effective classroom management to combine the principles from behavioural studies with those from other areas of research. In addition to influencing individual pupil management techniques and whole-class strategies, this publication and the Elton Report (DES 1989) also drew attention to the crucial importance of establishing clear and mutually agreed policies within schools for encouraging positive pupil behaviour. Again, principles from the behavioural literature, including the earliest emphasis on clear statements of rules and appropriate rewards and sanctions, were incorporated centrally into these recommended whole-school policies.

Generalization

Clearly, an intervention that demanded much in terms of the time of a teacher and psychologist would show relatively little return for this effort if its effects were to last only as long as the most intensive application of the intervention. Consequently, treatment generalization, or the extent to which improved behaviour is maintained and spreads after the ending of the intervention, became a topic of enduring interest. Five possible forms of generalization were envisaged.

Improved behaviour by the child generalizes beyond the intervention to other settings

Presland (1981) outlined 24 suggestions that might aid generalization of a pupil's changed behaviour. Drawing on the research literature, he included among his suggestions involving other children in providing reinforcement, involving the child in the construction of the programme and explaining to the child how improvements can be transferred to other behaviour and then encouraging these. Within such suggestions can be seen some of the precursors of the movement to take greater account of student participation in the development of strategies.

A little later, Gurney (1987) demonstrated, by means of a small-scale controlled study, that behavioural approaches could even be effectively employed in an area of interest traditionally seen as diametrically opposed in its focus, the area of humanistic psychology concerned with raising self-esteem. In this study pupils were taught, using contingent reinforcement, to make more positive statements about themselves and display more overt behaviours related to high self-esteem, and upon subsequent testing were found to have internalized these and to be displaying a higher level of generalized self-esteem. In terms of the potential to aid generalization, proponents of humanistic approaches would predict that pupils with increased self-esteem would be likely to display less difficult behaviour in a range of settings.

Improved behaviour in the target child influences the behaviour of other children

A few studies measured changed behaviour in pupils other than the pupil who was the target of the particular intervention. Harrop (1978b) demonstrated measured improvement in the classroom behaviour of two 15-year-old boys in what was then a school for ESN(M) pupils, when a third pupil in the class became the recipient of a standard teacher-administered behavioural intervention. The details of the programme were not communicated to the other two pupils by the teacher and Harrop argued that, although the pupil probably discussed these contingencies with his friends, as these friends were not themselves rewarded another type of explanatory mechanism was required.

Leach and Byrne (1986) demonstrated similar 'spill-over' effects of improved classroom behaviour on to 'equally disruptive control students' in a study of a home-based reinforcement scheme in an Australian secondary school. They argued that it was important to attempt to identify possible facilitative factors so that spill-over effects could be explicitly planned for and encouraged.

Changed teacher behaviour towards the target child extends beyond the intervention

The term 'generalization' has usually referred to the behaviour of pupils who were the subjects of interventions, although a case can be made for extending the concept to include the behaviour of teachers.

McNamara (1977) was one of the first to raise the question, based on his early experiences with behavioural approaches, whether all teachers wished to change their behaviour in the direction required by these interventions and, even if they did, whether they would all be able to.

Little in the way of data has been collected to provide an answer to whether teachers persist in the use of some or all of the procedures in a recommended strategy beyond its designated duration. Some teacher behaviours could become habitual and not consciously exercised, whereas other teachers might think they were still following certain recommendations when in fact they had deviated markedly from them, a phenomenon known as *treatment drift*. In neither sets of circumstances would teacher reports be very reliable sources of data for judging whether or not teachers continued to use aspects of interventions.

Changed teacher behaviour extends to other pupils

Presland (1978) followed up 27 teachers who had attended his workshops on behavioural approaches and found that 17 reported that they were using some of the techniques with pupils other than the study child. There is also a suggestion, of course, from Harrop (1978b) and Leach and Byrne (1986) that two of the teachers in their studies generalized their new management techniques to some or all of the other pupils in the class.

Target teacher influences the behaviour of teacher colleagues in directions related to the strategy

Although there have been published accounts of whole-school approaches to using behavioural strategies in special schools (e.g. Burland and Burland 1979; Fry 1980), there have been no published accounts of teachers in British primary schools influencing colleagues after taking part in a behavioural intervention. The special-school staff who published these accounts worked at establishments with a reputation for using such approaches and catered for what were then known as maladjusted pupils, where a special interest in behaviour management would be expected.

Presland in his early workshops for teachers made assiduous attempts to gauge the extent to which a ripple-like spread of new ideas could be expected within schools. After surveying teachers who had attended sets of workshops, Presland (1978) found that only five respondents out of 27 had influenced anyone else to use the techniques and one of these was in a special school where other staff were required to join in work with the target child. In fact, 'there were no clear accounts of influence leading to effective applications', and, Presland concluded, 'nor is there any support here for the hope that [course] participants might pass on the approaches to colleagues in an effective way'.

These studies suggest that practitioners have been concerned, from an early stage in the application of behavioural approaches, with understanding more fully the conditions for maximizing generalization of the effects of interventions. Although the issue remains complex, there are good grounds for concluding that various forms of generalization are attainable and that some of the necessary precursors have been identified.

Control and autonomy

Finally, the perception that behavioural approaches are inevitably bound up with the desire to *control* has been particularly persistent in some quarters. At the time of the earliest studies, the *Zeitgeist* within education was strongly in terms of 'child-centredness'. Whatever forms this ethos actually took in practice (Sharp and Green 1975), central aspects, at least of the rhetoric, involved a curriculum built around children's interests and varying abilities, teaching methods that aimed to encourage and support learning rather than teach directly and a room layout and timetable organization constructed around the principle of maximum flexibility. All of these sat uncomfortably alongside the widespread perception of 'behaviour modification'.

Interestingly, at the same time, behavioural approaches were gaining widespread credibility among psychologists working with an adult population in various clinical settings. Through experiments with creative adaptations, a range of adult problems and disorders as diverse as eating disorders, sexual dysfunction and agoraphobia were ameliorated. Techniques that were devised all retained the central characteristics of the approach outlined at the beginning of this chapter: the notion that behaviour is learned and that new behaviour can also be learned, the focus on setting events and consequences, the clear definitions of target behaviours and the careful recording of precise information. However, these approaches, which came to be classed under the title of 'behaviour therapy', did not suffer from the same connotations of control as their educational counterparts.

In fact, employed in a clinical context, behaviour therapy was in many ways far more 'democratic' and open than many of the 'talking therapies' with which it was in competition for professional acceptance. Whereas the latter were usually constructed around the premise that the therapist had greater insight into the client's problems and would decide how much of this to reveal as part of the treatment, behaviour therapists were to be found asking clients to be actively involved in planning and implementing the strategy – from determining target behaviours to changing antecedents and administering their own chosen consequences and recording schemes. In educational settings at the time, behavioural approaches retained a stronger aura of control, perhaps by being allied to the inevitable, if at that time sometimes unvoiced, need of schools to create and maintain a degree of order among their pupils.

Moves towards pupils having a more autonomous role within strategies came about as the result of attempts by some practitioners to extend the benefits of behavioural approaches to secondary school teachers and their pupils. This was generally found to be a far harder undertaking than similar work at the primary level. McNamara and Harrop (1979), for example, found that when they attempted to repeat for secondary staff the types of workshops that had generally proved welcome and successful for primary teachers, there was a much reduced benefit. Following a course for 100 probationary secondary teachers, there was only a limited response, compared with primary teachers, in terms of accounts of successful interventions supported by accompanying data. They concluded that these results, and the general paucity of studies in behavioural approaches in secondary schools, could mean that these schools did not easily lend themselves to such approaches.

A clear example of work at secondary level was provided by Wheldall and Austin (1981), who had persuaded the headteacher of a comprehensive school to carry out a rules–praise–ignore intervention with a fourth-year class identified as difficult by the staff. Using a signal of a random bleep, the headteacher was asked to make a judgement on whether the class was adhering to the particular four rules used in the study and, if so, to award a point that built into a system of free time for the class. From a baseline of 55 per cent on-task, the intervention achieved an increase to a 95 per cent rate. Although McNamara and Harrop (1981) gave this study a 'cautious welcome', they argued that the involvement of the headteacher showed how hard it was to enlist the efforts of the school staff in the intervention.

Previously, McNamara (1977) had offered a set of suggestions as to why working with secondary schools might be more problematic. These covered aspects of the organizational complexity of large schools and considerations of the older pupil group involved, for whom teacher praise might not in itself be reinforcing in the same way as it was for younger pupils, and might in fact have the opposite effect.

In order to overcome some of these factors and make the benefits from behavioural approaches available at the secondary school level, an interest grew in methods whereby pupils were responsible for monitoring and reinforcing their own behaviour.

A clear account of a detailed study of a pupil self-control strategy was provided by Merrett and Blundell in 1982. They reported on work involving a 13-year-old boy in what was then termed a remedial department of a comprehensive school, who displayed a very unsettled approach to many aspects of his work and also distracted other class members from theirs. Following a baseline period, an intervention was introduced that required the pupil to tally his on-task behaviour during the same periods that his teacher collected a similar record. A signal, audible to both the pupil and the teacher, was used to indicate when both should record the behaviour. It was explained to the pupil that only the tally marks of his that agreed with his teacher's would be counted towards a reinforcing activity – 10 jointly agreed marks could be exchanged for a two-minute period of colouring in a Doodle Art picture. The boy's on-task behaviour rose from a mean level of approximately 30 per cent during the baseline period to a mean level of more than 60 per cent during this intervention period.

In addition to reducing the aspects of control of pupils and increasing the extent to which they take responsibility for their own behaviour, this trend towards self-control strategies can also be seen as another attempt to encourage generalization by reducing the pupils' reliance upon externally delivered reinforcement.

The continuing legacy of research into individual behavioural approaches

From this discussion of significant themes, it is possible to see that the cruder stereotypes of 'behaviour modification' did not reflect the diversity and creativity that developed within practice. Rather than being over-concerned with control through the excesses of 'artificial' reinforcement schedules, teachers were encouraged through practice to take a more reflective stance towards pupil behaviour. The approach addressed the educational, social and physical environments, creating the potential to inform a comprehensive conceptualization of the difficulties both experienced and presented by some pupils.

The early stereotype of over-concern with controlling the 'on-task' docility of pupils through the heavy-handed use of punishments and rewards, if it ever existed to any significant degree, is not apparent in the published accounts of practice. The interest in classroom and school environments as 'setting conditions', the attention paid to matching pupils to educational objectives and, contrary to the stereotype, the creative and optimistic attitude towards teachers and difficult pupils have all made an impact upon the wider educational scene.

By the early 1990s, the stream of research publications had slowed to a trickle, if it had not dried up altogether. Similarly, there was a sense that psychologists had lost interest in these types of strategies that had originally embodied the practical edge of this wave of research activity. Educational psychologists, for example, became increasingly interested in approaches deriving from solution-focused and brief therapy (Rhodes 1993), approaches owing allegiance to a very different theoretical orientation and considered more compatible with the rising interest in consultative styles of working with schools (see later chapters).

However, despite the dated and perhaps tainted feel to the notion of behavioural approaches, many aspects of work with difficult student behaviour in schools still owe their origins, at least in part, to the extensive evidence base developed within this field of research and practice.

The increasing emphasis being placed on the voice of the student (Gersch and Nolan 1994; DfEE 2000b), the role of emotions (Long 2002) and the mental health initiatives referred to in Chapter 1 have led many practitioners who work with individual students in difficulty to extend their focus beyond what is merely observable – 'behaviour' – and to take account of thoughts and beliefs. For example, one of the earliest British pioneers of behavioural approaches in Britain, Eddie McNamara, has extended his work into 'motivational interviewing' (McNamara 2002), which incorporates a concern for thoughts, beliefs and emotions with a range of strategies deriving from a more behavioural tradition.

At the outset of this chapter, the point was made that current British legislation continues to display many characteristic elements of the early behavioural paradigm. Indeed, the fact that 'emotional and behavioural difficulties' have been seen since the Warnock Report (DES 1978) as a form of *learning difficulty* may be in no small measure due to formulations within the behavioural approach. Variations on early strategies also continue to find a prominent place within publications that aim to provide teachers and others with training resources for individual strategy planning, effective class management techniques and aids to whole-school policy development. Another major legacy has been in the shape of a concern and respect for evidence. Decades before the drive for 'evidence-based practice', and in an era when the pronouncements of many experts and pundits went largely unchallenged, advocates of behavioural approaches were engaged in a painstaking and unfashionable quest for data to demonstrate which of their interventions were achieving their aims, and which were not.

A final area, and one central to a major theme of this book, concerns the contribution of the behavioural tradition of research and practice to joint home and school initiatives, an area with very promising potential. Chapter 5 returns to this crucial topic.

4 Strategies with teachers and parents: an evidence base and a major challenge

This chapter looks at strategies to involve parents when there is a concern about a student's behaviour in school. Research into home–school approaches is reviewed and shown to yield a promising evidence base. This research is set against published accounts of the fraught and complex endeavour that attempting to set up such partnerships can often become. Details from the 'Successful Strategies' study are then introduced as a route towards understanding the complexities of home–school cooperation in this vexed area, and an agenda for later chapters is set within this discussion.

Introduction

The review of legislation in Chapter 1 referred to the complex and contentious area of parental involvement in cases of difficult behaviour in schools and classrooms. Home–school agreements, individual educational plans, and pastoral support programmes all exhort schools to secure the cooperation – preferably the genuine and enthusiastic cooperation – of parents. Who could argue against the desirability of this and who, working in a school, could not also attest to the extreme sensitivity and, in some cases, seeming impossibility of attempting to translate these fine words into practice?

It is clear that the radical changes in educational legislation from the late 1980s onwards – legislation that promoted the position of parents to give them, for example, a greater say in a choice of school, access to their child's National Curriculum attainments and a strong say in any assessment if their child is thought to have special educational needs – had less to offer in the area of 'difficult behaviour'. The present author attempted to sum this up in 1994 by stating that 'although "parental involvement" has swept through the educational landscape, seemingly leaving none untouched in its wake, the area of problem behaviour in school has been almost totally neglected and the question of how to work positively and productively with parents in such circumstances has largely remained unanswered' (Miller 1994b). Hence, the more recent legislation and guidance described in Chapter 1 attempts to define parental responsibilities (in addition to those of schools and LEAs) and to find workable methods for ensuring that these are adhered to.

The present chapter begins to address this vital and contentious area, first by looking at what is known from a research perspective. Details from a range of well conducted studies are described to show that, if a particular type of working alliance can be forged between teacher and parents, then strategies that build on some of the principles outlined in Chapter 3 can bring about considerable improvements in classroom behaviour. However, to underline that bringing about such working partnerships is a far from easy matter, a selection of extracts from publications by various experienced practitioners and researchers is quoted. Finally, the author's own 'Successful Strategies' research is introduced, with particular reference made to aspects involving strategies carried out jointly between teachers and parents.

The evidence base for home–school strategies

The classroom-based strategies described in Chapter 3 were usually expensive in terms of the time and effort required from teachers. Often they necessitated changes in teaching style and required the use of tangible rewards that were limited or alien within classrooms. It may well have been factors such as these that led to the limited levels of take-up referred to earlier. However, it was soon realized that, at home, parents often had access to a wide variety of privileges, rewards and treats. In home-based reinforcement (H-BR) approaches, which grew from the development of behavioural approaches in classrooms and now look remarkably like the types of strategies being promoted in recent government pronouncements, the teacher is responsible for specifying classroom rules, determining rule violations and communicating these to the parent. At home the parent is responsible for consistently dispensing rewards and sanctions to the child, based on the teacher's report.

In the USA, Atkeson and Forehand (1979) reviewed 21 papers that contained the results of 29 experiments or case studies using H-BR to influence the conduct or academic behaviour of pupils across the statutory school range. This review also scrutinized the methodology of these studies in order to evaluate the validity of the results, and concluded that 63 per cent had 'adequate designs'. The general conclusion from the paper was that H-BR was consistently effective in improving both academic achievement and disruptive classroom behaviour across a wide range of ages, in both ordinary and special classrooms.

In the same year Barth also reviewed this subject and considered 18 of the studies included in Atkeson and Forehand's paper. However, by taking a different emphasis, the two papers served a useful complementary function, especially as Barth discussed a number of the more elusive 'implementation' issues.

For example, he quoted from Hickey *et al.* (1977), who examined whether or not home–school programmes actually increased parent–teacher communication. They concluded that such interventions definitely did; in a programme involving five children and their parents no instances of parent-initiated contact were recorded during the baseline period but 20 such contacts were observed during the parent involvement stage.

Another study quoted by Barth, that by MacDonald *et al.* (1970), raised interesting questions related to the monitoring of such interventions, suggesting that this might not need to be as labour-intensive as might otherwise be imagined. In a programme involving 35 adolescents who were school phobic, two groups were randomly assigned to either a 'contact counsellor' or a 'contingency counsellor'. The contact counsellors made three times the amount of parent contact of the contingency counsellors, but the latter utilized daily notes home, with the result of significantly improved attendance for this latter group.

In conclusion, Barth was as enthusiastic about H-BR as Atkeson and Forehand, and stated that 'the wide-scale application of this system need wait no longer'. Despite such reviews and recommendations, however, the approach has not generated widespread discussion in the British research literature, although we may be seeing a less technical legacy in the form of government-recommended approaches.

Leach and Byrne (1986) carried out a successful H-BR study in an Australian secondary school with four disruptive pupils and extended their design to see whether any 'spill-over' effects could be observed in terms of improvement in the behaviour of non-targeted but equally disruptive pupils in the same class. Such effects were indeed observed in one class but not in the other, and the authors speculate on the possible reasons for this. Leach and Ralph (1986) provided a case study in an Australian setting that was successful in decreasing the classroom rule violations of a 16-year-old boy. Gupta *et al.* (1990) meanwhile reported on what they considered 'the only study which has been carried out in the UK which has attempted to assess the effectiveness of H-BR'. From a study of 24 children selected from two 'bottom-stream' Year 9 classes, Gupta *et al.* were able to claim that 'on the whole the implementation of H-BR improved these children's behaviour, attendance, motivation and the amount of work completed'. As a research design, however, this study would not fall within Atkeson and Forehand's criteria for acceptable methodology, thus compromising this particular study's legitimacy as part of a rigorous evidence base.

An account of a service application of home-based reinforcement in a British context has been provided by Long (1988). He described the work of educational psychologists (EPs) and behaviour support teachers in West Norfolk engaged in moving away from a system of off-site units for pupils with severe behaviour problems and towards supported home–school links.

In this work, the focus was placed upon the outside support professional taking responsibility for setting up and monitoring the home–school programme.

The approach used drew upon Topping's extensive (1983) review of provision for disruptive adolescents, the significant elements of the West Norfolk system being seen as being the use of a 'behavioural, problem solving approach, an emphasis upon the primacy of home–school liaison and . . . an effective home–pupil–school communication system'. Long argued, as have many writers on this subject, that a person outside both the home and school system 'can offer support, advice and apply pressure when necessary' in interventions that may well involve both home and school having to change significantly their perspectives on the nature of the 'problem' and on their respective responsibilities.

The particular tasks for the outside professional in this system were:

- To set up the school–parent interview. Long considered it important that this meeting was held at school because the precipitating events had occurred there and it might therefore be easier to air and clear up any early differences between home and school in the latter setting. The consultant also outlined the options available in terms of the possible routes, such as exclusion, special education or home tuition, and the negative aspects of these compared to the success rates of the recommended home–school report system. If the parents wished to be involved with the report system their suggestions regarding such aspects as possible home-based rewards were then used in the joint planning of the reporting system.
- The second task for the support worker was to visit home and school to ensure that the report was being implemented and to back up parental management. In the initial stages these visits were made at least weekly.
- The final phase for which the support worker took responsibility was the running down of the system. This was achieved by decreasing the frequency of reporting and visits when all agreed it to be justified.

Long evaluated the outcome for 44 cases treated in this way. Two support workers covering a secondary school population of 4700 worked with these pupils during an academic year, and they represent that 1 per cent or so whose problems had previously proved chronic and intransigent. The intervention was found to have achieved an 82 per cent success, or partial success rate. Full success (64 per cent) was defined as immediate improvements in attendance and behaviour at school as ascertained by a post-intervention school questionnaire, and partial success as attendance with a barely tolerable (but improved) level of behaviour.

Does 'parent training' lead to improved classroom behaviour?

Within the behavioural paradigm, another small but relevant set of literature is concerned with the possible generalization of the effects of a behavioural intervention carried out in a particular setting. This interest followed from the early work of psychologists who had achieved considerable success in teaching parents to use behavioural approaches in order to manage their children's difficult behaviour at home (O'Dell 1974). Two papers describe experimental approaches to determine whether a successful parent behaviour training programme, one that leads to a child's improved behaviour at home, will generalize so that positive changes also occur in the child's behaviour at school.

Forehand *et al.* (1979) worked with eight mother-and-child pairs, the children being aged between five and seven years. A control child of the same age and from the same class was also observed. Data were collected by independent observers before and after treatment in the home for the experimental group, and in each child's school for both the experimental and control group. In the home of the treated children both parent and child behaviours changed in a positive direction but no significant change occurred in the school behaviour of either group of children. Reviewing this study and others, McMahon and Davies (1980) concluded that:

> If the child is a behaviour problem in the classroom, then it appears that parent training is not the treatment of choice (except, of course, for the remediation of any concurrent home behaviour problems). Instead, appropriate classroom management strategies should be implemented.

This review of the research literature confirms the assertion made earlier that, if it is possible to unite parents and teachers in pursuit of strategies such as these, then it is reasonable to expect considerable improvements in the classroom behaviour of students. External consultants may sometimes have an important role to play in setting up such strategies, and we return to this issue in the next chapter. Finally, despite some popular calls for 'parent training' as the solution for classroom problems, early evidence does not support this as an effective course of action. Joint strategies appear to possess great potential, but there is no evidence to show that parent-focused approaches on their own will bring about changes in school contexts.

This highly promising evidence base for home–school strategies will count for nothing if the barriers to their execution are, for whatever reasons, impossibly high or the price of implementation is too costly. But what better focus of attention can there be for a book taking a psychosocial approach than to investigate and attempt to understand fully 'the interrelation of social factors and individual thought and behaviour' that might be cementing the sturdy foundation to these persisting barriers? Subsequent chapters address a range of factors likely to be implicated as obstacles to fuller and easier home–school cooperation but, as a starting point, certain published accounts that highlight the particular intensity and sensitivity surrounding these issues will be cited.

Barriers to home–school cooperation

The problem of antagonistic relationships between teachers and parents when pupils are experienced as difficult to manage has been graphically described within a range of research studies and accounts of practice. For example, a complex and ambitious British research project carried out by Kolvin *et al.* (1981) provided, among its findings, some empirical data concerning the relative effectiveness of certain types of home–school collaboration. Three forms of intervention with 'maladjusted' children (in the terminology of the time) attending mainstream schools were contrasted with each other and with a 'no contact' control group. Children from 12 schools were screened using several instruments to identify those with 'neurotic, antisocial, academic and/or peer relationship' difficulties and a group of 270 juniors (aged seven to eight) and 322 seniors (aged 11 and 12), who became the sample for study, were identified as definitely 'maladjusted'.

One treatment approach was psychodynamic in orientation, while a second derived from a behavioural perspective. Of particular interest to our discussion is the third group, which was described as representing the parent counselling–teacher consultation approach. In this approach specially trained social workers provided a service both to parents, in the form of short-term casework aimed at various social, financial and management issues, and to teachers, in the form of consultations over particular pupils. From work with this latter group, the project was made 'dramatically aware' of the 'extreme sensitivities' that can surround attempts to bring together school and home when a pupil is displaying difficult behaviour:

> Attempts were made to lessen mutual distrust and prejudice and ways sought to increase parental interest in the child's education and progress or, more generally, in school activities. Initially, the work consisted of carrying the teachers' ideas to the parents. Occasionally, it was necessary to reassure teachers that parents were concerned and interested . . . There was also the far more difficult operation of helping certain teachers to appreciate their personal impact on parents. This was perhaps the most sensitive area the school social workers had

to deal with; when it constituted an important issue, it had to be broached with great diplomacy and caution . . . Sometimes, before meeting, parents or teachers proposed angry confrontations with each other . . . Sometimes the teacher thought the school social worker was siding with the parents, while the parents thought the opposite.

(Kolvin *et al.* 1981: 194)

Similar points were also made in one of the most comprehensive British accounts of a consultative service to schools in respect of pupils exhibiting difficult behaviour. Coulby and Harper (1985) described and evaluated their work in a team consisting of support team teachers, an educational psychologist and a senior educational welfare officer, providing a service to some 80 primary and 15 secondary schools. Although there was a recognition that home and family factors would play a part in a pupil's school behaviour, Coulby and Harper were anxious not to minimize the findings from the literature of both school effectiveness and behavioural psychology. 'The thinking and rationale behind the team and its way of working indicate a preference to locate difficulties of classroom disruption within the school rather than ascribe it to the family of the pupil concerned.' On the other hand, where families were also deemed to require some form of intervention because of additional factors, the team was then able to suggest or arrange for the involvement of another agency.

Coulby and Harper offered a particularly graphic description of the potential for antagonism between home and school that many researchers and practitioners have noted in these circumstances:

There is still a tendency in many schools, after a particularly stormy episode, to summon parents to the head's office, in the hope that giving them a tongue-lashing will prove more effective than administering the same to their offspring. In such parental 'interviews' the values of the school and the home can be brought into sharp opposition. The results can range from sullen resentment to mutual blame. Even if the parents are prepared to wave a stick for the school, this can sometimes lead to absenteeism rather than reformation on the part of the pupil.

(Coulby and Harper 1985: 14)

Dowling and Taylor (1989) described outreach work from a clinic to a small number of primary schools. The outreach team consisted of a clinical and an educational psychologist and a teacher from the clinic. The purpose of the project was to reduce referrals to outside agencies by providing a way to address difficulties in school at an early stage. They provided a drop-in service for both parents and teachers as separate groups, as well as setting up time-tabled meetings for consultations with headteachers and other external support staff. Once again the delicacy of working between parents and teacher was addressed:

> Often a joint meeting with parents and teachers would seem the logical step to follow the drop-in session. However, careful and skilful handling is required in bringing the two parties together, as the situation can be so polarized that such an attempt could be perceived by the parent as a potential confrontation. The seemingly humble goal of reopening communication between parents and teachers must not be underestimated as it can lead to significant changes in perception of the difficulties and might release the child from the 'go-between' position.
>
> (Dowling and Taylor 1989: 26)

Many more examples such as these can be found in the published literature and the informal accounts of those professionals who work between homes and schools. Even where such relationships are of the highest quality, they can be severely tested by difficult pupil behaviour, again demonstrating that creating the conditions in which it is possible to launch home–school strategies, however strong their confirmatory research base, is a potentially delicate and complex undertaking.

However, it is certainly possible. The extracts in this section run the danger of exceeding their purpose, which is to highlight this delicacy and complexity, and turning over instead into a mood of pessimistic helplessness. It is time, then, to turn to a study of successful outcomes.

The Successful Strategies study

The Successful Strategies study was carried out as part of a series of studies at the University of Nottingham investigating psychosocial aspects of behaviour in schools. Twenty-four primary school teachers, who had all worked with EPs on strategies that they judged to have been successful, took part in detailed interviews. Different sets of findings from this study feature in a number of chapters, but for now the overall structure of the study and an outline of findings relating to cooperative work between teachers and parents is introduced.

The teachers were identified by contacting EPs in a number of LEAs and asking whether they could supply the name and address of any primary range teacher with whom they had devised an intervention deriving to a greater or lesser degree from a behavioural perspective. The pupil's behaviour had to be of an unsettled or anti-social nature and the intervention needed to have been judged by the teacher within the past two months as having been at least partially successful.

The teachers in the study

The 24 teachers so identified were drawn from eight LEAs spanning an area between the English Midlands and the Scottish border. They were nominated for the study by 20 different EPs (two EPs nominated three teachers each) and all but two taught in different schools. They had been working with primary age children for a mean of 11.6 years, the range being between two and 25 years. All the teachers interviewed except one were women, whereas they were identified by 13 female and seven male EPs. There were one teaching head, one deputy and three special needs coordinators in the sample.

The schools

The schools in which these teachers worked ranged in size from 71 to 484 pupils (excluding any nursery places), with a mean of 218. The percentage of the school population eligible for free school meals in these schools was between 3 and 67, with a mean of 21 per cent. National figures for a similar period (DES 1990) indicated average primary school sizes of 193 pupils and a take-up rate for free school meals of 13 per cent, suggesting that the schools in the sample were not untypical of the average in terms of pupil numbers but were probably slightly higher in terms of social disadvantage.

The interviews

The interviewing style was such as to encourage teachers to reflect and expand upon the points they made, and interviews were conducted in undisturbed settings after school, such as classrooms, the teachers' homes and the researcher's office. They were between 40 minutes and an hour in duration. In the main, the prepared interview comprised open rather than closed questions in order to elicit the maximum amount of data. The interviewing style followed the recommendations of Cannell and Kahn (1968) and aimed to 'create and maintain an atmosphere in which the respondent feels that he is fully understood and in which it is safe to communicate fully without fear of being judged, criticised or subsequently identified and disadvantaged'.

The pupils

The pupils were drawn from the full primary age range, with a bias towards the younger group, the mean age being 7.1 years. Of the 24 children only one was a girl. In terms of the perceived severity of the problem behaviour the majority of the 24 teachers gave vivid accounts of the type frequently found in popular discussions of discipline and behaviour in schools:

> I've been teaching 12 years and I've never met such destructive, such wanton . . . under tables . . . attacking other children under tables. (Boy aged 5)

> Aggressive and disruptive and he didn't cooperate in a group, anti-social with his peers. (Boy aged 10)

> He's very destructive, very aggressive, spitting, bad language and so on . . . just felt, well, it's not doing them [the children] any good and it's not doing me any good and it's not doing my family any good. I came home at night and I was so wound up. (Boy aged 6)

> Quite aggressive to teachers as well as children . . . if you refused a request of his . . . he'd be throwing chairs and leave the classroom, leave the school quite frequently as well. (Boy aged 10)

> A lot of physical abuse on teachers and people that were supporting him . . . an incident of arson and various other things outside school. (Boy aged 6)

> He was causing a lot of problems for her [his mother] at home in that he was having tantrums, refusing to do whatever she told him, throwing things, swearing, kicking, generally uncontrollable for her. (Boy aged 5)

In terms of perceived *severity*, ten teachers said the pupil was the most difficult they had ever encountered and eight said he or she was among the most difficult half dozen.

The relationships with the parents

Given everything that has already been said about the strain and tensions between school and home, it will be no surprise that the teachers frequently mentioned the parents of the children. In many cases, there was a perceived lack of support or 'back up' from home, and this was seen to be a serious impediment to some form of resolution. Quotes from five of the interviews illustrate the texture of these beliefs:

> Darren's mum had been very critical of how he had been handled . . . she's got a hair trigger. (Interview 18)

> Mum had caused so many problems here . . . she's a very bristly lady. (Interview 15)

> What we lacked before was cooperation from the parents. (Interview 20)

> We did try to get the parents involved. We got very little support from home at that time. (Interview 22)

> The mother had had such negative feelings about any involvement. (Interview 6)

Key features of the strategies

The strategies devised between the teachers and EPs contained a number of common elements, the most prominent of which appeared to be variations on themes introduced in Chapter 3, with some deriving directly from the original, classic study by Madsen *et al*. (1968). So, increased use of praise, the ignoring of certain behaviour and closer attention to and elaboration of classroom rules all showed prominence. However, the other major feature was the involvement of the EPs with both teachers and parents. In 18 of the 24 cases, meetings involving these three parties were arranged, whereas in the other six cases, the EPs made visits between home and school, as some form of 'shuttle diplomacy', carrying information between each party and setting up common approaches. A number of different methods for recording progress towards targets and exchanging information between home and school also featured in many of the examples.

Clearly, either all the participants must have been extremely calm and highly motivated, given the fraught relationships between home and school reported frequently to surround difficult behaviour, or much more was happening here than the setting up of seemingly simplistic behavioural strategies. This issue is subjected to much closer examination in subsequent chapters.

Perceived changes in pupils' behaviour

The sample consisted of teachers who judged the behavioural interventions devised with the EP to have had positive outcomes. A selection of their comments, again from the first three and last three interviews, as above, gives a flavour of these responses:

> Quite honestly I can say I was knocked for six because it had worked and it has worked ever since. (Interview 1)

I think now that he's found that it's easier for him if he cooperates in school. (Interview 2)

I can honestly say he's not like the same child. (Interview 3)

I think he was finally motivated to do something about it [behaviour] and it was quite evident he was very involved in this. (Interview 22)

Towards the end of last term I felt very positive about what had been achieved . . . but this term the last couple of weeks for some reason have been awful. I'm hoping it was just Christmas . . . and yesterday was a very good day. (Interview 23)

It was one of those wonderful ahh, this is great, one of those wonderful success stories. (Interview 24)

In total, six interviewees expressed the view that the intervention had been successful but had some reservations, such as that there might be a deterioration again in the future (as in Interview 23). Eleven saw a definite improvement with no qualifications (as in Interview 1), and seven saw such a degree of success that it made a strong emotional impact on them (as in Interview 24).

Perceived changes in teachers' relationships with parents

Interview 18
> *Before:* Darren's mum had been very critical of how he had been handled . . . she's got a hair trigger.
> *After:* Mum came in every single night to check . . . I think she feels the more help she gets the better.

Interview 15
> *Before:* Mum had caused so many problems here . . . she's a very bristly lady.
> *After:* Mum and I got on quite well . . . I feel she's got some respect for what I'm trying to do for him.

Interview 20
> *Before:* What we lacked before was cooperation from the parents.
> *After:* Any time I meet the parents they're very enthusiastic now.

Interview 22
> *Before:* We did try to get the parents involved. We got very little support from home at that time.

After: The head, after her conversations with the parents, would then come to me and say, 'They're really pleased, you know.'

Interview 6
   Before: The mother had had such negative feelings about any involvement.
   After: She said, 'You don't know how much you've achieved with him' . . . she's so positive about the improvement.

In terms of the whole sample, 16 of the 24 teachers volunteered that they had experienced a significant change in the level of 'back-up' from home during the strategy, with seven of these seeing this as an extreme change. It is important to add here that the interviews did not directly ask about perceptions of collaboration with parents, but instead raised the more general question about the factors to which the teachers attributed the successes of the strategies. In view of all that has already been said about the barriers to setting up effective home–school strategies, clearly something, or some things, have happened within many of these case studies that merit closer attention, a scrutiny that takes place in a number of subsequent chapters.

School-based advice and support or external consultants?

Before we take a closer look at the Successful Strategies research, it is necessary to say a brief word about EPs as external consultants to schools. Clearly, schools cannot be reaching for external assistance every time a problem with student behaviour is encountered. Even if the required level of resourcing of external personnel were ever to be available, this would be highly undesirable. Much current legislation requires schools to develop and extend the skills of staff in this area, and the discussion of 'generalization' in Chapter 3 emphasizes the repeated finding that new skills in managing pupil behaviour have not easily spread among staff or to new but similar challenges for specific teachers.

This book does not make simple or definitive pronouncements about when it is desirable for school staff to be solely responsible for effecting strategies and when the perspective of external professionals may best, or should, be sought. Instead, it attempts to provide a full and honest exposition of the psychosocial processes surrounding difficult behaviour in schools, so that teachers may proceed in collaboration or independently with a confident understanding of the subtle complexities surrounding successful strategies.

5 Consulting with teachers – and parents

This chapter takes a closer look at the nature of the working relationship that is formed when teachers and EPs work together to devise and implement strategies, drawing again on data obtained from the Successful Strategies study. The emotional consequences for teachers attempting to manage difficult behaviour in their classrooms, and the additional demands when acting in partnership with parents, are illustrated with data from the study. The delicate and ambiguous territory between school and home is illustrated by teachers' comments and, employing the concept from systems theory, discussed as a set of 'boundary issues'. The important and useful features of the collaboration with the EPs, as identified by the teachers in this study, are examined and utilized as an introduction to some of the more theoretical accounts of the process of 'consultation'. The chapter concludes with a wider review of the published literature on consultation in schools.

Introduction

Chapter 4 introduced a study of successful practice involving teachers, parents and EPs. It also reiterated the common caution against assuming that such interventions can be easily implemented in the tense atmosphere that often surrounds difficult behaviour. The key aspects of the strategies outlined, although supported by the respectable evidence base outlined in Chapter 3, are hardly novel or revolutionary. In fact, strategies such as these in the form of 'tips and techniques' are to be found in a host of publications aimed at teachers. With a common perception that difficult behaviour in schools is on the increase, clearly these publications have failed to have an effect, either because they have remained unheeded (which is unlikely given the huge programmes of training in behaviour management that have been provided for teachers ever since the publication of the Elton Report), or because these key aspects themselves are far from the whole story when it comes to successful interventions.

One major difference between using suggested strategies from a textbook and engaging in a professional consultation is obviously the personal contact afforded by the latter. Given the high emotions that can surround difficult student behaviour, it is likely that successful consultations will also be effectively addressing these in some way. Consequently, this chapter opens with a review of the data from the Successful Strategies study, referring to emotional aspects for those teachers taking part.

Emotional consequences of having to manage difficult behaviour in classrooms

In Chapter 4, we considered the frustrations expressed by teachers about the difficulty of obtaining parental support or 'back-up'. Feelings of mutual suspicion, recrimination and blame were also voiced in other studies quoted. In this section we examine the data from interviews with the 24 teachers in order to identify, at a slightly more detailed level, the emotional consequences of attempting to manage difficult behaviour in the classroom.

For some, such as the deputy headteacher from Chapter 4 faced with a most challenging six-year-old, the original *stresses were transferring into life at home*. Another said, 'Quite honestly, never having met a child like this in 12 years of teaching, I would go home some days and say "I don't know what to do next"' (Interview 1). Additionally, these stresses provoked doubt among some of the teachers about their *professional competence* in general:

> I really was upset because I felt that I was failing, and I mean I've taught for a long time and I can honestly say I've never felt like that before. I just felt that I couldn't cope. (Interview 3)

> You sometimes think, will they [colleagues] think it's me, that I'm inadequate? (Interview 21)

A third emotional component, experienced by most of the teachers, was a sense of *feeling alone and solely responsible* for the pupil's behaviour, *even in schools where colleagues were seen as generally friendly and supportive*. This feeling was conveyed strongly in 10 instances and in a more mixed fashion in another nine:

> It's a fairly strong feeling, you know, you keep your problems in your classroom. (Interview 10)

> I don't think anyone else was that interested to be honest . . . he's my problem, Lee. And I don't think anyone thought that much about it. (Interview 14)

There was a lot of feeling from other [staff] that he shouldn't be [in our school] . . . When he was naughty in assembly I was the one who always had to fetch him out . . . I always had to have him. Nobody ever said to me, 'Look I'll take him for you while you get on with what you're supposed to be doing.' (Interview 17)

I was very aware that the rest of the staff . . . would blame Darren for anything because they always have done . . . I was having a lot – no, a fair amount of opposition from the head . . . any kind of misdemeanour on Darren's part was just jumped on . . . you can feel quite isolated in a school. (Interview 18)

These are strong emotions. Support from within schools, both through formal, hierarchical channels and informal staff interactions, as well as that available from outside agencies, will need to recognize that 'difficult behaviour' often gives rise to intense and unpalatable feelings. This presents a set of dilemmas and challenges. How legitimate is it to acknowledge such feelings? Will teachers feel like failures or that they are being judged as 'unprofessional'? How can feelings be expressed safely, without spreading a sense of pessimism and help-lessness? If the formal, espoused aspects of the organization (as outlined in Chapter 2) do not, or cannot, address these issues, will a less tangible and morale-sapping culture arise to assume this function?

If a student's classroom behaviour is experienced as difficult to manage, this can be construed as a form of strained relationship, in the form of an absence or loss of an easy understanding between student and teacher, for whatever reason, about certain basic classroom expectations. A high degree of anxiety or antagonism between teacher and parent is also very likely.

Boundary tensions between school and home

Relationships between teachers and parents, which always have the potential to become confrontational or, at least, discordant, are usually never more stretched than in the case of difficult pupil behaviour. In recognition of this, some of the legislation discussed in Chapter 1 attempts to delineate respective responsibilities. But a close examination reveals that this is desperately ambiguous territory. Where does the responsibility for taking action begin and end for the school? Chapter 2 highlighted the importance afforded by systems theories to boundary issues and the interviews in the Successful Strategies study brought to light much of the finer detail of these when a student is perceived in school as displaying challenging behaviour.

Throughout the interviews the issue of an original 'lack of support' or 'back-up' from home was cited. The teachers perceived it to be impossible to feel a unity of purpose and action with parents over the difficult classroom behaviour of their children; a barrier was perceived and attributed to the parents:

> What we lacked before was cooperation from the parents. (Interview 20)

> We did try to get the parents involved. We got very little support from home at that time. (Interview 22)

The interviews reveal four different types of boundary issue between school and home: the system's internal functioning; the negotiation of shared meanings across the boundary with the environment; uncertainty over the predictability of aspects of the environment; and uncertainty over the actual location of the boundary itself (Rice 1976).

Internal functioning

Maintenance functions within a system enable its members to contribute towards the primary task rather than having to divert their energies unnecessarily into preserving homoeostasis. (see Chapter 6) These maintenance functions take the form of administrative procedures and a common identification with a set of beliefs, values and norms.

In the interviews, administrative procedures were not seen as a barrier to working with parents, except in one case where the teacher said, 'To be honest, I didn't actually see a great deal of the parents, they usually went straight to the head' (Interview 22). More significant was the teacher's obligation to share the responsibility for the way the school had previously responded to the child or parent, either in terms of being unable to acknowledge the possible legitimacy of a parent's claim or by being the recipient for angry feelings originally engendered in respect of another member of staff.

> [Mother] was very critical of how he'd been handled in the past . . . You have to handle her very carefully in a certain manner. I think in previous years that hadn't been done. (Interview 18)

> [Mother] was very anti Miss Roberts [headteacher]. (Interview 15)

The negotiation of shared meanings

In order to function, an institution must arrive at shared definitions of problematic situations. Particularly in the case of difficult behaviour, where the sense of individual threat to teachers' professional competence is so high, it becomes imperative to have an explanatory framework that will command collegiate acceptance. However, such definitions are often unacceptable to parents and apprehension or uncomfortable experiences in this area form a frequently cited barrier to working with parents.

> His mother said he never misbehaved in the home and that was the biggest stumbling block because he was 'good at home' and she was blaming the school. (Interview 2)

> She was very protective of Gary, in her eyes he can do no wrong. (Interview 22)

> I didn't think the mum thought he was a problem. (Interview 14)

Such definitions, which evidence does or does not require attention, the actual descriptors used and the explanatory mechanisms to be assumed, implied or elaborated – all these are derived during a process of socialization into an institution. To members of the institution they become part of the shared, taken-for-granted, common-sense knowledge (Berger and Luckman 1966). However, parents, in addition to having different perspectives and interests, are also not party to this institutionalizing process. It is little wonder therefore that attempts to include parents within the teacher's or school's definition by means of a few meetings, or even one, lead to such angry exchanges:

> Mother is very, very nervous and flares up at the slightest thing. (Interview 18)

> [The parents] were very, very touchy. (Interview 23)

> Mother had caused so many problems here. She's a very bristly lady. (Interview 15)

> The mother had come in and had a row with the supply teacher in front of the whole class . . . shouting and screaming at her. (Interview 7)

In these examples the emotional interactions are all attributed to characteristics of the parents, usually 'the mother'. However, although less common, there was also some recognition that a barrier to communicating effectively might also originate from the school's side, in the form of a lack of certain interaction skills. These are sometimes alluded to during answers to questions about the particular abilities that seem to be possessed by the EP:

> Maybe we didn't talk as straight as Tina [EP] would have wanted us to. I know she goes into the homes and seems to have a good rapport . . . but I think perhaps we flannelled a bit. (Interview 7)

> She's [EP] had training in listening as well as talking and in also the sort of questions she wanted to ask. (Interview 4)

Interestingly, in these latter examples the differences that the teachers see between themselves and the EPs are in terms of interactional skills, whereas the parents were all construed in typifications concerning emotional instability. In considering the parents, the psychologists and themselves, no teachers construed the interactions as reflecting the various role positions of each party with respect to the other.

Uncertainty over the predictability of aspects of the environment

In systems theory, uncertainty in the environment, the inability to predict the nature of interactions across the boundary because of the possible range of behaviour that may be encountered in sections of the external world, is taken to be a major contributor to decreasing homoeostasis of the system. Working with the parents of pupils exhibiting difficult behaviour provides ample scope for such uncertainty and examples have already been provided of this in the construction of parents as emotionally unstable.

Another major aspect is a teacher perception of parents having an alien lifestyle or set of mores. Although this aspect is often linked to a possible explanatory mechanism for a pupil's behaviour, there is also a sense that it exists in some teachers' eyes as a barrier to working together:

> He's got no dad but there's a man living there. (Interview 14)

> She [mother] has a series of boyfriends . . . she talks about different men being there. (Interview 9)

> She watches adult films and has a lot of adult vocabulary on occasions. (Interview 20)

The uncertain status of a parent's (always the mother's) sexual relationships is often referred to as though it automatically makes conversation or problem-solving more contentious. Other teachers in the sample, however, also make very favourable comments about the effects of a new partner on the pupil under discussion.

A final source of the perceived barrier derives from judgements about the intellectual ability or maturity of a parent: '[Mother's] really like a girl of about 14 . . . not very bright but she means well' (Interview 3).

Uncertainty over the location of the boundary with the environment

Another common uncertainty concerns the degree to which parents and teachers might construe differently the extent of each other's responsibilities and thus lead to difficult boundary transactions – in fact, to a difficulty in deciding upon the exact location of the boundary itself. Teachers sometimes expressed a lack of confidence about the extent to which they would or should be allowed to inquire about events at home and offer advice and suggestions:

> I think sometimes they think 'Oh you're . . . Because [EP] is involved, somebody official, it's not so much like prying, it's not like prying from school.' (Interview 9)

> The mother came in looking for assistance originally and said 'Smack her if she needs it, she needs a good wallop sometimes.' But to me some attention from the mother would have gone a long way to assuaging some of the difficulties we were having with the child. (Interview 20)

> I wouldn't like to start involving parents with things like money if I didn't know it was going to be profitable(!) (Interview 11)

> I don't remember us actually saying 'Look, he needs a wash!' (Interview 7)

There is also a belief that the home culture is such that any comments from school about a pupil's behaviour will only contribute to a downwards spiral for the child or parent or both:

> I'll say to her sometimes, 'What's he been like at home?' and she'll say, 'Oh, he's been terrible,' and I'll say 'Well unfortunately he's not had a good day at school either.' It's *extremely* difficult, you know, the fine balance. I tend to give him . . . average [ratings on a chart]. (Interview 13)

> I think she just dreaded coming in because of what we would say about him. (Interview 16)

In addition to all the immediate classroom and school-based challenges for teachers in managing difficult behaviour, this discussion of boundary issues demonstrates that boundary tensions between school and home will also make an emotional impact – perhaps in some cases a huge one – upon teachers.

How consultation is more than giving advice

Given the feelings expressed by the teachers above, and the delicate and ambiguous boundary between school and home, any effective process of consultation over difficult behaviour will have to go some way beyond the pupil management strategies typically found in the textbooks. It will also have to travel the potentially unsettling territory of emotions such as anxiety, threat and shame. Yet we, as a society, occupy an uncomfortable position in relation to help-seeking. At one end of a spectrum we envisage the overly precious self-absorption of the 'therapy generation' and at the other the cold and clipped pragmatism of the emotionally neutered. Neither of these caricatures is helpful but both cast a long shadow over the search for effective ways of working together productively in emotionally charged circumstances. In most forms of human conflict, from international tensions through to strained intimate relationships, it is recognized that effective mediation by an external person or body is sometimes the best or only hope for reconciliation and agreement on ways forward.

In order to develop a greater insight into the face-to-face consultations in the Successful Strategies study, the full set of transcripts was analysed and every comment referring to the EPs' behaviour, suggestions or manner was coded and categorized. Four broad categories emerged: knowledge, skills, personal qualities and aspects of role.

The knowledge base

The teachers in this study made frequent reference to the knowledge they perceived their consultant EP as possessing. While consultants may aim to impart new knowledge, it is instructive to examine the recipients' perspective in terms of salience and effectiveness.

Many of the teachers felt that the psychologist had had *experience of successful interventions with other pupils*:

> She gave some examples of how she'd tried it with other children and they had been very successful. (Interview 11)

> She's seen it so many times in so many different places. I mean she's drawing on all her resources, isn't she, from previous experiences? (Interview 7)

One teacher also expressed the view that this experience would be much broader than could be gained by a teacher, even one working in a specialist capacity within a school:

> It was quite obvious that Carol had come across the situation, had lots of information at her fingertips and could actually cheer you up with the news that this child wasn't the worst behaved one in the world. Whereas a member of staff may not have come across the same situation, [even if] they were the special needs expert. (Interview 20)

There was a more mixed view among those who commented upon the exact nature of this *specialist knowledge*. A few felt critical that this knowledge did not seem to be any more technical than their own:

> I thought perhaps she was looking at it a bit too simplistically. I was expecting something . . . I don't know how to say it, perhaps a little bit more technical. I didn't expect it to be quite so simple. I think I expected a lot more hype . . . perhaps something that she would have from her research or whatever. (Interview 18)

The majority, however, saw the knowledge that informed the strategy as characterized by a sense of timing and appropriateness:

> He was a professional so he knew what to do . . . he was very specific about exactly what I should be doing, the length of time I should be doing it, and so therefore I felt that must be the right thing to do. (Interview 8)

An area of practical knowledge that many of the teachers appreciated seeing in their psychologists was a recognition of the *constraints* imposed upon their time by the realities of classroom teaching. This was a subject that sometimes elicited accounts of other much less successful encounters with psychologists, or stories about the experiences of other teachers they had known:

> It was very simple what she did. Because there was no way I could keep reams and reams of notes. (Interview 16)

> I think she was very realistic about the programme. I know I have dealt on several occasions with educational psychologists who have a rather rosy view sometimes of classroom existence . . . I have been given tick sheets for how many times they do this or that . . . quite honestly it's impossible to do in a class of that size. There was no way I could note down the time they did something or how long they did it. (Interview 20)

The main way in which these constraints could be appreciated was by the psychologist spending some *time actually in the classroom*:

> He'd been in, he'd watched them, he'd seen me working with them. (Interview 3)

> I was quite cross that she was talking about this child on a piece of paper, that she hadn't actually got to know Brian and come to work with him in the classroom. I can remember going home feeling quite angry about that. And that's when I actually asked her if she would come in and see him. (Interview 15)

> It's really just to get them to say, 'Yes I can see what you mean' or a bit of . . . I don't know . . . it probably wouldn't be any better . . . I just think it might put a different slant on it. I don't know to be honest, now I've talked about it, it sounds a bit silly. (Interview 14)

In general, although there are some indications that teachers perceive psychologists as having a theoretical and research base that may prove helpful, their comments are hedged in with a number of qualifications and reservations. This suggests that actual specialist knowledge *per se* was not seen as the main contributor to these particularly successful interventions. Real examples of interventions that had been devised by the EP and proved successful, and at least some direct experience of the classroom context and the pupil, were accorded far more credibility. Although the more theoretical issues raised by this are not discussed here, the interested reader may refer to Miller (1996).

The skills

Three main skill areas emerge from the interviews – listening, questioning and problem-solving – and all are commented upon in far more unequivocal and positive terms than aspects of the knowledge base. *Listening* was seen as an active process, sometimes akin to a counselling procedure, that aided problem-solving:

> The most valuable thing for us is for somebody to listen to our problems, like talking it through and trying to help us see one thing at a time. (Interview 6)

> She listened. Teachers have an awful habit of chipping in, don't they? . . . She listens and I'm sure she picks up lots of vibes [with parents]

just by listening, whereas we don't because we're thinking of the answers to the next question. (Interview 15)

Intimately linked up with an active listening approach is the use of *questioning*:

She's had training in listening as well as talking and in the sort of questions she wanted to ask. (Interview 4)

I think the way she questioned me, she got that information and the way she spoke to me, she encouraged me to talk . . . I think I almost discovered something of what I was doing myself, and probably I didn't even know I was doing it. (Interview 18)

Both of these skills feed into the *joint problem-solving* that subsequently takes place:

There was that kind of emphasis of looking and exploring ways of developing strategies . . . there was sort of a tone of careful step building . . . it was more analytical I think than the way a teacher would handle it and perhaps more objective. Less waffly, perhaps. (Interview 23)

Many of the teachers in the sample commented favourably on the fact that during this planning procedure, the psychologist had *avoided adopting a dogmatic stance*. This point was often made with a sense of relief, as if there had been an expectation of a different type of approach.

She doesn't dictate, she doesn't say, 'Do this.' (Interview 7)

I'm delighted to say that I've never been in a situation where I've been told what to do, you know, just like a child. (Interview 6)

I don't think she was trying to teach me, my job or whatever. (Interview 13)

Another closely related aspect that emerged from the interviews was that many of the teachers appreciated the working relationship being one in which they could feel at *liberty to challenge* the psychologist's suggestions:

One thing she said that encouraged me was . . . 'Some of the things that I'm going to suggest to you will really get up your nose as a teacher.' She said, 'I will tell you that now,' and she said, 'I want you to say . . . "it won't work for me".' So that was really good because we had the relationship and I then felt the freedom to say to her, 'No, I can't do that.' (Interview 1)

On one occasion I think I just said to him, 'It's all right you saying this, that and the other, but it's different when I'm in there and I've got the parents queuing up outside the door complaining' . . . We just talked round it, we didn't . . . we always got on very well. (Interview 17)

Personal qualities

The interviews revealed a complex interaction between what might be termed the personal qualities of the psychologist and the skills already considered above. Although no definite dividing line can be drawn between the two, it is possible to add some clarity to the understanding of successful consultative behaviour by attempting to make finer distinctions.

The most frequently occurring and most widely appreciated of these qualities was the psychologist's *encouraging approach*:

> The first thing she did for me, if nothing else, she made me feel that I was worthy and she made me feel that I was doing the right thing. She made me feel that all was not lost and she gave me more confidence to go on and to persevere . . . she was really sort of heartening and she sort of spurred you on to do more. (Interview 18)

Another feature identified by a number of the teachers was the psychologist's *empathy* with the emotional reactions produced in the teacher by the pupil's behaviour:

> He said he would have it all on to cope with these two. I mean he'd been in, he'd watched them, he'd seen me working with them and he said, 'It's enough to drive anybody round the bend, you're doing well' . . . Obviously, as a psychologist he was boosting my morale but it's still nice to be told. (Interview 3)

> The feeling that there's somebody else who knows . . . If you got so desperate, there's somebody else in the authority who knows what's going on. (Interview 17)

A slightly different personal quality was the ability to act as a *facilitator of social interactions*, especially in meetings that also involved parents.

> She smiled a lot . . . she was just a very calm, collected person. (Interview 16)

> She seemed calm and always positive . . . she would never get cross. When we had the small group [of staff] she wouldn't get cross with people and everything she said brought the positive side out of them. (Interview 19)

Aspects of role

In addition to the knowledge and the various skills and qualities that the teachers identified as being important, there was also a range of comments alluding to aspects of the role of the psychologist. Some teachers referred to the psychologist as an *'authority figure'*, although the nature of this authority was variously construed:

> He had the authority to make suggestions and he also in a way was taking some of the responsibility. (Interview 3)

> Because it was an outside agency perhaps one feels that you have to respond a little bit more positively to what they are going to be saying. (Interview 22)

By being external to the everyday life of the school, the psychologists were also seen to be more *detached from the emotional effects* of the difficult behaviour:

> He was more detached, he didn't obviously have the same level of panic that I was getting into. (Interview 5)

> It's nice to meet and talk to someone who's not involved with the day-to-day turmoil, or can look at it in a detached manner. (Interview 21)

Another characteristic of this more detached position is that it *allows basic information-seeking questions to be asked*. A special educational needs coordinator explained how it was far less easy for her to ask the same questions about a pupil of whom she would have at least a fleeting knowledge:

> It takes somebody out of the situation. You see if I went in and said to a member of staff, who might be much more mature than me and have a lot more experience, 'Now what do you mean by badly

behaved?', if I said that, it could come over as me saying, 'You don't know what badly behaved means,' or taken another way. But because it's coming from an objective situation, not having seen the child, and trying to get a clear comprehensive picture, then it's taken in the manner in which it's intended. (Interview 6)

The external position was also seen to contribute to the psychologist being able to act as an *arbiter*, especially between school and parents.

> Mum and dad sat over there, Sandra sat there, and I sat there and Miss Jones sat here . . . It was an 'us and them' situation. She was very quiet, she listened a lot . . . [and] acted as a judge and jury in a way. (Interview 15)

> Quite often if you've got an interview between a parent and a teacher, it starts off at an aggressive . . . If an interview is set up with a psychologist, because they are obviously not to blame, there's no element of blame there. It's somebody removed from the situation . . . We still get a starting off by accusing the school to a certain extent but then it breaks down and you get to look more into the home side of things because the psychologist is there . . . and delves into it. (Interview 24)

Within these examples of the knowledge base, skills, personal qualities and role positions of effective consultants, there are clearly some character-istics that can apply equally to personnel inside a school – special needs coordinators or senior management team members, for instance – and some that belong more appropriately to external professionals such as educational psychologists and behaviour support teachers. Which belongs where may vary slightly depending on the circumstances of each particular case. However, where there are evident boundary tensions, then an external professional whose skills include those of effective mediation may well make an important, or even essential, contribution. The priority is an understanding of the full nature of the consultative process. With such knowledge, a more informed decision about who should do what will then become possible in each particu-lar case.

Models of consultation

A number of writers have offered definitions of the term 'consultation'. Conoley and Conoley (1990) describe it as a problem-solving relationship between professionals from different fields, having aspects in common with psychotherapy and advice giving. Unlike psychotherapy, however, they argue that consultation only focuses upon work-related problems and avoids 'intra-psychic' material. And although advice may be given by a consultant, the primary purpose is to enhance the problem-solving capacity of the consultee, the teacher in this instance. Merely providing answers to questions is not seen as the most likely means by which this may be accomplished.

According to Conoley and Conoley (1990), consultants aim to provide:

- new knowledge;
- new skills;
- a greater sense of self-efficacy;
- a greater degree of objectivity in the consultee.

West and Idol (1987) make a number of similar points in defining consultation as a technique that always possesses the following six characteristics:

- it is a helping, problem-solving process;
- it occurs between a professional help-giver and help-seeker, the latter having responsibility for the welfare of another person;
- it is a voluntary relationship;
- the help-giver and the help-seeker share in solving the problem;
- the goal is to help to solve a current work problem of the help-seeker;
- the help-seeker profits in respect of future problems.

Many of these features, but not all of them, are apparent in the teacher comments from the Successful Strategies study.

West and Idol (1987) provide a simple but extremely useful model for illustrating the skills and knowledge required by successful consultants (see Figure 5.1). In this model, there is a separation between the knowledge base that informs the interaction between the consultant and the consultee (Knowledge Base 1) and the base that provides the techniques and insights used by the consultee in working with the client (Knowledge Base 2). In the context of

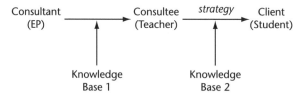

Figure 5.1 West and Idol's model of the two knowledge bases that inform consultation in schools

difficult behaviour in schools, one major area of evidence informing Knowledge Base 2 is the research into classroom-based strategies reviewed in Chapter 3. The teachers above identified consultant factors such as experience of successful interventions elsewhere and specialist research knowledge, and these may be seen as examples of Knowledge Base 2. However, West and Idol also drew attention to a Knowledge Base 1, which could include many of the other examples above. Listening, questioning and problem-solving skills, encouraging and empathizing can all be necessary contributors to the working relationship between the teacher and EP, rather than techniques to be used directly with the student.

Working within the coherent framework from Figure 2.3, consulting to teachers and parents together requires a slightly different model of consultation. Because of the extreme sensitivities that can surround this area of work, a consultant working without a clear framework runs the risk of exacerbating an already tense situation and escalating a barrier into a barricade. West and Idol's model can be extended to provide guidance and structure for a consultant in these circumstances, as in Figure 5.2

In this, Knowledge Base 2 remains focused upon strategies that will be used this time with teachers and parents working together with the young person, as happened in many of the interventions in the Successful Strategies study. Here elements of home-based reinforcement approaches, in turn based on the earlier strategies described in Chapter 3, may be found. Knowledge Base 1, however, now becomes potentially more complex, referring as it does to the consultant working not only with a teacher and a parent individually, but also with the changing relationship between them. Again the teachers' remarks above draw attention to many of these, including all the factors already mentioned, with skills in arbitrating and facilitating interaction also perhaps coming especially to the fore.

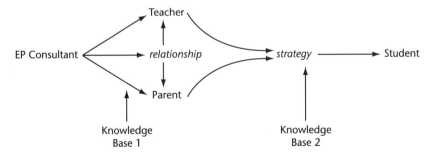

Figure 5.2 A model of the two knowledge bases that inform teacher–parent consultations

Other perspectives on consultation

In order to understand the process of consultation more fully, this chapter now turns to a brief review of what others writing in this area have had to say about these particular ways of working. Although it is seemingly simple and straightforward at one level, effective consultation can also be seen as a subtle and delicate undertaking, steering a course between thoughts and feelings, the professional and the personal.

The earliest studies

The earliest reference in the literature to working jointly with schools and families in instances when children are showing unsettled or disturbing behaviour is to be found in Tucker and Dyson (1976). These professionals were, respectively, a family therapist and educational consultant with a family psychiatry department and a senior administrator for a school district in Pennsylvania. They described a pilot project with two elementary schools, the purpose of which was to test the feasibility of utilizing the processes of family therapy to reverse the maladaptive school behaviour of children and facilitate constructive interactions both between the school and home, and among school personnel. They were concerned that parents and teachers seldom met outside formalized contact times unless there was a severe problem, and that under such circumstances these meetings became a confrontation between adversaries in an atmosphere of 'alienation, scapegoating and blame'.

A major intention was to find a way to diminish this mutual scapegoating by helping parents and teachers to understand each other's motives and actions. One major method used was a series of weekly meetings involving three or four teachers who taught the same children, the principal, the school psychologist and the family therapist. It was reported that, in these discussions, teachers frequently gained greater insights into the ways in which they might be encouraging some of their pupils' provocative behaviour. Tucker and Dyson, perhaps showing their background in family therapy, commented that as the group proceeded it became apparent that it was functioning in ways frequently observed in families, with the teachers often acting as a group of siblings.

In a later stage of the project, families of children who were having difficulties in school were invited to meet with the principal, the psychologist, a member of the teaching team and the family consultant. By using principles deriving from family therapy practice – the definition and observation of boundaries, clarifying roles, creating a non-critical atmosphere – the authors claimed to be able to provide the security that permitted and encouraged individuals to share relevant material within agreed parameters. Some of these meetings were held with the expectation that a family would accept a referral for family therapy, but many were intended solely to serve the purpose of exchanging information, modifying perceptions and sharing ideas and suggestions. Tucker and Dyson claimed that the project produced substantial benefits for the schools, the families and the body of professional knowledge.

Following this work, Aponte (1976) illustrated the approach in action with a case study of a 10-year-old who was frequently involved in fights with other boys at school. In this example the therapist brought together for an initial meeting in school two therapists, the three teachers who taught the pupil, the principal, mother, father and child (they had wanted to include the boy's five siblings as well!). Important role implications for the therapist, consultant or whoever is responsible for the intervention are pointed out:

> The teachers . . . do not expect to be treated as clients. The prospect of being interviewed with the child and his parents brings into question the school staff's status in relation to their pupil. And yet the therapists are being called upon to accomplish something neither the family nor the school could do and thus must lead the three-way effort . . . to solve the problem.

Subsequent studies

Taylor (1982) described the responsibility placed upon a pupil to act as 'go-between' when the two systems of family and school fail to mesh: 'As the lynch-pin between them he is the focus of the greatest stress and any indications of a bad fit are going to manifest themselves in him.'

Using two case studies, Taylor outlined a method of working that involves an initial family interview in school followed by continuing consultations with school staff. In one case study, she described involving two of the school staff for the first half-hour of the family consultation, 'to voice the complaints of the school and to have an initial response from the parents and [the pupil]'. This understandably generated strong feelings in the parents and these then became the focus for much of the rest of the meeting. In this way Taylor was working to some degree along the lines described by Aponte but had pulled back from a full application of his ecosystemic approach. Aponte acknowledged the difficulties as well as the benefits posed by working with members of the two systems always physically together, and Taylor opted for some separation between the two.

Taylor saw the theoretical roots of this type of practice as lying within a number of fields:

> The would-be consultant . . . owes a debt to many approaches in the field of mental health . . . a psychodynamic understanding of the life

cycle; systems theory, learning theory and crisis theory; techniques of brief therapy, family therapy and consultation and, for work in schools, at least a nodding acquaintance with the literature of organizational development. Trying to determine which is the major influence in this or that tactic can lead to the proverbial problem of the centipede.

She argued that it was imperative to find early in the interview an explicit focus to work on that is accepted by the family and has meaning for them: 'Tasks which involve the school and the family can help to change the dysfunctional interaction between the two systems and can be regularly monitored by the consultant on his regular visits to school.' In 1983, Fine and Holt again reviewed the approach advanced by Tucker and Dyson and Aponte, and, drawing on their experience of such work, cautioned others against unrealistic expectations by highlighting a number of important considerations.

They drew attention to the sophisticated and dynamic nature of consultation with a systems orientation. It was far harder to draw up a set of repeatable procedures for a consultant, they argued, than it was in the use of behavioural approaches where standard formats and manuals were in existence. Because of this, some consultants felt less comfortable, by virtue of their own temperament, with work with a far less predictable course of action and outcomes. Problems with identification of the 'client system' were also raised. Within a more traditional mental health consultation position, 'the client, that is, the child with a problem, is seen as the responsibility of the consultee, the teacher . . . When the consultant views the client system as the child in interaction with the teacher and the classroom environment, then the consultative relationship is likely to change.'

In 1985, Dowling and Osborne's book *The Family and the School: A Joint Systems Approach* (revised in 1994) brought together a collection of papers by practitioners associated with the Tavistock Clinic. In the opening chapter Dowling sets out the theoretical framework for the 'joint systems' approach, adding to earlier formulations that drew mainly upon concepts from family therapy by drawing parallels with the systems thinking developing in relation to educational institutions. In particular, she points to notions such as decision-making executive subsystems within both family and school systems and to the prominence and nature of rules in the form of both ground rules and meta-rules, the former referring to the specifics of the way a system functions and the latter to the meaning of the ground rules.

At the same time, in the American context, Power and Bartholomew (1985) presented in some detail a case study aimed at intervening between a school and family system, 'getting uncaught in the middle' as they termed it. These workers, a psychologist and a consultant, drew upon the family systems approach of Minuchin and Haley to provide a model for their intervention planning with a 10-year-old boy whose school was concerned about his poor academic performance and his facial tics. This paper went further than the earlier examples of ecosystemic approaches by providing a more detailed assessment of the problem in terms of symmetrical relationships and hier-archical problems, and joint meetings with staff and parents were planned and conducted in the same way as family therapy sessions.

In this particular case the home–school conflict was seen as providing an issue on which the parents could collaborate and thus afford a partial solution to their own relationship problems. To become 'uncaught' the team needed to understand how the family–school pattern mirrored the family pattern, establish a clear boundary between the home and school domains, validate the authority of each party in their own domain and provide a new way for the parents to unite their energies.

In addition to recognizing the need to work with this dynamic, Power and Bartholomew acknowledged a dilemma common to school consultants: 'Since the team was contracted by school personnel, in effect they were mandated to validate the school's position in the conflict. If the team had not sanctioned the school's position, any power they had as consultants would have been lost.' Notions of the client and lines of accountability thus intervene directly to determine the types of strategy that are acceptable to some or all of the parties concerned, *early acceptability* being the *sine qua non* for any successful action.

Returning to the British context, Campion (1984) describes her use of a family therapy approach as an educational psychologist. Clinic-based sessions were organized for families where children had been referred for various school-based problems deemed by the author to have their origins within the family background. She does not detail the form of work undertaken with the schools but states that for many of them a 'joint systems' approach was attempted, with an intervention at school 'which would complement the intervention in the family system'. Of the 72 children worked with, Campion's evaluation, based on reports from school, showed that 42 had made more satisfactory progress and the main reason for referral had disappeared, 27 had made a partial improvement and three had shown little or no improvement.

Subsequently, Cooper and Upton (1991) published a series of articles extolling the benefits of the ecosystemic approach as a new method for conceptualizing behaviour problems that opens up exciting new avenues for intervention. They argue that these approaches, using interventions such as 'reframing and positive connotation', are in many cases suitable for autonomous use by teachers without the need for expert supervision. Although they recognize the value of consultation with external professionals, Cooper and Upton (1990) believe that there are many situations in schools in which these techniques could be used independently by teachers or within the context of peer support groups.

Finally, in recent years Wagner (2000) has been particularly influential in promoting, especially among EPs, forms of consultative working that incorporate and extend many of these approaches to working with schools and parents.

The challenge for the consultant

This brief review of the development of consultation to teachers and parents together has shown that it is possible, in both the USA and the UK, to bring together parents, students and teachers and to achieve outcomes that are valued by each party. The studies also indicate the range of skills and knowledge that a consultant may need to contribute in order to achieve these results.

However, the studies also frequently refer to the delicacies surrounding the roles of the parties involved. The teachers and consultants are both 'professionals' and the latter will need to validate the school's position, in terms of accepting the school's definition of the nature and severity of the problem being experienced. However, the consultant at the same time will have to demonstrate somehow that she or he also accepts the parents' interpretation of events as a legitimate understanding from the parents' perspective. Helping everyone to break out from any unproductive, recursive patterns such as those described in Chapter 2 will require a careful and sensitive negotiation of roles between all involved, and particularly the professionals. In a position to be easily perceived as 'taking sides', the consultant will sometimes need to exercise considerable skill to ensure he or she remains 'uncaught in the middle'.

For these reasons, and given the powerful emotional consequences for teachers having to manage difficult behaviour referred to earlier, successful consultation will have to consist of more than providing tips and techniques. While carrying out joint tasks will be an important aspect of the building of a positive working relationship between parents, students and teachers, crucial to many occasions will be 'Knowledge Base 1' interpersonal skills, such as listening, questioning, problem-solving, inviting challenge, encouraging objectivity while legitimizing feelings, arbitrating and social facilitation.

So far, much of the discussion in this book has considered work with individual teachers, parents and students. But this is not the whole story. Part 3 turns to the less tangible features of the psychosocial framework in Figure 2.3 to demonstrate why teacher and pupil cultures must also be brought within the scope of study as appropriate and necessary arenas for intervention if we are to achieve positive outcomes for all.

PART 3
Teacher and Pupil Cultures

6   Teacher culture and difficult behaviour in classrooms

This chapter explores the informal system of rules and expectations among teacher colleagues – the teacher culture – found in the Successful Strategies study. A closer exploration of the interview data reveals what seems like a paradox. Although the students in question are usually well known to other staff because of their behaviour, and although the positive outcomes resulting from the strategy are often recognized by others, little or no discussion about the strategy used to achieve these effects takes place between these colleagues. In fact, some teachers in the study suggest that strong sensitivities surround the issue and any such conversations could be extremely delicate. Following this preliminary analysis, a return to the research literature examines organizational culture in general, schools as organizations and the experience of individual teachers, and the nature of boundaries within systems thinking, in order to arrive at a deeper understanding of these psychosocial phenomena. Armed with concepts from these areas, a return is made to the teacher interviews and a further level of analysis leads to an explanation for this paradox and the lack of generalization of effective strategies. Finally, implications for intervening with teacher cultures are raised, pointing the way to the contents of later chapters.

Introduction

The Successful Strategies study was exploratory in nature and looked in minute detail at many aspects of the 24 interventions carried out in different parts of England. The common factors at the outset, the criteria for selecting the sample of teachers to be interviewed, were that each of the teachers worked in a primary school setting and had developed with an EP a successful strategy for managing what they had been experiencing as the difficult behaviour of a particular student. Given the complex psychosocial settings in which difficult student behaviour is located (see Chapter 2), explanations of behavioural approaches in terms of social learning brought about by the manipulation of antecedents and consequences (see Chapter 3) seemed incomplete and simplistic. Consequently, the major intention of the study was to explain at a more satisfactory, psychosocial level how these interventions came to achieve their effects. To carry out this type of investigation a method known as grounded theory was employed.

Using a grounded theory approach

A full account of the use of grounded theory, which is a detailed methodology generating its own debates and schools of thought, is not provided here. A range of publications may be consulted (e.g. Strauss 1987; Hutchinson 1988; Henwood and Pidgeon 1993; Strauss and Corbin 1999) and the author has written more fully on the method as employed in this particular study (Miller 1995a, 2003). Here, a flavour of the approach is provided in order to give a general impression of the means by which the arguments and accounts, especially those in this chapter, have been developed.

The interview transcripts were analysed by the 'open coding' procedure from grounded theory, which is achieved by what is known as 'the constant comparative method'. This involves a line-by-line, or even word-by-word, analysis of the data during which the researcher gives each discrete incident, idea or event a name or code, aiming for the code to be at a higher conceptual level than the text. Proceeding through the text, the researcher generates new codes and finds other examples of already existing codes. Strauss (1987) has detailed the methods whereby these codes can be developed in terms of their properties and dimensions by asking questions about their frequency, extent, intensity and duration. In this study the analysis of the first interview transcript took place over a period of weeks, yielding over 80 different open codes, with many examples of these being repeated at various places and in differing combinations within this interview.

Level II codes, also known as categories, are derived from condensing level I codes – the open codes. Decisions about categories are made by asking certain questions of the data and then comparing the incident with all others in the fieldnotes or transcripts. The researcher asks what categories other similar incidents would fall into and compares each emerging category with all others to ensure that they are mutually exclusive and cover all the variations. Academic and professional knowledge then supplies theoretical constructs to form level III codes, so that they give meaning to the relationship between themselves and the level I and II codes, 'weaving the fractured data back together again' (Glaser 1978).

The impact of interventions on other staff

In this particular study, a number of the discussions about teacher colleagues seemed to contain paradoxical and contradictory items and strong feelings. In total, 24 open codes relating to other staff were found to occur and recur within the transcripts, and these are listed in Table 6.1. This set of open codes is returned to for further analysis later in this chapter, but first a number of common and striking themes that emerged early in the interviews are presented.

Table 6.1   Total set of open codes relating to other staff

Pupil impinging on other staff
Role of head
Staff agreement with the need for referral
Consultation within school
School policy on managing the day
Other staff's knowledge of pupil
Previous teachers' strategy with pupil
School culture re problem-solving
Support as the opportunity to talk
Teacher alone/not alone with problem
Staff's/head's support strategy
Reluctance/lack of reluctance to seek support
Valuing/not valuing colleagues' expertise
Staff consensus over presenting problems
Other staff's role in strategy
Consistency of strategy across staff
Individual staff's consistency within strategy
Other staff's knowledge of strategy
Staff's general agreement with strategy
Staff's reluctance re time factors
Staff's reluctance re equitability
Staff's original perception of likelihood of progress
Staff's ongoing perception of progress
Staff's enthusiasm for/interest in strategy

Despite the very positive outcomes described in Chapter 4, many of the teachers were very reluctant to tell their colleagues about the details of the EP's suggestions:

> I was a little unsure and I didn't want to say anything – stick my neck out if you like and say, 'Look we're doing this and it could prove wonderful.' I wanted to go very tentatively and then when I could see

> some sort of hope I turned to the staff and said, 'This is what we're doing, will you please bear this in mind.' (Interview 18)

This reticence is being expressed in a school where the general atmosphere is perceived by the teacher as positive: 'a very happy school . . . staff are very nice and . . . all quite happy to help'. The tension between her optimism ('it could prove wonderful') and caution ('I didn't want to say anything – stick my neck out'), a tension present in a dramatic form in many of the interviews, is partly explained by her subsequent comments, which reveal something of the texture of staff room culture:

> I didn't want to offend Margaret [pupil's previous teacher] in any way by saying, 'I shall keep him in the class no matter what.' So it was only very gradually that I explained to her what was happening . . . [she's] the deputy head . . . [it's] very, very delicate.

Whereas it may be relatively easy to understand this reticence, it is harder to believe that a school staff member could perceive positive changes in a pupil with a previously notorious school-wide reputation, be aware that some form of intervention had taken place yet express little interest in the nature of this intervention. Yet this phenomenon occurs clearly in more than a third of the 24 interviews. The point is perhaps best illustrated by considering sets of three quotes from a number of interviewees. The first in each set refers to the previous reputation of the pupil, the second the class teacher's and the other staff's perceptions of change, and the third the staff's curiosity concerning the nature of the intervention responsible for this change.

Interview 13

> The other staff were very aware of Brian . . . they'd all met him in the playground and in the dining hall. He would get into trouble with all the other teachers on playground duty and the dinner ladies as well . . . He would get very cross and throw himself on the floor and bang his fists on the ground and scream his head off, and he actually did that to the head once, which amazed me. You don't very often do that to the headmaster.

> Brian is a changed character. I think everybody's noticed . . . I'm absolutely astounded in the change in Brian.

> No one's really questioned it as such. They obviously think it's just happened. You tend to take things for granted I suppose if you're not directly involved. No one's actually said to me 'How did you do it?' or whatever.

Interview 20

The parents have had meetings with class teachers, special needs teachers . . . throughout the child's stay in school . . . She was infamous throughout the school for the things she did . . . She had chopped up the duvet cover and the curtains [at home]. We had the Bishop in . . . and she went up to his table and sort of 'Oh my name's Chloe!' Most of the other children were quite deferential.

Her behaviour showed, over the last six weeks roughly a dramatic improvement. Her standard of work did as well and her reading came on in leaps and bounds . . . [Staff] who knew I was doing it they'd say, 'Ooh she's behaving herself, I didn't have to tell her off in the yard.'

One or two of them did ask me what recommendations she (the EP) had made, one infant teacher who had her before especially. I didn't make a big issue of it . . . If anybody asked I did, but quite honestly at the end of the term it was quite chaotic.

Interview 15

Teacher: Oh, he had a tremendous reputation, yes . . . the chief education officer was at school that day and he cried . . . screamed all day . . . he was really quite a handful . . . He was the topic of conversation in the staff room but now he's rarely mentioned . . . They've remarked how different he's got.
Interviewer: Did they ask what you'd been doing with the ed psych?
Teacher: No.
Interviewer: Did you tell them?
Teacher: No, I didn't.

In total, among other staff, some or all were aware of definite improvements in 17 cases, only one teacher felt that others were unaware of changes and six did not comment on this aspect.

Although this pattern of a high-profile pupil, a recognition of considerable improvements and a lack of interest in the possible reasons for this is explicit in nine of the 24 interviews, in many of the remaining cases there is still a clear schism between the teacher's enthusiasm and achievements and the general staff culture. Although staff are more aware of the nature of the recommended interventions, this does not mean that they are encouraging or positive in their attitude towards them:

Generally the feeling was why should this child have this sort of treatment . . . why should he be seen to be getting special treatment just because he's naughty . . . I think it went against the grain as teachers. (Interview 1)

A lot of people felt that you've got to treat everybody the same . . . We had quite a few discussions . . . Basically it was, 'Well that's all right but are these things fair on the other children?' (Interview 17)

I think we all felt the same. We all felt that maybe ed psychs should come in here and have the class on their own. (Interview 21)

In summary, in all but two of the 24 cases, the teachers felt that their colleagues were uninterested in their actions, negative about the EP's recommendations or doubtful about the likelihood of their success.

However, in work with the EP a totally contrasting sense of supportive attention is relayed in many of the interviews:

I think he was seeing it as I was. I think he was seeing that I just couldn't take any more . . . I suppose he had the authority to make suggestions and he also in a way was taking some of the responsibility I suppose and it was nothing to do with the rest of the staff really. They just breathed a sigh of relief that it wasn't their problem. (Interview 3)

She didn't quiz me. She was lovely, she would just sit there and I could ask her questions, like 'I am trying this particular thing, is that alright?' . . . She would sort of say, 'You're doing well. Yes, you are doing the right thing.' So yes, I appreciated that part of her . . . as the professional . . . [The other teachers] would have said . . . 'Oh go on, he'll be all right' . . . but it meant more coming from her . . . She was trying hard to get Brian out of this negative situation. (Interview 15)

Within the 24 interventions investigated, 18 resulted in teachers and parents working in some form of partnership. In many of these, the EP's contribution to the formation and/or direction of this working relationship is readily apparent. In some, the EP's effect, in terms of teachers feeling legitimized to operate in a different way, is very much present even when the EP himself or herself is not actually physically present, as the following excerpt illustrates:

Teacher: Theresa [EP] also suggested talking to the parents as well.
Interviewer: Had you not done that before?
Teacher: Yes, I'd spoken to them in an informal way but not actually had them in and talked to them formally. She recommends that a lot.

> *Interviewer:* Did she suggest any particular things to say to Gary's parents?
>
> *Teacher:* Yes, to try to stress the positive side of Gary and the head and I had a very interesting chat . . .

Later:

> *Interviewer:* Do you think you would have got to know the parents anyway like that or do you think it was because Theresa suggested these things that it helped you to get to know the parents better?
>
> *Teacher:* I think maybe it was a little bit of both. We see the parents at the beginning of the day for five minutes, five minutes at the end, but when we had that formal interview with the head, myself and the parents, I think we got a lot more into the background, that maybe she wouldn't have said as much – they wouldn't have said as much just picking the child up. So we got to know a little bit more of what it was like at home and that was one of Theresa's suggestions. (Interview 7)

In the usual sense of the word, procedures that are *formal* could be invoked by a school if, for example, exclusion of a pupil was being considered or an assessment made of special educational needs within the Code of Practice. However, there is no reference in the interview to any procedures of this nature. Instead, the term is used here as a frequent reminder that the head and the teacher are behaving untypically, 'delving into home backgrounds', and that this has apparently been recommended by the EP. Presumably they are quite capable of asking such questions of their own volition and of giving advice concerning praise and encouragement. There is nothing particularly 'expert' about either. Similarly, if the parents were to take great exception to this, it seems highly unlikely that justifying themselves by saying they were acting on the EP's suggestions would save them from the immediacy of the parents' criticisms.

The EP's influence appears to remain in an almost reified form to govern the interactions taking place, which are clearly perceived as a departure from the normal form of interaction that takes place between parents and teachers when there is a difficulty associated with a pupil's behaviour. Just as some of the teachers experienced a sense of supportive attention from their EP that contrasted so sharply with their colleagues' response to the negotiated strategy, so too they were aware of construing some parents anew in a way that departed from normal school procedures:

> Mrs Roberts [mother] had caused so many problems here. She's a very bristly lady, very much on the ball, but in her own way she really did

care for Barry. Maybe not the way that you and I would care for our children but she did . . . she really was a caring mum. (Interview 15)

The involvement of the EP in some way allows the generally accepted view among the staff, that Mrs Roberts is very 'bristly' and causes 'so many problems', to be departed from but to continue to coexist with a more positive, if perhaps slightly patronizing, view of her as a 'caring mum'. This temporary escape from the dominant view is also sometimes expressed in terms of privacy and ownership:

I think a lot of the time when teachers are working with a psychologist they keep it very much to . . . it's their property almost. It's strange teachers are very possessive of the children in their class and they don't want to share things. (Interview 24)

This phenomenological experience of 'possessiveness' and secrecy, of not 'sticking one's neck out', may be understandable in the example from Interview 18 in which the teacher initially found the prospect of success after the relative 'failure' of the deputy head in the previous year 'very, very delicate'. Even after successful completion, when the results are visible to the others in the school, the notions of teacher-effected change with difficult pupils will not fit easily into the staff culture:

I mean I've come back to teaching after 15 years' break and they've been super, they've been really helpful . . . I can't come into the staff room and say, 'Aren't I good?' . . . It's very big-headed isn't it? (Interview 15)

We're a very close school . . . we do talk in the staff room and say, you know, 'What do you think? How can you help?' . . . When I found that it was working then I thought that as I felt so good about it everybody had to know . . . I think they all got fed up of me keep saying, 'Richard, Richard, Richard!' (Interview 21)

The analysis so far has identified and explored to some extent the discouraging reactions of colleagues to a teacher's successful interventions. It has contrasted this with very different working relationships with EPs and identified a changed style of interacting with parents.

For obvious reasons, the presentation in lectures and seminars of this particular set of findings has sometimes provoked controversy among teachers and others. The author's main professional responsibility is for the training of educational psychologists and some audience members have viewed these findings as a crude and partisan attempt to present this particular group as professionally virtuous and to denigrate the actions of teachers and schools. I hope it will already have become apparent that one of the major messages of this book is that the vexed area of difficult student behaviour is suffused with notions of blame, that people are stuck, demoralized and set against each other as a result of it, and that any attempts to add to these accusations is the very opposite of what is so desperately required.

The teachers in this section are raising a curious phenomenon, potentially a very important one, and it deserves consideration. Understanding is not the same as blaming, however sensitive the issues may feel. Understanding has the potential to inform effective intervention, and effective intervention is surely needed in this area.

'Common-sense' explanations

In the Successful Strategies study a group of 24 teachers, with an average of nearly 12 years' experience, brought about considerable improvements in the classroom behaviour of students experienced by half of them as *the* most challenging they had ever encountered. Many of the others interviewed described the particular pupils as among the most difficult half dozen they had ever encountered. Trying to manage this behaviour had produced strong emotional reactions, often undermining the teachers' sense of professional competence and even leading some to question whether they could continue in their career. These students were usually widely known within their schools as being difficult to manage, thus presenting a challenge to the whole school rather than just the particular teacher in the study.

In view of these factors and the national level of concern, the policy- and law-making referred to in Chapter 1, a reader removed from school contexts might reasonably ask why others are not desperate to learn from the experiences of their successful colleague. Why is there a recurring sense of exactly the opposite reaction in a sample of schools spread across half of England?

Is this not an ideal opportunity to examine an approach that might be of direct practical benefit to other colleagues within a school? Might there not be clues as to how to solve a persisting national problem, to find a glimmer of optimism in an area sometimes beset with a sense of hopelessness? It is true that these results have been obtained from a small sample of 24 teachers. But these teachers do at least show what is possible and there is no reason to think that they may be wildly atypical of the profession as a whole. Chapter 4 describes the characteristics of the teachers and schools in the study, and shows them to represent a range of teaching experience, urban and rural schools, large and small, the socially disadvantaged as well as the relatively privileged.

A number of explanations for this apparently curious phenomenon suggest themselves. The sensitivity around embarrassing a colleague who had previously struggled with the student in question has already been raised. Although this may well be a powerful psychosocial factor in some cases, can it really be such a pervasive experience that it accounts for the same findings in almost all of these 22 schools?

Perhaps another explanation involves the maxim of 'not counting one's chickens before they have hatched'. Compare the situation when a teacher helps to bring about considerable improvements for a pupil with literacy difficulties, or almost any other form of academic difficulties. Once substantial progress has been made, there will be a general expectation that most, if not all, of these gains will be maintained, that the student will not find himself or herself back where they started. This is not the received wisdom concerning behaviour, where there is a sense that gains can rapidly disappear for a variety of reasons, that the problem can get far worse rather than better. Allied to this may be the reservation expressed above about appearing 'big-headed' in front of colleagues.

An unfortunate consequence of acquiring a reputation for succeeding with difficult students, and this applies to schools as much as individual teachers, is that there is an increased likelihood of being allocated further challenging students in the future. Whereas academic, artistic and sporting successes bring accolades and a valued recognition, it can easily appear that making progress with exceptionally challenging students will go unrecognized, or bring further stresses as its reward.

These are some possible explanations for why successful strategies may not become picked up within a school and widely treated as exemplars and learning opportunities. However, they are 'common-sense' explanations, views that have a certain status through being 'taken for granted' as plausible by particular groups. To be really useful, an explanation needs also to incorporate a clear and consistent theoretical rationale. Theory, especially in pressing social issues, has the tendency sometimes to irritate practitioners seeking pragmatic solutions. But it is good theory that can bind together otherwise disparate strands of knowledge and explain the forces and factors that lie beneath the changing surface features of problems. It can highlight the bigger picture, illustrate the common links between seemingly different phenomena and ultimately present a greater range of options and possibilities.

The next section of this chapter summarizes areas of the published literature that are pertinent to arriving at a theoretical understanding of the relationship between staff culture and student behaviour. This is more technical in conceptualization and language. But, I hope, as the chapter then returns to the teacher interviews, it will be possible to gain a deeper understanding of the paradoxes raised above. The three areas of research and theory to be examined are: the general concept of organizational culture; schools as organizations and the experience of individual teachers; and the nature of boundaries within systems thinking

Organizations and cultures

Definitions of organizational culture were quoted in Chapter 2: 'what we experience as the "way things are" in an organization, the written and unwritten rules that regulate behaviour, the stories and "myths" of what an organization has achieved, the standards and values set for its members' (Dalin 1993), and 'the system of informal rules that spells out how people are to behave most of the time' (Deal and Kennedy 1982). Also highlighted was Argyris and Schon's (1978) distinctions between 'espoused theory' and 'theory-in-use'. The former represents the formal, publicly available statements about how an organization functions, while the latter refers to more hidden, cultural aspects. Argyris and Schon also pointed out that a consultant external to an organization will not be in a position to understand and help that organization (and these psychologists were commenting on organizations generally, not specifically on schools) without an appreciation of the exact nature of the gaps between its espoused theory and theory-in-use. Again, this is not intended as an act of blaming, although many may initially see it as such. The assertion is that this gap is a property of organizations – all organizations. And 'well practised and effective defensive routines' are always brought into play when there is a danger of the gap being revealed, not necessarily deliberately or with Machiavellian motives, but perhaps as a consequence of complexity, competing priorities, ambiguous terminology or whatever.

Henning-Stout and Conoley (1988) have argued that the success of a consultant working with a school depends equally upon the characteristics of the consultant and those of the organization. They identified three aspects of an organization that are implicated in the outcomes of consultative practice: the organization's history with previous consultants, organizational stresses and the prevailing ideology of the organization. These are factors usually found in discussions about the properties of systems and the interactions across their boundaries (e.g. Glatter 1989), including the literature on organizational cultures (Morgan 1997) and on teacher cultures specifically (Hammersley 1984; Woods 1984).

Although ethnographic research in schools has mainly been concerned with classroom practice, a few researchers have looked particularly at staff rooms. Woods (1984) examined the nature and function of staff room humour and Hammersley (1984) looked at the subject of staff room 'news'.

In the latter study, Hammersley described staff room news as serving both a referential and a rhetorical function. Because this work was carried out in a secondary school, in which pupils move from teacher to teacher, staff room conversations gave teachers the opportunity to know what to expect from particular pupils. Hammersley found that the conversation focused predominantly on the difficult behaviour of pupils and consisted of the trading of 'summary typifications'. Because teachers employ typifications of pupils to guide their actions in the immediacy of the classrooms, Hammersley argued that through the exchange of classroom news teachers supplement their own information with that of colleagues in the construction of these typifications.

However, Hammersley also detected aspects of teacher conversations that served a dismissive rather than a descriptive function. In this rhetorical form, conversations were concerned with hypothesized characteristics of particular pupils rather than detailed descriptions of their behaviour. Hammersley found that in all the examples of conversation he collected, the context of any pupil behaviour – that is, the setting, the teacher's expectations and actions etc. – was 'taken for granted' and did not need explanation or discussion in terms of its possible contribution to pupil behaviour. The recurrent topic for comment and discussion in the staff room was the 'failure' of pupils in various contexts, a failure seen as due to the typifications given to pupils by the teachers. These typifications, consisting of psychological characteristics, were such that they could be seen to produce typical behaviour in diverse contexts, irrespective of the contexts themselves.

Individual teachers and schools as organizations and cultures

A number of commentators have drawn attention to the sense of isolation that characterizes the professional role of the teacher. For example, Lieberman and Miller (1990), writing about the American scene, have stated that:

> loneliness and isolation are high prices to pay but teachers willingly pay them when the alternatives are seen as exposure and censure . . . By following the privacy rule teachers forfeit the opportunity to display their successes; but they also gain. They gain the security of not having to face their failures publicly and losing face.

Similarly, Little (1990), reviewing studies of teachers working in a 'collegial' manner, also sees 'a devastating picture of professional isolation among experienced teachers and trial and error survival of beginning teachers'. She does find examples of genuine peer support and joint effort but concludes that it is 'a remarkable accomplishment: not the rule, but the rare, often fragile exception'.

It is not that teachers do not necessarily enjoy the company of their colleagues but that colleagues do not serve the function of being stimuli and agents for each other's professional development. 'Many teachers are satisfied with their peer relationships, but few claim that those relationships make their way into the classroom. Many schools offer congenial work environments, but few offer a professional environment that makes schools as educative for teachers as for students' (Little 1990).

This point was dealt with at greater length by Lortie (1975) in his socio-logical study of teaching. He referred to the ambivalence for the teacher, in respect of colleagues, between what he called 'the wish for boundedness and the search for assistance'. Lortie discovered in his study that the major reward for teachers was in the form of interactions with *their* pupils and satisfaction with their learning and development. Although various administrative duties – lunchtime supervision etc. – were seen as requiring collaborative efforts between teachers from the point of view of equitability, these 'costs' were balanced by the 'profits of psychic benefits' from working alone with pupils. Lortie describes teachers as 'entrepreneurs of psychic profit' working to maxi-mize positive interactions and feedback from their pupils, while attempting to reduce the organization's influence on them and ensure that they have no more bosses than already exist.

However, these teachers also reported that they saw their colleagues as a powerful source of ideas and, sometimes, as mirrors in which to assess their own performance. Lortie's analysis, much more than the previous two papers, sees teachers as more positively involved in maintaining the boundedness of some important arenas of their work despite the cost of professional isolation.

These three studies identify a number of factors that contribute to this phenomenon:

- the ecology of most schools, with their separated classrooms;
- the major reward for teachers, the development and responses of pupils, being something most easily earned away from colleagues;
- the lack of a technical language with which teachers can discuss their work with each other;
- the lack of commonly agreed standards by which teachers can meas-ure their competence (especially away from centrally set targets and in areas such as student behaviour), leading to a lack of confidence through an inability to judge their own worth;
- the high value placed upon being able to keep a class under control, leading both to a wariness of being observed and a desire to keep a class within a more bounded space where it can be more easily managed.

Sharp and Green (1975), in their ethnographic study of a 'progressive' primary school, argued that teachers utilized a 'child-centred vocabulary' to account for their classroom actions to significant others, but that these actions were themselves guided far more by the principle of 'ad-hocing' and following tried and tested routines to cope with the immediacy, frequency and changing nature of classroom demands. In such circumstances, even if teachers possessed a shared technical language in the form of the child-centred vocabulary, the fact that it did not link to their actions can clearly cause a situation in which conversations with colleagues about purposes and methods grounded in practice could become extremely difficult.

Despite these barriers to a shared professional culture, teachers need reference groups from which to derive norms and values for their practice. Chapter 2 introduced the research carried out by Nias (1985), in which she interviewed 99 teachers from various parts of England who had been teaching for between two and nine years. In particular she was concerned with the role of reference groups in the 'defence of the self', through a normative function in which individuals identify a group against whose norms and values they wish to evaluate themselves. The reference group also serves a perceptual function whereby the group's norms are used as anchoring points in structuring the perceptual field, in helping to make sense of events by indicating which events to pay attention to, and what degrees of saliency to ascribe to each. 'Thus once one has internalised the particular outlook of a reference group, it becomes a "frame of reference" which is brought to bear on all new situations' (Nias 1985: 107).

Many of the teachers appeared to need the referential support from only one other: a colleague, a headteacher or a visiting professional. Nias comments that the amount of support provided by such a group was out of all proportion to either the size of the group or the time spent in communication. Further, the majority of teachers interviewed found themselves at some stage working in schools where they had no adult reference group and then they often sought it in outside courses or from 'like-minded' friends. Interestingly, especially in respect of Lortie's findings concerning the primary rewards for teachers, the most frequently invoked reference group in Nias's study was pupils. In other words, they were the group whose positive reactions the teachers claimed to be most concerned to stimulate. 'As long as classroom processes remain largely hidden from all other participants, pupils may be invoked as a reference group to justify many different decisions and types of behaviour' (Nias 1985: 109).

Nias extends Lortie's argument concerning the lack of a common technical culture and language among teachers. She considers that teachers construct their views of themselves and of reality within schools via conversations with their own reference groups. Outside these groups they do not share a language with which to attach meanings to their common experience. Attempting to create such a language with others outside the reference group would actually be destructive of the processes that create and sustain their 'substantial selves'. Hence, teachers actively do not enter into conversation about fundamental aspects of their work with many of their colleagues.

However, it is recognized that teachers also have certain affiliative and affective needs in respect of their colleagues, 'especially in circumstances where they feel themselves to be under threat from pupils'. Consequently, open conflict is often avoided by arriving at a 'false consensus' in the staff room while the teacher continues to follow a course of action in the classroom more consistent with the norms of a reference group.

Drawing together a range of perspectives, including rational-emotive therapy and cognitive-behaviour therapy, Wagner (1987) has developed the model of the 'knot' in teacher thinking. This is the situation when the dominance of 'self-imperated cognitions' – beliefs and messages to oneself couched in the form of 'shoulds, musts and oughts' – prevent a form of thinking that leads to problem-solving. As part of a six-year study in Germany, Wagner showed how teachers' thinking was often characterized by going 'round in circles, posing questions without resolving them, jumping from one issue to another and considering goals and strategies without ever putting them into practice'. Most importantly, and this was found to be a dominant feature of knots, there appeared to be no recognition of the many contradictions contained in these modes of thought. The other consequence was a strong emotional component, often involving anger, anxiety and attachment, and seen as the result of vain attempts to resolve these dilemmas or knots.

One section of the study most pertinent to this discussion concerned the in-depth analysis, using a rigorous and original methodology, of the knots occurring in the transcripts from interviews with seven teachers about their school life. There were 62 issues that teachers talked about at least 12 times or more and four that contained significantly more knots than the others. Surprisingly, these were 'fellow teachers' (83 per cent), the principal (81 per cent), giving permission as opposed to forbidding students to do certain things (70 per cent) and students paying attention rather than being absent-minded or distracted (65 per cent). The issue that produced the least knots was the actual content or subject matter of the teaching.

In other words, issues relating to immediate teacher colleagues produced more inconsequential and contradictory thinking, with high levels of emotion, than did either the curriculum or even the management of student behaviour.

Systems and their boundaries

There has been considerable interest in systems theory approaches among those who have studied schools as organizations. Hoy and Miskel (1989), for example, described schools as open systems interacting with their environments, and discussed the ways in which uncertainty in the environment affects the internal structures and processes of organizations. Similarly, Rice (1976), discussing open or 'socio-technical' systems, described how systems seek to define, or validate, and then maintain a definition of their boundary during transactions across it with the environment. (See Chapter 5.)

The purpose of the boundary is to distinguish those tasks and responsibilities belonging to the system from those that do not. Within a system's boundary, norms and procedures are then arrived at to guide such activities as interacting with others inside the system, dealing with internally disruptive events, carrying out joint tasks, presenting the system's stated aims and objectives to the environment and communicating across the boundary. There will be rules within the system's boundary that do not apply outside. There will also be secrets. There may well be rules about the rules and secrets about the secrets. And the boundary may even also hold in rules about the secrets or secrets about the rules!

In addition to boundary validation and maintenance, another important aspect of systems is their orientation towards *homoeostasis*, a tendency to maintain internal stability. Systemic family therapy (Palazzoli *et al.* 1978). has drawn upon similar theoretical roots, with the nature of the boundary, its maintenance and the interactions that take place across it again yielding important conceptual tools to inform the practice of therapists. A particularly significant notion deriving from systemic family therapy is that of 'the rules about the rules': the principles, often informally defined and communicated, concerning who is permitted, and by what means, to generate, challenge, change and make exceptions to the norms and procedures of the system.

In the context of family therapy, De Shazer (1982) has argued that 'when the system under consideration is defined as the open system of the therapy situation, then the boundary is drawn around the therapist and the family subsystems of the therapeutic suprasystems'. This new system then develops its own norms and values but is temporary in the sense that its existence depends on the continuance of the therapist's involvement.

Ball (1987) has also criticized systems approaches and accused their adherents of by-passing and obscuring the realities of organizational life in schools in favour of 'the abstract tidiness of conceptual debate'. Instead, he advocated that schools as organizations would be better understood through the study of 'the micro-politics of school life'. Frederickson (1990a) has helped to clarify this discussion by pointing to the confusingly broad range of professional practice that has often been uncritically included under the rubric of 'systems approaches'. Particularly helpful here is her distinction between systems theories that derive by analogy from a biological perspective, such as those employed in systemic family therapy and the socio-technical approach, and those having their origins in a technological perspective, such as soft systems and hard systems methodology.

Hard systems methodology is the area concerned with work addressing the formal structure of organizations, as developed within professional educational psychology by Burden (1978). It is the biological tradition that gives rise to concepts such as boundary maintenance and homoeostasis, concepts that, as Frederickson points out, can elucidate processes within organizations by analogy but should not be developed too literally.

So far this chapter has identified a number of processes relating to schools as organizations and cultures that may be implicated in ambiguous and problematic relationships between teacher colleagues in the context of difficult pupil behaviour. Similarly, systems theory derived from a biological perspective may also offer conceptual tools with which to elucidate those factors influencing the interactions that take place between teachers and parents in such circumstances. With this theoretical sensitivity, the transcripts were further examined to allow categorization and theory building to proceed.

A further analysis of the level I codes relating to 'other staff' (see Table 6.1), using the grounded theory methods, enabled two major categories to be derived at a relatively early stage. These could be identified as the espoused theory and the theory-in-use as far as the responses of these schools to difficult pupil behaviour were concerned. The former was often manifested in the form of a written policy document, whereas the latter was often referred to much in the manner of Deal and Kennedy's (1982) definition of staff culture: 'the system of informal rules that spells out how people are to behave most of the time'. What is more, this analysis revealed that, in almost every school, there was a conflict somewhere within the relationship between espoused theory (policy), theory-in-use (culture) and the teacher's preferred method of handling the pupil.

Policy–culture conflict

In this study, the term 'policy' is taken to include both written statements accessible to the staff and less clearly articulated procedures that are generally recognized as institutionally approved, usually by originating from the head or other policy-makers. Despite these explicit public policies, however, teachers were still able to identify prevailing and incompatible attitudes and assumptions on the part of staff – the staff culture – *in respect of pupil behaviour*. For example, one of the special needs coordinators said: 'we started a system of rewards . . . in the school generally, yet, at the same time, I felt guilty that these problems [a particular pupil's difficult behaviour] simply weren't being addressed and that it was down to me in my role and the class teacher' (Interview 5). A number of interviewees described the procedure whereby teachers with a difficult pupil would consult with either the head or the special needs teacher:

> I think if I had a real problem with a child I would see the head and then she would say, 'Well, try this, have you tried that?' Or she would say 'Right, we'll call in the ed psych.' (Interview 9)

> I normally go to Rachel [SENCO] for help and advice on problems like this one. I spoke to her originally and said, 'Look I've got a real problem here and I need some help,' and she tried to give me some help. (Interview 13)

However, despite the existence and recognition of such procedures, the staff culture, in these same cases, lies in marked contrast to this problem-solving and advice-giving approach:

> I think that sometimes you just get in the staff room and think, you know, you don't want to talk. I mean really you just want to moan about your children, you don't want anyone to tell you anything because you don't want to listen. You just want to get it out of your system. (Interview 9)

> I think a lot of the time when we talk to each other in the staff room we can be a bit negative, you know, doomy about things. We don't always make each other feel 'Go on, you can do it!' (Interview 13)

In these examples the teachers have a positive attitude towards the formal policy but at the same time experience an unsupportive culture, unsupportive in the sense of not taking a positive approach towards a difficult pupil. In other examples the reverse is the case: the official way of dealing with difficult behaviour is not highly regarded but the informal support received from colleagues is positively experienced.

For example, one teacher describes her opposition to the headteacher's preferred method of dealing with a particular pupil: 'I fought very strongly because the head . . . just wanted him removed' (Interview 18). Although the rest of the staff were described as having lost much of their patience with this boy, the culture is nevertheless perceived as positive: 'This is a very happy school and the staff are very nice indeed and they were all quite happy to help' Interview 18).

To summarize this section, for these particular teachers there was seen to be in eight cases a tension between staff culture and stated policy, whether it was in a written form or not, no tension in six and an indeterminate relationship in 10. Any actions on the part of a teacher that were likely to point out this disparity between espoused theory and theory-in-use would be likely to be met by one of the organization's 'well practised defensive routines' (Argyris and Schon 1978).

Policy–teacher conflicts

In other interviews it was possible to detect a strain between the school's formal procedures and the teacher's preferred method, without there necessarily being such a clear or obvious clash between policy and culture. A deputy head who had taught for 25 years described her reaction to the strategy of placing a difficult pupil in her class because of her seniority and experience:

> Well, the head, I think she just thought, 'Well, I know you'll cope,' you know. Well, I didn't. In fact, I could cope but I just went in saying I'm not prepared to any more ... I really did feel that as long as I coped I could be left to do it ... In fact people used to send him out from things, out of assembly or a story, and back to me. (Interview 3)

Another teacher who did not feel comfortable with the school's procedure for approaching difficult behaviour said:

> Now the head communicates very, very well but she communicates only with the person she needs to communicate with. She doesn't communicate generally in the staff room if there's a problem with the children and really we don't delve into backgrounds too much. If it's necessary we do ... Maybe my one criticism would be that it [the school] is very, very secretive. (Interview 7)

While this criticism is rather guarded and set within a generally positive approach towards the main policy-maker – the head – other teachers expressed their disagreement in stronger terms:

> The head ... knew the best way to do it and he would have him in his office working at a little table but then all of a sudden he'd have to go to a meeting so he'd have to pile him on to someone else or he'd have the odd private phone call or show someone around the school so Darren was left by himself in the office ... You don't discuss it with the head, he hasn't got a clue ... In our school you don't send them to the head because it just causes more hassle for you. (Interview 16)

In the remaining interviews six teachers indicated weak strains in relation to policy (making nine in total who experienced a negative reaction to the school policy), eight (one of them a teaching head, and two special needs coordinators) described their policy in either a positive or non-judgemental fashion and the remaining seven made no reference to standard procedures in relation to difficult behaviour.

Thus, strains in the relationship between policy and the teacher may be seen to be a factor in nine of the 24 cases, and a powerful one in three of these.

Culture–teacher conflicts

The *general* staff culture within a school may be positively perceived by a teacher, irrespective of the prevailing views specifically concerning difficult behaviour, and this was the case in 10 interviews. In these positive instances comments were usually very general and to the effect that the school was 'very happy' or 'open' and that staff were very 'supportive' or 'sympathetic'.

More critical judgements of the culture usually existed where the teacher felt that a rejecting or 'doomy' attitude prevailed in relation to difficult pupils (as in Interviews 9 and 13 above). The teachers in the study perceived this as clashing with the positive approach they were trying to adopt with the pupil in question.

However, these attitudes were expressed more intensely in some of the sample:

> [The staff] felt they [difficult children] shouldn't be here if they're going to behave like that . . . they should be somewhere else. (Interview 17)

> They thought that he was really a lost cause and they thought he was extremely obnoxious and aggressive and a very naughty boy . . . His previous teacher was still smarting quite badly from his behaviour. (Interview 18)

Whereas here the culture is being created and maintained by the staff's verbal reactions, it is possible for it to be communicated in equally powerful but far less tangible ways:

> *Teacher:* I've gone in as an acting deputy in lots of different schools . . . and [in] several schools I've been in its 'The children are in your class, your responsibility, you look after them, you deal with them, if there's a problem you handle it.'
> *Interviewer:* Who's saying that?
> *Teacher:* Oh no, it's *there* when you walk through the door.
> *Interviewer:* So nobody's actually saying it?
> *Teacher:* No, it's *there*. (Interview 24)

Even though a negative general culture was only perceived in six cases, a sense of feeling alone with the responsibility for a pupil's difficult behaviour was to be found throughout many of the interviews. It was stated strongly in 10 instances, and in a more mixed fashion in nine.

The following examples are all from schools where the general culture is perceived as positive.

> People need to know, really do need to know, that they're not bad teachers. I needed to know that after 12 years I wasn't being gotten the better of by a five-year-old child. (Interview 1)

> You always do as a teacher tend to think it's your fault. (Interview 3)

> They all thought I was fighting a losing battle. (Interview 15)

> You sometimes think, 'Will they [colleagues] think it's me, I'm inadequate?' (Interview 21)

In summary, the teacher perceived the *general* school culture to be negative in six cases, positive in 10 and a mixture of both in three. In only four cases was no judgement conveyed. However, as far as the culture specifically in regard to difficult pupils is concerned, there was a widespread feeling among the teachers interviewed of being solely responsible for the solution, and sometimes for the causes, of a pupil's problem behaviour

Theoretical explanations: the creation of a temporary overlapping system

In total, in only three of the 24 cases were there seen to be no initial strains in the relationship between policy, culture and the teacher's view in respect of a particular difficult pupil. It is important to emphasize that this does not mean that the schools were in a perpetual state of disharmony. What it does mean is that when the teachers in this study found themselves with a difficult pupil, then, from their perspective, there was an internal strain within the system. If there was no intervention then homoeostasis could be restored by changes in policy, in culture or in the teacher's attitude towards the pupil in question.

Change in policy requires the time and commitment of a large number of staff and is unlikely to arise as a response to a single pupil. Change in culture, by definition, is extremely difficult to arrange even if time and commitment are available. For a particular teacher, holding attitudes or acting contrary to policy and/or culture in the fraught area of extreme pupil behaviour, however, would normally lead inevitably to increasing alienation. Yet this does not occur in these interviews. So what processes are at work encouraging positive outcomes for the teacher and child while at the same time avoiding an increase in internal strains?

The interviews reveal a frequent teacher perception of a temporary and overlapping system deriving from the involvement of the EP. This system always includes the teacher, pupil, EP and mother and often also contains other family members and staff, particularly dinner supervisors and non-teaching assistants. It takes the form of the 'therapeutic suprasystem' described by De Shazer (1982) in the context of family therapy, in which the boundary is drawn around both the family and the therapist to create a new system. This new system develops its own norms and values but is temporary in the sense that its existence depends on the continuance of the therapist's involvement.

In these interviews, the new system is seen as temporary; it originates with the 'formal' involvement of the EP and it ceases with the ending of this involvement. While the system is in place it allows the teachers to step outside the values and norms of behaviour imposed through membership of the school system. Looking again at two of the earlier quotes, it is possible to illustrate some aspects of this new boundary, perceived by the teachers as a seemingly paradoxical combination of the fragile and intangible with the authoritative and reassuring.

> I think he [EP] was seeing it as I was. I think he was seeing that I just couldn't take any more . . . I suppose he had the authority to make suggestions and he also in a way was taking some of the responsibility, I suppose, and it was nothing to do with the rest of the staff really. They just breathed a sigh of relief that it wasn't their problem. (Interview 3)

> She didn't quiz me. She was lovely, she would just sit there and I could ask her questions, like, 'I am trying this particular thing, is that all right?' . . . She would sort of say, 'You're doing well. Yes, you are doing the right thing.' So, yes, I appreciated that part of her as the professional . . . [The other teachers] would have said . . . 'Oh, go on, he'll be all right' . . . but it meant more coming from her . . . She was trying hard to get Brian out of this negative situation. (Interview 15)

'She didn't quiz me . . . she was lovely' is language more appropriate to a reference group (Nias 1985), and many of these teachers' accounts of working with the EP are couched in similar terms. Within this new system, the norms and support of a reference group allow the teachers to construe pupils and parents differently, to escape from the typifications identified by Hammersley, in which difficult behaviour was seen only in terms of fixed personality characteristics.

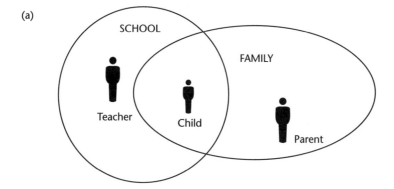

Each boundary includes the norms and rules for:

• interacting with individuals within the system;
• dealing with internally disruptive events;
• carrying out joint tasks;
• presenting a 'common front';
• communicating across the boundary.

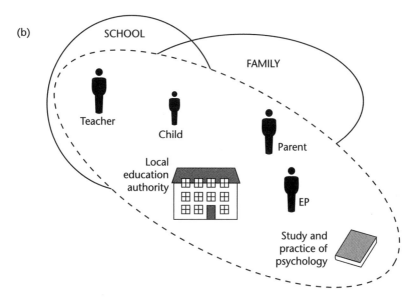

Figure 6.1   The location and nature of the temporary overlapping boundary: (a) the child as a member of the family and school systems; (b) the introduction of the temporary overlapping system (from Miller 1994a)

Systems boundary maintenance

The new temporary boundary achieves two functions. First, it defines a new system within which norms and expectations more typical of a reference group can be encouraged. Usually this new system includes at least the teacher, the mother and the EP. In a minority of cases the system is comprised of only the teacher and the EP, but the same degree of intersubjectivity can still be detected in these accounts. As a result of these new norms it becomes possible to reconstrue children and parents. In discussing family therapy procedures, Dallos (1991: 142) comments that

> a dialectical approach . . . emphasises repeatedly that action and con-
> struing are inextricably connected . . . Change involves a shift at both
> levels – action and construing . . . we need to be wary when there is
> only evidence of movement in one area and not the other. It is easy
> enough to talk about things in a different way and to act in a different
> way, at least for a while. However, in order for change to be sustained,
> shifts in both areas are necessary.

Not only, then, does the new system create a partnership that will implement a joint strategy, it also creates a level of personal relationships within which it is possible for members to reconstrue each other, thus adding to the strategy itself in the manner Dallos sees as essential for sustained change within a system.

However, the temporary boundary also serves a function in respect of one of the major systems: the school. Normally, transgression of the rules and norms of the major system would lead to an increased internal strain – a decrease in homoeostasis – within that system. But the new procedures are seen to exist *only* for the life of the temporary system. When it is removed, when the mechanism that brought it into being, the 'official' involvement of the EP, ceases to operate, the major boundary of the school system with its norms and procedures can be seen to have been preserved intact. Even when not physically present, the EP was still seen as responsible for the temporarily new way of responding to pupils and parents.

The school system will preserve its norms concerning the extent of tolerable difficult behaviour and the procedures for relating with parents in circumstances where it seems as though dialogue has broken down. Although the experiences of the teachers in this study will have demonstrated that their own actions, aided and mediated by an outside consultant, can have a very positive effect even in extreme circumstances, the need to protect both policy and culture remains. As these reflect the boundary of a system's responsibilities in uncertain relations with its environment (Rice 1976), they serve to increase internal collegiate support in times of professional threat. The nature of future threats is unpredictable, and therefore it is unlikely that the experience of one particular case will lead to the teacher involved making great efforts to disrupt the system's homoeostasis by pushing for new school procedures, permanently altering the location of the boundary because of one particular event.

Consequently, the lack of interest on the part of the rest of the staff may not originate solely from them. For the teacher in question to bring into the staff room accounts of teacher-initiated change would threaten the organization's homoeostasis. Hence, the teachers in this study would be as likely to 'talk down' their achievements in order to preserve affiliative links with colleagues, as the rest of the staff would be diffident in enquiring about them. The teacher also avoids being on the receiving end of the organization's 'defensive routines' by not highlighting any mismatch between espoused theory and theory-in-use in relation to problem behaviour. The intervention can be accommodated precisely because it is separate and distinct from the activities of the major system. The school has maintained its boundary, changes in policy, culture or practice have not been required and possible inconsistencies between them have not been illuminated.

The need for a 'blame-free' understanding

This chapter has examined in some depth the relationship between the system of informal rules operating among staff and the difficult behaviour of some pupils. It has not argued that these factors *cause* difficult behaviour but it has suggested that the relationship is complex and that staff culture can act to obstruct positive outcomes for teachers and students, and deny schools exemplars and learning opportunities.

These findings may, at first sight, seem highly critical of teachers. But I hope the point has been made that the processes described by the teachers within the Successful Strategies study are characteristic of a range of organizations, including but extending well beyond schools and other public sector institutions. Difficult student behaviour may be particular to schools (with parallels in a few organizations) but it should be seen as engaging with psychosocial processes that are endemic to organizations of many shapes and forms. This suggests that coherent attempts to address student behaviour in schools ought to include, among other considerations, the issue of staff culture, and Chapter 9 returns to this subject.

However, as the hidden and informal aspects of schools as organizations have been considered in this chapter in terms of staff processes, the next chapter turns to the mirror image in the psychosocial system presented in Figure 2.4, the pupil culture.

7 Pupil culture and difficult behaviour in classrooms

This chapter acts as a mirror image to the previous one, being concerned with the informal and more hidden aspects of the social interaction between pupils – the pupil culture – and its place in the fuller psychosocial system. It begins with a brief look at an early study that conceptualized pupil culture as a bulwark for some students against school policies and procedures perceived as alienating, before turning to some of the ideas arising from the more recent literature on bullying in schools. Following this, interventions and studies that attempt to work with pupil culture, as a potentially positive process, in particular the Circle of Friends approach, are outlined. Returning to interventions that involve teachers and parents working collaboratively, an examination is made of the possible relationships between pupil culture and such interventions, in the form of a survey of students' views on the likely efficacy of such approaches. Finally, data from the Successful Strategies study are drawn upon to give insights into the 'texture' of pupil culture around actual home–school interventions.

Introduction

Chapter 6 considered the subtle yet powerful ways in which the staff culture within a school interacts with the difficult behaviour of some students, not as a cause of the behaviour, but as a feature of schools as organizations with their own distinctive dynamics. In Chapter 2, the important notion of circular causality was introduced to explain the complex of interactions that can be seen to be taking place within the school as a psychosocial system. Clearly, challenging behaviour has the potential to reverberate around this system, impinging not only on staff culture but also on its mirror image from Figure 2.3, the pupil culture.

Once again it is wise to avoid making simplistic assumptions about causes, and to accept that there may well be a whole range of recursive relationships between an individual student's behaviour and the sets of informal rules within groups of pupils that spell out 'how people are to behave most of the time' (Deal and Kennedy 1982).

Early studies

A classic study from a social psychology background is that conducted by Hargreaves (1967) and reported in his book *Social Relations in a Secondary School*. Adopting an ethnographic approach, Hargreaves spent one year in what was then a 'secondary modern school' studying fourth-year pupils and collecting data by means of multiple choice questionnaires, sociometric techniques and informal interviews with all pupils in the age group. He also asked teachers to complete questionnaires and carried out direct observations. In addition, numerical data from school, such as attendance rates and house point allocations, and from home – socio-economic class, family size and housing conditions – were assembled. Pupil tastes and preferences were even investigated in the extent to which they preferred 'long-haired' or 'other' pop groups, a measure of rebellious dissent now quaintly assigned to the time capsule.

A major outcome from Hargreaves's study was his description of an anti-school subculture that he attributed to the school's streaming system and the creation of a group of pupils rejected as public examination candidates. The description of the structure and membership of various cliques among pupils and the relationship between these and the teaching groups into which these pupils were organized, enlivened as they are by pupil quotes, brings a vividness to the social complexity of school life that is still pertinent and worthy of study today.

Bullying and the psychosocial system

More recently, considerable attention has been directed towards bullying in schools. As well as being a matter of widespread concern to students, teachers and parents, this phenomenon has attracted considerable media attention and government initiatives, and Smith (1999)'s international review indicates the pervasive nature of this abusive behaviour. Of particular interest to the discussions within this book are the ways in which research and policy developments may be seen within the coherent psychosocial framework proposed in Figure 2.3.

In a comprehensive review of developments in England and Wales, Smith (1999: 69) declared that 'the climate of opinion on the matter has shifted significantly over the last eight years; bullying is discussed much more openly, and many schools now have anti-bullying policies'. Within the framework, this may be described as an aspect of pupil culture, hidden but powerful, that has now become more public and addressed within the arena of 'leadership, policy and procedure'.

Salmivalli (1999) has devised a method for recording the extent to which different roles are carried out within student groups around bullying: victim, bully, assistant to bully, reinforcer to the bully, outsider, defender of the victim and 'no clear role'. As a result of investigating the incidence of these varying roles within different age groupings, she has argued that the power of the peer group should be fully recognized and used to combat bullying in schools. She advised that peers should be encouraged to take action against bullying both informally in their spontaneous everyday interactions, i.e. within the peer culture, and formally as peer counsellors, a type of pupil organizational grouping that may be set up by the school.

Cowie (1998) conducted interviews within seven secondary and two primary schools in the UK where peer support systems had been well established as part of a school anti-bullying policy. The systems included informal befriending schemes, a conflict-resolution scheme and counselling-based schemes – all of which required training for the students and support or supervision from staff. Cowie found that all peer helpers reported great personal benefits as a result of their involvement, most especially in terms of the interpersonal skills and teamwork acquired in the course of training.

She noted that teachers involved with the schemes were unanimous about the benefits for the students directly involved and for the whole school, but also reported that teachers not directly involved did not view the 'empowerment' of the young people in such a positive light, echoing those aspects of staff culture explored in Chapter 6.

Circles of Friends

An increasing range of approaches attempting to utilize the power of the peer group may now be found in educational practice (e.g. Cowie and Wallace 2000). Probably the most widely known and employed as a regular curriculum activity with all members of a class is Jenny Moseley's Circle Time (Moseley 2001)

In work specifically to aid the inclusion of students who experience difficulties that can lead to their alienation in mainstream contexts, there has been an increasing use of the Circles of Friends technique. Developed originally in Canada by Forrest et al. (1996), this approach was subsequently pioneered in the UK by Newton et al. (1996), who were working as educational psychologists in Nottinghamshire. These authors reported on 20 examples of Circles of Friends for pupils aged between four and 14, primarily pupils with severe emotional and behavioural difficulties. Where other approaches had been tried and failed, Newton *et al.* managed to prevent permanent exclusions from school and to avoid segregation into special education. The technique was subsequently evaluated using a carefully controlled experimental design (Frederickson and Turner 2003) and was again shown to increase the social inclusion of students aged between six and 12 years who were displaying emotional and behavioural difficulties.

Circles of Friends facilitates the active participation of the peer group in supporting the focal pupil in the search for realistic – and often highly unconventional – solutions to the inevitable problems faced by any child who is rejected or alienated within the school. Within the psychosocial framework from Figure 2.3, the technique may be seen to be working towards the creation of a friendship group for a specified student as an attempt to turn alienation within the peer culture towards acceptance.

A case example

The approach is illustrated here through the presentation of a case example in which the author worked with 11- and 12-year-old students and the special educational needs coordinator from a secondary school.

Billy (not his real name) transferred at 11 years of age into secondary schooling with a Statement of Special Educational Needs from a junior school where he had made good progress after being placed for some of his time in a special class with favourable teacher–pupil ratios. Billy had been diagnosed as having dyspraxia and underdeveloped motor skills, which showed especially in his difficulties with writing. His reading skills were more commensurate with his age, and the junior school staff described him as popular and well motivated.

However, in his new school, which had successfully helped previous students with a range of relatively serious difficulties, Billy soon began to challenge the management skills of many of his teachers. In subjects where he experienced particular difficulties, class work was differentiated and he was allocated a non-teaching assistant. Near the end of his first term in this school, comments were collected from all the staff who taught Billy, as some had already raised concerns with the SENCO that they were experiencing great difficulties with him. From these collected comments it was clear that in a minority of lessons Billy's behaviour presented no challenge, but that in the majority it definitely did. For example, he was described by one teacher as argumentative with her and other pupils, another said that at times he refused 'point blank' to do anything he was asked to do and a third related an incident in which he had begun to repeat 'this is boring', first under his breath and then with increasing volume. Many commented on rudeness and a refusal to carry out tasks, and he had once whispered *sotto voce* of his non-teaching assistant that he was going to acquire a buzzer that signalled to her 'to ****** off!' In exasperation, the deputy head in charge of pastoral and disciplinary matters, a teacher generally respected by students as being 'firm and fair', had spoken to Billy, who, at the end of his admonition, responded with an exaggerated military salute and a crisp 'Aye aye, sir!' – a career first for this experienced senior teacher!

Despite an awareness of the comic nature of some of Billy's style, and the hints of a deeper distress or discomfort that might be fuelling some of this, the continuing failure of staff to help Billy to settle and cause less disruption to their lessons was leading some within the school to question whether he was most appropriately placed with them. When other strategies had failed to improve the situation, the author suggested the idea of a Circle of Friends approach to Billy, his mother and the SENCO. This was described in detail and approval was sought from, and given by, Billy and his mother for this to take place.

The next stage of the process consisted of the facilitator working with Billy's class in his absence. An attempt was made to engender a tone of serious application by the facilitator stating that the purpose of the session was to try to find ways to help Billy. The approach was also introduced as being highly unusual, in that a member of the class was to be talked about behind his back, but reassurance was given that this was being carried out with the full knowledge and approval of Billy and his parents.

The first task was then introduced by the facilitator, who asked the class to describe the things that Billy was good at and his positive qualities. These were written up on a flip chart sheet. While this list was being generated one student asked if she could say how some other students described Billy, and a second list was commenced. The contributions made here were far more tentative at first, although there was an atmosphere of intense and serious participation. After a short while, one boy asked whether it was all right to use swear words, and after being told that on this occasion it was permissible if these were things that had actually been said, a steady stream of contributions was made. A small degree of embarrassment was shown within the group at first, but a sense of solemnity was soon induced among students, the SENCO and facilitator alike as the mounting list revealed the heavy social burden that Billy carried.

How others describe Billy

thick	alien	stupid
der-brain	spastic	imaginative
dense	gay	mental
queer	demented	dickhead
mongol	creative	different
prat	plonker	

Although the SENCO had been aware that Billy might sometimes be socially ostracized, it was not until these descriptions were being volunteered that the full severity of aspects of the peer culture, the more hidden aspects of 'the ways things are around here', became revealed.

The facilitator then asked the class to describe how Billy acted in class and around the school:

How Billy behaves

talks to his watch/his cat/himself	tries to kiss boys	swears
makes funny actions/noises	pretends he's a policeman	hits people
pretends to have sex	has imaginary friend	unpredictable
tries to start conversations	backlips teachers	takes the mickey
tries to be funny	tries to get attention	copies people
sometimes talks nonsense	mardy	short-tempered

The next part of the approach turns from a focus on Billy to a more general discussion about the role of friends for everyone. A set of four concentric circles are drawn and the facilitator explains that the innermost circle can be thought of as containing the people about whom we care most deeply. In most cases this will include family members and perhaps pets and very close friends. The next circle contains good friends, while at the third level are acquaintances, people who might almost have been included in the second circle. Finally, the outer circle contains the people who are paid to be in our lives; for example, teachers, doctors, crossing patrol people and others.

In this example, the facilitator drew these circles on a flip chart and then filled in the initials of people whom the class suggested might be in a hypothetical person's life. This procedure was completed slowly and with elaboration and discussion to ensure that everyone understood the basic principles. When the circles were amply populated, the facilitator asked the class to imagine who would be in their own personal circles.

Following this, the facilitator encouraged the class to imagine what their lives would be like if there was no one in circles two and three, if their lives consisted only of their close family and those people whose paid employment brought them into their lives. As with all of the Circles of Friends approach, care and sensitivity is necessary in the presentation of this, but experience suggests that even young children are able to participate positively in the process. The class was then asked how they would feel, and the recorded replies, which were readily provided by the group, are shown below:

How would you feel without anyone in circles 2 and 3?

sad	left out	alone
inferior	upset	depressed
empty	weak	lonely

insecure	rubbish	guilty
hopeless	lost	dejected
feel it for the rest of your life	broken-hearted	confused
no confidence	suicidal	wish you'd never been born
stuck	nowhere to go to	no one to talk to
blame yourself		

The facilitator then asks the class members how they would act if they had no one in these circles of friendship and Newton *et al.* (1996) describe this as 'the turning point in this whole class meeting'. In this example, this was certainly also the case. As the group suggested the items listed below, one girl's hand shot up and she fixed the facilitator with a look of determination. 'This is what Billy does,' she said.

How would you behave?

act stupid	talk to yourself	become ill
kill self	wouldn't get up in the morning	get attention
not go to school	cry/scream at people	make an imaginary friend
try to move school	do things like Billy	

This list was then compared with the earlier one detailing Billy's current behaviour and the same girl volunteered that 'It's because he's got no friends.' Newton *et al.* (1996) report that considering the overlap between the two lists, and whether the focus child's behaviour could result from a sense of having no friends, 'can be a spine-tingling moment', and in this example the level of intense participation and empathy with Billy's situation was certainly striking and impressive.

The final part of the whole class meeting then consisted of suggestions about the ways in which members could be of help to Billy and an impressive list was forthcoming:

Ways to help Billy

listen	talk to him	comfort him
treat him the same as you	try to be his friend	start conversations with him
let him join in with you	help him to have more friends	stick up for him
offer to be his partner	give him a chance	hang around with him
encourage others to be his friend	help him with his work	say 'well done'
make him feel special	praise him	spend time with him
include him in your group	recognize when he's trying his best	
try to carry out his good ideas		

The session with the whole class concluded with a request for volunteers to make up a small group to meet on a weekly basis with Billy, the facilitator and the SENCO to try to devise and carry out various plans along these lines. All but about half a dozen students readily volunteered and it was agreed that the names would be drawn from a hat. It was also acknowledged that it was not necessary to be within this small group to be involved in various ways in some of the plans soon to be developed.

The planning group, the Circle of Friends, ended up consisting of five other boys and two girls and met for the first time over lunch the following week and then for nine more sessions through that term. At the first meeting with Billy, each member was asked why they had volunteered. The genuine positive concern expressed, and the pragmatic approach towards planning, impressed the two adults in terms of its lack of sentimentality and condescension. Billy too seemed very pleased with the arrangement. The group was then asked to point out what they liked and valued about Billy and to talk about the focus for the various plans they might develop together:

Things to help Billy with

stop making noises	quick temper	learn how to ignore people
do some more mature things	stop being cheeky to teachers	have control over tone of voice
think before you act	learn others need teachers' attention	respect more people
accept that you can't always have your own way	use the right nicknames	do what you agree to do

For the first week, the facilitator selected the item concerning the use of nicknames and asked Billy and the group to consider ways in which Billy could be helped in this respect. A number of strategies were selected and plans made for their implementation over the following week. In subsequent weeks, Billy and other Circle members were encouraged to select the areas to develop, and a series of inventive plans were developed, plans often characterized by an intimate acquaintance with the subtlety of the peer culture. In addition to their creativity, these plans were also often bold and ambitious in scope and, with some facilitation, detailed in terms of who would what, when and with whom.

Some Circle members took responsibility for seeking out different teachers to appraise them of certain plans, even to elicit their participation. In addition to strategies taking place actually within lessons, Billy was included in break time activities and games, he received phone calls at home, and one boy made enquiries about whether he could become a member of his scout troop. Both the SENCO and the facilitator were frequently struck by the maturity and commitment shown by the Circle members. Levels of sensitivity, diplomacy and creativity were displayed that exceeded all previous expectations of students of this age.

The sessions were not, however, without some difficulties. In particular, after four or five weeks, Billy was experienced as having had a bad week in some lessons and some Circle members felt that Billy had taken their efforts for granted and had shown far less commitment to certain strategies. These feelings were explored within the next Circle and again members impressed with their ability to steer a careful course between being patronizing, rejecting and unduly understated. This careful but assertive behaviour led to a level of discussion in which Billy seemed genuinely more engaged and positive, and subsequent sessions witnessed a widening range of achievements, with no further reservations.

Some commentators have voiced concerns about the extent to which the Circles of Friends approach draws attention to a student experiencing difficulties and the potential for vulnerabilities to become exploited or mishandled. Commenting on this in their own work, Frederickson and Turner (2003) observe that 'these pupils were already negatively labelled and rejected by their peers, so the Circles of Friends in assisting them and their classmates to learn more constructive ways of relating to each other, was judged to outweigh the possible risks'. In Billy's case, he continued through school (whereas originally exclusion seemed a real possibility), he made various positive contributions and subsequently he enrolled in further education. The original intensity of his rejection and distress within his peer group, which surfaced during the early class session, had already set in motion a set of recursive processes within the peer culture that would have been unlikely to abate of their own accord. Similarly, the exasperation of many of his teachers was in danger of setting up a dynamic within the staff culture that was likely to build in pressure for exclusion. In this case, as in other documented instances, not only did the Circle of Friends approach bring substantial benefits, it did so when other possibilities showed little likelihood of halting the momentum of these powerful psychosocial processes.

Pupil culture and home–school interventions

A major focus of this book is on home–school interventions. Given the repeated assertion that recursive or circular influences are likely to ripple through a school's psychosocial system far beyond the visible or most obvious point of an intervention, it seems reasonable to ask about the possible role of pupil culture in interventions such as these.

Will other pupils in a class understand the need for such strategies, sympathize with their rationale and be optimistic about success? Or might they not resent what they see as special treatment for that one student, or sense that the authority of their teacher is undermined in some way, with the potential for deterioration in the behaviour of others following as a consequence?

In order to answer questions such as these, an investigation involving 206 students aged between 10 and 11 was carried out in three schools drawing from mixed socio-economic catchment areas in the north of England (Miller and Black 2001).

In order to gauge student reactions to a proposed home–school strategy, a vignette, or case study, was constructed by combining aspects from the accounts of two of the teachers in the Successful Strategies study. This amalgamation was carried out in order to capture some of the most common and most distinctive features from the 24 strategies investigated. This 'case study' was then presented to the class groups of pupils in stages, after each of which the pupils were asked to respond to certain questionnaire items, in an attempt to reflect the unfolding nature of real-life cases. A parallel study, using exactly the same materials and approach, was also carried out with teachers in the schools and the results from this are reported in Miller and Black (2001). The vignette included the more practical aspects of the strategies, such as targets, ticks and rewards, but also alluded to interpersonal processes to be found within consultation, such as mediation and resolution of blame and suspicion (Chapter 5).

So, this first part of the vignette was read to each class group:

> John is a 10-year-old boy who usually arrives at school late. He finds learning difficult and doesn't do much work. When he is given work that he can't do, he pushes it across the table and refuses to do it. When he *is* able to do it, he thinks it must be too easy and again pushes it across the table.
>
> John's teacher finds having John in the class very difficult. Instead of working, he wanders around the classroom hitting other children and banging objects together. His teacher finds it hard not to lose her temper with him and she gets very frustrated. John is quite aggressive to teachers as well as to children. If people don't do what he wants them to do, he can 'blow up'; even throwing chairs around and running out of the classroom. In fact often he leaves the school as well. His teacher feels that she doesn't get much support from his mum and dad, as they don't go up to school much and she hardly ever sees them.
>
> John's mum seems very protective of him. In her eyes John never seems to do anything wrong. John's dad has just come out of prison.

Then, the students were asked to turn to their accompanying questionnaire, which contained an 11-point rating scale, where '1' represented the 'worst behaved pupil I have ever known' and '11' the 'best behaved pupil I have ever known'. The students were asked to ring the number between 1 and 11 that they felt best represented their reply to the question: 'How well behaved is John at school?' The mean response for the 206 pupils is shown in Table 7.2.

The students were also asked at this stage whom they thought was most able to bring about an improvement in John's behaviour: his parents, teacher, John himself, other pupils or someone else. The replies to this question are shown in Table 7.1. Interestingly, the pupils viewed 'parents' and 'the pupil himself' as significantly more able to help effect solutions (and this is a statistical significance) than any of the other agents suggested, including teachers. This belief in the potential positive contribution that parents are able to make should augur well for home–school interventions, in that other pupils can be expected to be sympathetic to their rationale. This finding should also counter teachers' fears that other pupils will resent a teacher's attempting such an intervention. This result appears further to complement and consolidate the findings of the 'reward preference' studies (Chapter 8), in which pupils consistently rate positive information sent home as the most powerful reward at the disposal of schools.

Following these opening questions, a further section of the vignette was read, outlining the proposed home–school strategy:

> The educational psychologist came to school a few times to sit in John's class and watch what was going on. One of the times she came to school, she had a joint meeting with John's mum and dad and his teacher. As somebody who didn't usually work at the school, she was not so close to what was going on, and so she was able to listen to all sides of the story (mum's and dad's views and the teacher's view). She made sure she really understood what they were all saying. It was clear that John's parents did not want him to go to a special school.

Table 7.1 The number and percentages of pupils choosing each agent as the person most able to help improve behaviour

	No.	%
Parents	79	38.5
John himself	57	27.8
Teacher	24	11.7
Someone else	23	11.2
Other pupils	22	10.7

The educational psychologist made some suggestions to John's parents and his teacher of things they could try at home and at school in order to help John. Together they worked out a behaviour plan. The plan involved John's teacher choosing three of the classroom rules for John to try to concentrate on. She chose: put up your hand, work hard and listen carefully. She told John which rules she had chosen and explained that at the end of each lesson, they would sit down together and talk about how well he'd managed to stick to these three rules. He would get one or two ticks depending on how well he had done. If he hadn't stuck to the rules at all he wouldn't get any ticks for that lesson.

John was keen to try this behaviour plan and very confident that he'd be able to get lots of ticks. At the end of each week John and his teacher would count up his ticks, and if he had enough of them he would be allowed to choose where he wanted to go and work; for example, to go and use the computer.

The ticks also went into a home diary, which John took home at the end of each week to show his mum and dad. They looked at the diary to see how well John had stuck to the rules by counting his ticks. When he had lots of ticks his mum and dad allowed him to do certain things that he wanted to do. They also paid him five pence for each tick he got (though the school did not know about this). Since the start of the behaviour plan, John's mum would go up to school quite often to say how pleased she was that he had got so many ticks for a particular day.

After this section of the vignette the classes were again asked to turn to their questionnaires, and to respond on an identical 11-point scale to the question 'How well do you think John will behave now?' The mean score for the 206 students in the study is also shown in Table 7.2.

A final and much shorter section of the vignette was then presented: 'When the behaviour plan was being used, John's behaviour in the classroom improved a lot.' This was then followed by two questions, one on John's likely behaviour one month into the plan and a second relating to six months later, as in Table 7.2, and each in turn required a response on the questionnaire in exactly the same format as previously. The replies to these questions are also shown in Table 7.2.

Table 7.2 shows that, after the first section of the vignette, which detailed aspects of John's difficult behaviour, the pupils rated his behaviour as being at a level of some severity. After the second section of the vignette, this group showed a significantly optimistic view of the likelihood of improvement. Although some of this, and especially the estimates of medium- and longer-term outcomes, might be partly attributed to a naivety about the likely course

Table 7.2 Pupils' predictions of the probable degree of success likely to derive from the home–school intervention

	Pupils' mean score
Vignette 1 Description of 'presenting problems'	
A How well behaved is John at school?	1.87
Vignette 2 Outline of intervention	
B How do you think John will behave now?	6.08
Vignette 3 Brief account of outcome of intervention	
C How do you think John will behave after one month of the behaviour plan?	7.98
D How do you think John will behave after six months of the behaviour plan?	9.67

Rating scale: 1 = worst behaved pupil I have ever known, 11 = best behaved pupil I have ever known.

of interventions in respect of complex educational problems, this positive energy is there to be capitalized upon as an extra resource (Leyden 1996). The frequently voiced concern by teachers that other pupils are likely to resent or suffer in some way from interventions aimed at individual pupils displaying difficult behaviour is not, therefore, supported by this study.

However, it can be argued that these results derive from students responding to hypothetical scenarios and that, in real classrooms, real attempts to implement home–school strategies may produce very different responses within the student body.

Pupil culture and the Successful Strategies study

Fortunately, the Successful Strategies study can shed some light upon the actual responses of students to the implementation of real interventions of this type. From the teacher accounts in this study, it is possible to ask whether the pupil culture seemed to play some part, positive or negative, in the strategies or was in turn affected or altered by them. Put less theoretically, what effect, if any, do interventions involving teacher, parent and pupil have upon the other members of the pupil's class?

To answer this, it is useful to consider the peer group's response to the difficult behaviour before the instigation of the strategy in question. Although the study sample was not specifically chosen to include children who had engaged in physical attacks on other children, but only asked more generally for problems of 'an unsettled or anti-social nature', the teachers' accounts made frequent reference to this:

> Hitting children for no apparent reason. She had been standing at the corner and as kids came round she flailed them across the face with her skipping rope. (Interview 20)

> Knocking everybody else's bricks down and annoying everybody, very into kicking . . . he would kick all the other children and spit at them, virtually non-stop. (Interview 13)

> Hitting out, injuring other people . . . he was considered too dangerous to be in the classroom. (Interview 4)

Teachers and schools are vulnerable to accusations from parents and others that they are not carrying out their protective function *in loco parentis*, and physically aggressive behaviour of this order inevitably increased the pressure in some cases:

> He would throw tables and chairs, attack other children, really quite violent . . . you've got a safety aspect . . . we had to think about the other children because we'd had complaints from their parents about his behaviour. (Interview 15)

In total, 16 of the 23 teachers (70 per cent) referred to physical assaults on other children.

The pupils who were the subjects of these interviews were also seen by their teachers to have a direct and deleterious effect upon their classmates in another four cases (17 per cent). Although there was no mention of actual physical violence in these cases, the children all exerted a disruptive effect on the efforts of some or all of the other children. Sometimes this interference was direct in its nature, at other times it had a more diffuse effect:

> Where the children were all sitting together maybe on the carpet for a story or just a bit of discussion or whatever . . . he would want to get the attention of all the children and sort of do like cartwheels across the circle or something. (Interview 23)

In only three (13 per cent) of the interviews did the teachers not construe the problem behaviour as having a tangible effect upon the other children. In these cases the problems were described more in terms of the child being disorganized or reluctant to work, or of being oppositional to the teacher in some way. In the majority of cases, then, the target pupil's difficulties are very much seen by the teachers as having a classroom-wide effect in terms of impinging upon the other children.

The planned involvement of peers in the strategies

In six of the cases, teachers had included other pupils within the strategy in the class and in one other outside the class. In two of these strategies, the children were encouraged to ignore certain aspects of the child's behaviour:

> I tried to talk to the other children about [ignoring naughty behaviour] . . . And the children became very sensible and caring towards Brian because it worked so well that his personality just changed after a period of time and they actually like him. (Interview 13)

> We talked about how . . . they could just ignore him if he was doing that and if they laughed at him how that might encourage him. (Interview 23)

In another two cases, the class involvement was in terms of supplying information when there was a need for the teacher to make a judgement about degrees of responsibility:

> If he's hurt someone and it's an accident, and they [all the children present] admit that it could have been an accident, then he still gets his smiley face. (Interview 8)

The further two cases in which peers were included involved only more general exhortations to them to be helpful. The one intervention that elicited help outside the class did so in the form of feedback information:

> They came and told me that he'd been good. I think they probably made allowances . . . they all rallied round him in a way . . . they were all there, you know, 'Is he going to get a sticker today?' and they were just happy when he did. It was nice. (Interview 14)

The unplanned involvement of peers in strategies

However, the study revealed that there were also nine cases in which the pupils, of their own accord, initiated actions in sympathy with the aims of the interventions. (Two of these were cases in which peers also had planned roles.) These include occasions on which the pupils had, as it were, attached themselves to the strategies and those during which their praise and encouragement had generalized to other activities:

> The diary . . . some are . . . they always used to come up and praise him
> if he got a star – some of them – and if he'd had a good day they'd say,
> 'Oh, Peter's done well.' (interview 12)

> They would pat him on the back when he'd achieved something, they
> were wonderful. I didn't have to ask them to do that, it was there. And
> they would say, 'Well done, Brian, that's really good.' Maybe they
> heard me doing it and were copying me doing it but a lot of it I really
> felt came from them. They were genuinely – they shared his triumphs
> with him, they were lovely. (Interview 13)

Another teacher found herself speculating about the possibility that pupils
were not imitating her behaviour as much as seeking some of the extended
teacher availability or teacher praise for themselves. She nevertheless found
the mechanism elusive to identify:

> I don't know, maybe it was to please teacher. I don't know. I'm sure
> that they were more protective and more helpful towards him . . . It's
> so subtle that they may not have realized that he was getting extra
> attention. (Interview 21)

In some interviews, new social dynamics developed among the pupils. The
teachers saw these as being unambiguously outside the teacher's sphere of
direct influence:

> They also started to include him in class activities . . . they also
> included him in their games a little; they tried to tolerate him . . . I
> noticed he was chosen to be with a group. You know, when you say,
> 'Will you form yourselves into groups.' (Interview 18)

> I think, because of the way his attitude changed, the other children
> were more responsive to him. And he wasn't sort of pushed about as
> being 'Oh, it's only Ian!' And I suppose they showed him more
> respect. (Interview 11)

In total, there were 10 interventions in which the teacher did not involve
pupils or did not think that pupils had found some way to involve themselves.
In all but one of these, however, the pupils were none the less aware of some
elements of the strategy. There was clearly a concern for a number of the
teachers that other children, if they knew, would expect to be treated in the
same way as the pupil who was the subject of the intervention. Only two,
however, felt that they actually had to make a response to this, although for
one of them this took a somewhat dramatic form:

'Why has Ben got a book and I haven't?' We got that one . . . Particularly the children who were on his table, so I sat down and talked to them about it . . . I just said that it was a special book that went home because his mummy didn't always come to school . . . and they were quite happy with that. (Interview 15)

The turning point came when one of the other children came and said, 'If I'm a naughty boy will you do for me what you do for Lee?' And at that point I went to the head and said, 'That's it. This child has had too much of my time!' (Interview 1)

Despite their initial apprehension, however, none of the other teachers encountered such problems:

I haven't yet fortunately seen anybody who thinks they're going to be naughty so they can have a contract! I was quite worried about that . . . I think that the children know that what Adam does is wrong. And they really know that the contract is trying to help Adam. (Interview 6)

They knew about the charts . . . they didn't see that as anything special. (Interview 17).

A number of teachers felt that the other children tolerated the different management regime because they saw it as linked to a classmate's unacceptable behaviour:

I think they just thought, 'Well, yes, she's telling Darren [the rules] because Darren is Darren.' (Interview 3)

The children accepted it very well . . . they knew that he had his chart to fill in and they knew why – because his behaviour was so obviously different to theirs. (Interview 17)

This theme – the concern that making exceptions will lead to a deterioration in the teacher's ability to manage the whole class – is a prevalent one. The general reaction of the other pupils, however, runs counter to these expectations and the phrase 'they just accepted it' recurs very frequently.

As if to add to the fears of insurrection within a class group, some of the teachers in the study also found the strategies they were attempting to implement undermined by parents or colleagues who once again introduced considerations of other pupils:

It was the parents more who wouldn't accept that he was going to be treated differently because I had people in saying, 'Why is he getting more stickers than other people?' or 'We hope you're not rewarding bad behaviour.' (Interview 17)

I think they [colleagues] wondered how much damage it was doing the rest of the children in the class, and in the school. (Interview 15)

In summary, the Successful Strategies study has shown that all but one of the 24 teachers recognized that the interventions, although primarily involving home and school, also impinged in various intended and unintended ways upon the pupil culture. Put more theoretically, the individual teacher, student and parent strategies also displayed various recursive relationships with the pupil cultures (as they were shown in Chapter 6 to do with the staff cultures).

Despite the teachers' initial concerns, these 'side effects' were seen as positive, or no worse than neutral, in all but one of the cases. Apprehensions that treating one pupil differently would lead to overall class management problems were common but unrealized, although other staff and parents occasionally exacerbated these fears.

The relationship between pupil culture and the other subsystems

This chapter has examined various aspects of pupil culture, both in relation to home–school behaviour strategies and in terms of interactions with other psychosocial processes in schools. Recently there has been an increasing focus upon the capacity of peer cultures to act in a 'prosocial' fashion. Utilizing the power of peer cultures, whether in the form of bully courts, peer counselling schemes, Circles of Friends or other approaches, has, however, proved controversial or of some delicacy at times.

To implement such approaches usually requires changes to pupil organizational groupings, possibly backed up by new policies and procedures. Some of these suggested changes may impinge upon staff culture, creating anxiety about the capacity of fellow students to act with the sense of care and responsibility required. This caution is a sensible reaction, given the sensitivities involved and the consequences of abuses of trust. However, as the evidence base continues to grow, so too may optimism about the potential of many of the approaches, provided they are not construed simply as isolated techniques to be pasted into the curriculum, but are seen in interaction with other formal and informal aspects of the psychosocial nature of schools.

Even where strategies predominantly involve only a teacher, parent and individual student, recursive relationships with pupil culture have been shown to exist. Teachers' accounts from the Successful Strategies study reveal that a classroom is no place to keep secret the details of such interventions. Despite some teachers' understandable reservations, sometimes fuelled by parents and colleagues, other pupils will accept these individualized approaches and will participate productively and enthusiastically in them – whether invited to do so or not!

8   Teacher, student and parent perspectives on behaviour: clash *and* concordance

Having explored the ways in which informal group belief systems arise within schools for both teachers and students, in this chapter I turn more specifically to studies of individuals: teachers, students and, for the first time in the book, parents. The studies described present an evidence base that demonstrates the fundamental differences between these three parties over the ways in which they make sense of various aspects of the behaviour issue. The reasons for these genuinely held perspectives are related to the psychosocial nature of schools and the particular challenges presented by student behaviour deemed to be difficult. Clashes in perspective are shown to exist in at least four areas: the identification of which students and which types of behaviour are judged to be problematic; the assumed causes of difficult behaviour; effective rewards and sanctions; and views about whose responsibility it is to take what action, and its likely efficacy. The case is made that these various differences may give rise to many of the intense emotions surrounding attempts to achieve productive partnerships between teachers and parents. On an optimistic note, the evidence base also shows that there is concordance between teachers, students and parents. The detailed pattern of clash and concordance shows that simplistic attempts to blame one party or another are both incorrect and counter-productive and that, with a deeper understanding of these phenomena, attempts at mediation stand a much stronger likelihood of bringing about positive outcomes for all.

Introduction

Previous chapters have examined in detail the hidden and informal processes that help to shape collective beliefs about student behaviour for both teacher and student members of a school community. Although such cultural phenomena are not usually stated explicitly, their influence on policy development and especially on everyday practice has been shown, in Chapters 6 and 7, to be considerable. Chapter 4 has outlined the evidence base that supports the potential of certain strategies involving teachers and parents and

Chapter 5 has detailed the ways in which an external mediator can assist in the implementation of these.

However, the barriers to effective strategies seem, in the light of developments outlined in Chapter 1, to remain strong. As high profile cases and political pronouncements pour into the national consciousness in a sometimes indiscriminate and ill-considered fashion, these barriers escalate. Whereas research and practice have shown that challenging behaviour can be successfully improved by careful professional intervention, intemperate public airings can all too easily raise barriers into barricades. The task of this chapter is to bring these discussions back into a rational examination of the legitimate boundaries between school and home, in terms of the respective responsibilities of each, and to look carefully at the ways in which the escalation into barriers and on into barricades may be prevented.

In order to do this, four areas of evidence are considered, beginning with the fundamental issue of whether there is an initial perception shared between teachers and parents as to what constitutes difficult behaviour in schools.

Teachers' and parents' identification of problem behaviour

A number of carefully conducted surveys have asked teachers to identify the intensity and frequency of different types of difficult and/or disturbed behaviour among their pupils. These have normally required teachers to complete schedules or checklists specifically devised for this purpose. Some of the studies have also asked parents to complete similar instruments designed to detect problems in the home context. The same finding occurs in each study – that the *majority* of children identified as problems in one setting are not seen as such in the other.

For example, in an Isle of Wight survey of over 2000 children – one of the most thorough studies of childhood problems ever carried out – standardized questionnaires completed by teachers and parents proved extremely effective in screening out children with psychiatric disorders (Rutter *et al.* 1970). However, there was surprisingly little overlap between the two sources, with only one child in every six or seven in the 'deviant group' being identified by both parties.

This lack of a close correspondence between teachers' and parents' perceptions of behaviour problems was also demonstrated in the longitudinal study of 343 London children by Tizard *et al.* (1988). At the end of the top infant years teachers saw 34 per cent of the children as having a mild or definite behaviour problem and parents identified 22 per cent. However, only 30 per cent of those seen by teachers as a problem at school were also seen as problems at home and only 34 per cent of those identified by parents were similarly perceived as difficult by teachers.

This is not just a phenomenon confined to British society; similar results have also been obtained from a study conducted in New Zealand (McGee *et al.* 1983). This recurring finding suggests that either some forms of behaviour are context-specific in that they are more likely to occur either at home or at school but not at both, or that some forms of behaviour have far more salience for teachers and others for parents. For example, Tizard *et al.* (1988) suggested that some types of behaviour, such as lack of concentration, may be more of a problem in the school setting than at home and that other types, such as fooling around or nervousness and withdrawal, may simply be more likely to occur at school.

The studies have enormous implications for the types of initial discussions that parents and teachers may have when a school is concerned about a pupil's behaviour. Parents may be seen as being 'unwilling to accept that there is a problem', whereas they may genuinely not be experiencing the same difficulties in the home setting. The scenario in Chapter 2 illustrating circular causality hypothesized just such a parental perception and illustrated how this could become linked into a set of recursive beliefs and consequent actions extending far into the public and hidden aspects of school and family functioning.

Similarly, parents who mention difficulties with their children at home, when these children are models of conformity at school, may be inaccurately perceived as 'fussing unnecessarily', 'neurotic' or 'incompetent' as parents. The relatively high probability of such judgements being made as a result of differing problem identification on the part of teachers and parents is likely to be one reason why some attempts to set up mutual strategies quickly become confusing and mutually antagonistic.

Of course, it is not necessary for teachers and parents actually to meet for such perceptions like this to arise. Misconceptions can flourish in the absence of contact and communication. 'It's the ones who never turn up that you really want to see' is a common complaint in many staff rooms and also the title of a chapter by Bridges (1987). This describes the results of a series of interviews in Cambridgeshire with parents who were regular non-attenders at parents' evenings and social events at schools. Rather than mere indifference and apathy, the interviews identified a range of reasons, from practical difficulties such as transport, family ties and shift work, through to a concern about not being as confident as some other parents in discussing educational matters. But the most recurring theme in the interviews was a dread of school, often associated with their own childhood experiences, this being most prevalent among those parents who had minimal or no contact.

It is not hard to imagine such a parent, avoiding contact with the school, however welcoming the invitation. If the situation arises when the school wishes to discuss any matter, especially behaviour, it is also not hard to imagine this parent's manner, fuelled by adrenaline and defensiveness, coming across as 'aggressive' or 'belligerent' or, at the very least, 'uncooperative'.

Attributions for the causes of difficult behaviour in schools

Another area where a huge potential for early misunderstanding exists is in the attributions that the various parties – teachers, students, parents and others – are likely to make for the causes of difficult behaviour in schools. In Chapter 2 it was argued that, once patterns of recursive causation are in motion, the beliefs and behaviour of any one party may be construed as the cause of, or stimulus to, the thoughts and actions of the other. Hence, the search for the 'original or one true cause' or 'what started this in the first place' may become fruitless and a distraction from finding ways forward. But engaging in such searches is a deeply human pursuit and, *outside of systems where there are likely to be high degrees of recursive causality*, an eminently sensible course of action.

Hence, if there is a strong tendency to make attributions for the causes of complex events, it becomes extremely important, given this book's subject matter, to ask how teachers, students and parents attribute the causes of difficult behaviour in schools, and whether there is a clash or concordance between their various views.

Before we look at some of the research evidence concerning these attributions, however, it is also necessary to note that the very notion of 'cause' becomes more complex when applied to difficult behaviour and in a system where there is a high likelihood of recursive patterns of causation. At least four types of cause may be envisaged:

- *Predisposing.* These are factors that may be distant in time and space from the actual behaviour but be construed as contributing to the likelihood of the behaviour occurring in certain circumstances. Predisposing factors might include experiences in early life, insufficient sleep or uninspiring curriculum planning.
- *Precipitating.* These may be thought of as 'triggers', perhaps a chance remark, a sense of frustration or a dispute amongs students over an item of equipment.
- *Prolonging.* As the term implies, included here might be responses or consequences that lead to maintenance of the behaviour for longer than might have been the case, such as the reactions of others or an experience of having some need temporarily met.
- *Perpetuating.* Included here would be other consequences that might make the behaviour more likely to occur again at some time in the future, perhaps a change in the student's peer status or a particular change in a teacher's class management strategy.

Clearly, when discussing whether different individuals and groups agree or clash in their judgements about the causes of difficult behaviour, or just attempting to understand as an individual, it may be extremely important which type or types of cause are being envisaged or discussed.

Teachers' attributions for the causes of difficult behaviour in schools

Early study of teachers' attributions for difficult pupil behaviour can be found in that area of literature concerned with labelling theory. In British accounts this was usually approached more from an ethnographic perspective and tended to yield accounts that were mainly descriptive in nature.

For example, Hargreaves (1975) approached the subject of attribution via the concept of implicit theories. He argued that individuals form implicit theories about what personality traits occur together, deriving these partly from common elements within the culture and partly from various forms of social learning peculiar to the individual. He went on, however, to argue that the attribution of motives or intentions was of greater importance than just personality traits and described how this might take place, concluding that 'once Person has developed a fairly consistent picture of Other he will tend to resist new information which threatens this consistency' (Hargreaves 1975: 25).

In their ethnographic study of a primary school, which drew upon data collected by interview and participant observation, Sharp and Green (1975: 179) set out the processes that such a study would need to examine:

> It would appear that parents should not be studied atomistically but in relationship to other facets of the interactional nexus within the school itself . . . it seems important to adopt a dynamic perspective to see how teachers' and parents' typification of each other are generated over time as each attempts to negotiate a meaningful symbolic reality and further their ends in response to the situation they confront. Thus categories of good and bad parents, or good and bad teachers, have to be seen in relationship to the past and present biography of the actors concerned in the ongoing process of their mutual encounters. Similarly, there is a need not merely to look at attitudes but also actions as teachers and parents develop strategies which both derive from and serve to stabilise the complex systems of meaning generated in specific situations.

Within an extensive survey of primary school teachers' attitudes, Croll and Moses (1985: 42) argued that

> Teachers' ideas about the causes of special needs, particularly learning difficulties and behaviour problems, are likely to affect the attitudes

they take towards children with special needs and so too influence the ways in which they react towards them in the classroom. When considering teachers' explanations of the special needs of their pupils, it is of interest to set them in the context of the different, and at times competing, explanations available for children's academic failures and behaviour difficulties.

Croll and Moses (1985) examined mainstream teachers' knowledge and practice in respect of special educational needs, and asked 428 teachers to give their explanations for the special needs of children in their classes. Causal factors such as 'IQ or ability', 'attitude' and 'concentration' and others were grouped under the general heading of 'within-child', whereas those such as material circumstances at home, parental attitudes or pathological social or emotional conditions were categorized under 'home'. This survey found that behaviour or discipline problems were seen to be due to home factors in 66 per cent of cases, to 'within-child' factors in 30 per cent of cases and to any school or teacher factors (including previous schools or teachers) in fewer than 4 per cent of cases.

Similarly, the Elton Report (DES 1989: 133) commented that 'Our evidence suggests that teachers' picture of parents is generally very negative. Many teachers feel that parents are to blame for much misbehaviour in schools. We consider that, while this picture contains an element of truth, it is distorted.' In fact, after reviewing the pronouncements of a wide range of interested parties – policy-makers, teaching staff and organizations, parents' groups, academics and others – Hood (1999) concluded that models of parents as 'problems', rather than 'partners' or 'consumers', were likely to dominate in situations where there is concern about student behaviour in school.

Given the picture emerging, the Successful Strategies study sought to get beneath the surface of descriptions such as 'home factors' or 'within-child' explanations and to explore the more 'fine-grained' detail of the attributions that teachers make about causes. As part of the analysis, the transcripts of the teacher interviews were subsequently 'combed' for all suggested or hypothesized causes of the original behaviour. These are listed in Table 8.1.

Perhaps, the most striking aspect of Table 8.1 is the number of different items it contains. Unlike some political pundits and sections of the media, these teachers clearly perceive causation to be a complex issue, influenced by a web of characteristics belonging to parents, teachers and pupils themselves.

Eiser (1978) has argued that the degree of differentiation within a set of attributions represents the extent of the conceptual elaboration of that set and hence its perceived importance:

> When we make an attribution about another person . . . we are essentially trying to interpret or explain his behaviour, and in doing so

Table 8.1 Teachers' attributions for the origins of difficult behaviour

Attributions made to pupils	Attributions made to parents	Attributions made to teachers
Need for praise (7)	General management of child (8)	Interest level of work set (4)
Lack of acceptance of social norms (7)	Punitive/violent home (7)	Work expectations/steps set (3)
'Physical/medical' (7)	Absence of father (6)	Negative attention to pupil (2)
Temperament/personality (6)	Lack of attention to child (6)	Teacher's anxiety (2)
Not feeling valued/self-esteem (5)	Divided loyalties re: separation/divorce (5)	Lack of incentives/tangible rewards (1)
Attention-seeking (4)	Management of difficult behaviour (4)	Lack of record-keeping (1)
Lack of acceptance of school rules (4)	Geographical problems re: separation/ divorce (1)	Lack of specific management techniques (1)
Lack of maturity (4)	Lack of encouragement (1)	Lack of affection/sympathy for child (1)
Attention span (4)	Atmosphere of disharmony (1)	Teacher not making an exception (1)
Lack of motivation towards school work (3)	Adoption issues (1)	Pressure from other parents (1)
Intelligence (2)	Parent illness (1)	
Lack of awareness of effect on other children (2)	Grandparents' influence (1)	
Knowledge of specific school rules (1)	Lack of affection (1)	
Knowledge of general social norms (1)	House move (1)	
Lack of respect for teacher (1)	Geographical isolation (1)	
Comprehension level (1)		
Lack of awareness of effect on parent (1)		
'Tough guy' self-image (1)		
'Clutter in head' (1)		
Lack of trust in others (1)		
Effect of bad previous school experiences (1)		

render our social environment that much more predictable and intelligible. The size of the vocabulary at our disposal is evidence of the importance we attach to doing this.

In Table 8.1, there are 21 mechanisms attributed to pupils – that is, 21 different ways in which pupils were seen as being implicated in the origin of their own difficult behaviour – 15 ways attributed to parents and 10 to the teachers themselves. Pursuing Eiser's argument, this might suggest that the teachers in this study had a relatively large 'vocabulary' with which to construe pupils' contributions to their own behaviour. This makes intuitive sense, in that the behaviour is most immediately located in the young person, and teachers' thinking and discussion with colleagues will help to elaborate this range of mechanisms. The set of mechanisms attributed to parents is also developed to a relatively high degree, with those to the teachers themselves less so. What is being discussed *here* is not whether pupils, parents or teachers are seen as ultimately more responsible. Instead, the relative extent to which a set of attributions is elaborated is taken as an indicator of the degree to which a particular type of discourse has been developed.

So, these findings suggest that teachers are more used to thinking and talking about the detail of the varied ways in which pupils, and then parents, may act as the causes of difficult behaviour. These are highly elaborated discourses.

However, there is another, less immediately obvious feature of these lists that has significant implications for practice, and that is the extent to which these possible causes are seen to be under the *control* of the parties to whom they are attributed. If, for example, people were to view a student's 'attention span' as something beyond that young person's conscious control, then they would be likely to be relatively sympathetic towards any difficulties arising from this. Alternatively, however, behaviour judged to be within conscious control, perhaps a parent's 'lack of attention to a child' or a teacher's 'lack of record keeping', is far more likely to elicit feelings of blame and disapproval.

The lists in Table 8.1 were examined item by item by a group of seven teachers training to become educational psychologists. They were asked to make judgements about the degree to which each item might be considered to be under the control of the 'actor' to whom it had been attributed. Each interview transcript was then read again and note was taken of every *high controllability* attribution made by the teachers to parents, pupils or themselves.

Table 8.2 summarizes the number of teachers making high controllability attributions to each actor for the causes of the difficult behaviour. When only the items commonly agreed as being highly within the control of each actor were compared in this way, then a clear majority of the 24 teachers judged the difficult behaviour to be the *fault* of parents. However, half of this sample of teachers also assumed some responsibility themselves.

Table 8.2 The number of teachers making *high controllability* attributions to the three agents for the causes of the difficult behaviour

High controllability attribution to	No. of teachers
Parents	17
Teachers	12
Pupils	9

Attributions of cause, it is worth repeating, are not 'objective truths'. They are the results of our human capacity to infer cause in complex social situations. When circumstances are distressing or threatening, it is often on the basis of our attributions, rather than other sources of information, that we tend to act. The studies reviewed in this section suggest that there has been a longstanding tendency on the part of teachers to see difficult classroom behaviour as being caused predominantly by parents and other home circumstances. In the light of the injunctions contained in legislation and policy for teachers and parents to engage in 'genuine discussion' over issues of pupil behaviour (DfEE 1998a), it is not difficult to appreciate just how significant an impediment such attributions will almost certainly be.

And this may not be the end of the story. What of the attributions for causes that parents and students make? If these are at odds with those of teachers, the stage will be set for dialogue of a very superficial nature, in which differences of deep fundamental assumptions are not acknowledged. Just as with the research showing teachers and parents often coming to different conclusions about who and what is actually construed as 'difficult', so too with theories of who or what are to blame. These psychosocial factors may have the power to undermine and destroy the best-laid plans and policies. Hence, the next section of this chapter examines research into the attributions made by pupils and parents for difficult behaviour in classrooms.

Students' attributions for the causes of difficult behaviour in schools

In order to investigate how students attribute the causes of difficult behaviour in schools, a two-part study (Miller *et al.* 2000) was carried out in an inner city secondary school in the north-west of England. This involved a total of 125 Year 7 pupils (predominantly 12 years of age), comprising essentially that entire year group for the school.

The investigation was carried out using a questionnaire about the possible causes of difficult behaviour in schools, the items for this questionnaire having been derived from a number of prior small group interviews. The students who generated the questionnaire items were selected by the head of year as being representative in terms of ability, behaviour and gender, and were seen by the researcher in four small groups. In these groups, the students were asked to think back to their time in primary schools and to remember the types of misbehaviour they had witnessed, and perhaps engaged in. Primary, rather than the current secondary, school settings were examined because that is the sector examined by the corresponding research on teacher attributions. The researcher was careful not to suggest answers, but provided a set of prompts to encourage the students to think of all possible reasons why there might be misbehaviour in schools.

A questionnaire was then constructed incorporating all the possible reasons provided by the groups using, wherever possible, the actual terminology of the students. One or two items, such as the possibility of sexual abuse, were omitted from the questionnaire, despite being raised in each group, because it was felt that, presented on a questionnaire, they might cause distress or anxiety. The resulting questionnaire consisted of 27 items (as in Table 8.3, but presented in a randomized order) and students were asked how important they judged each to be as a cause of difficult behaviour in schools.

In the second part of the study all pupils from the year group who had not participated in the preliminary discussions, 105 in total, filled in the questionnaire. This was administered in class groups, with the researcher reading out the questions one by one in each class, providing reminders about the method of responding and encouraging students to ask about any items where the meaning might be unclear or ambiguous.

The data obtained from this study were analysed by means of exploratory factor analysis and further details of the statistical analysis carried out may be found in Miller *et al.* (2000). In essence, this approach identifies clusters of items that are perceived by those completing the questionnaires as belonging together in some way as 'psychological entities'. Table 8.3 shows the four factors emerging from the analysis. Factor 1 was termed 'unfairness of teacher's actions' and appears to attribute misbehaviour to injustices on the part of teachers. The second factor was termed 'pupil vulnerability' and reflects misbehaviour attributed to certain children being vulnerable to pressure from other pupils, their own emotional turmoil or difficulties with school work. The third factor was termed 'adverse family circumstances' and reflects attributions for misbehaviour being located within families' inability to control their children and general family problems (financial hardship, drink, drugs etc.). The final factor represents another teacher factor but this time reflecting on the 'strictness of the classroom regime' in terms of the amount of class and homework set and the rigour with which the teacher manages the class.

Further analysis of the data showed that these pupils rated 'teacher's unfairness' and 'pupil vulnerability' as statistically significantly more important causes of misbehaviour than either family problems or how strictly

Table 8.3 Pupils' perceptions of the causes of difficult behaviour in schools

Factor 1	Factor 2	Factor 3	Factor 4
Teachers shouted all the time	Other pupils wanted pupil to be in gang	Too much classwork was given	There were fights and arguments at home
Pupils were picked on by teachers	Other pupils told pupil to misbehave	Too much homework was given	Alcohol/drug abuse by family members
Teachers did not listen to pupils	Pupil was unable to see mum/dad	Teachers were too strict	Parents let pupils get away with too much
Teachers had favourites	Pupils were worried about other things		Families did not have enough money to eat or buy clothes
Pupils were unfairly blamed	Pupils liked misbehaving		
Good work wasn't noticed	Other pupils wanted to copy work		
Teachers were rude to pupils	Pupils needed more help in class		
Teachers had bad moods	Classwork was too difficult		
Teachers gave too many detentions	Other pupils stirred up trouble		
Teachers were too soft			
Pupils didn't like teacher			

the classroom was managed. There were no significant differences between the results obtained from boys and girls.

This study shows students to attribute to teachers a significantly greater responsibility for pupil misbehaviour than they attribute to parents. This is in dramatically marked contrast to the findings from Croll and Moses (1985), in which teachers attributed pupil misbehaviour to home rather than school factors by a ratio of 17:1, and is a finding likely to prove unpalatable to teachers and many involved with educational policy-making.

This ongoing strand of research is, however, showing that other groups of students identify home and family factors as being equally implicated with 'teacher unfairness' as causes of misbehaviour in classrooms. There is also emerging evidence that these attributions vary between students with differing patterns of academic abilities and psychological characteristics (Ferguson et al. 2003). While this new research 'softens' the previous finding somewhat, there is still a strong conflict with the patterns of teachers' attribution and, whatever the 'truth' of the situation, this has the potential to remain an enormous obstacle to the search for agreement between teachers and students.

Parents' attributions for the causes of difficult behaviour in schools

Given the drive for parents to be involved in genuine home–school agreements and in acceptance of some responsibility for their children's school behaviour, it becomes imperative to know whether their attributional styles will resemble more closely those of teachers or of students. In order to investigate this question, a study that paralleled many of the procedures from the study of pupils' attributions was carried out with parents in an inner-city primary school (Miller et al. 2002).

This again consisted of two parts, the first being a series of intensive small-group interviews designed to elucidate scenarios that would form the basis of the questionnaire. The second, and main, study was a quantitative survey of parent attributions regarding pupils' misbehaviour in schools. The group interviews eventually yielded 61 different items, including the 27 previously obtained from the small-group discussions with pupils, all of which were seen by these parents as possible causes of student misbehaviour in schools.

Two copies of the resulting questionnaire and a covering letter were then distributed to all 165 families represented in the school. The researcher also spoke to all the children about the project in assembly the same day and asked them to encourage their parents to complete the questionnaires and to return them to school. Either one or two questionnaires were returned by 114 families, a response rate of 69 per cent. Although the full 61-item questionnaire was administered to the parent sample, the analysis concentrates only on those items also presented to pupils in the previous study, to allow for a direct comparison between these two groups.

Factor analysis of the parent responses produced a three-factor model. Factor 1 was again termed 'fairness of teacher's actions', as in the pupil study, and appears to attribute misbehaviour to perceived injustices on the part of teachers. The second factor was termed 'pupil vulnerability to peer influences and adverse family circumstances' and reflects a view of misbehaviour as originating with pressure from other pupils, or from families' inability to control their children, and general family problems (e.g. financial hardship, discord, absent parent). The final factor, 'differentiation of classroom demands and expectations' comprises school-based elements related to the appropriateness of, and the degree of support provided in respect of, the curriculum demands placed upon pupils.

The factor structures for pupils and parents reveal a number of interesting comparisons and contrasts (as in Table 8.4), which are discussed in detail elsewhere (Miller *et al.* 2002). First, the same factor, 'fairness of teacher's actions', emerges from the study of both parents and pupils. For both groups this is also seen as one of the most prominent causes of misbehaviour. The two studies were conducted in cities about two hundred miles apart and this result cannot therefore be interpreted as a reflection of local circumstances common to both groups.

Second, a factor concerning 'pupil vulnerability' rates equally highly for both parents and pupils as a major cause of misbehaviour. However, this study also shows that parents do agree with teachers that certain adverse home circumstances can equally be seen as a major cause of difficult student behaviour in schools.

These findings may be interpreted as a cause for either optimism or pessimism. Although teachers express a 'lack of parental support' as a major barrier to being able to implement successful behaviour plans (see, especially, Chapters 4 and 10), this study shows that parents do concur with teachers over certain aspects of the influence of home background. Therefore, it should not be assumed that parents automatically start from a different set of beliefs from teachers in this respect. The converse, however, seems to be the case when it comes to considering the possible influences of teachers on the behaviour of pupils, with parents and pupils far more likely to share a common opinion concerning the influence of actions by teachers that they deem to be unfair.

The sequence of studies described in this chapter so far has drawn attention to the potential importance of issues of attribution to an understanding of the strained and contentious nature of home–school relationships that surround instances of difficult behaviour in schools. This area of psychological study could well be seen as the 'missing link' between legal and policy imperatives on the one hand and workable, 'real world' strategies on the other. The implications for policy and practice are examined at the end of this chapter,

Table 8.4 The most important causes of misbehaviour deriving from factor analytic studies with parents and pupils

Pupil factors	Parent factors
Unfairness of teachers' actions	*Unfairness of teachers' actions*
Teachers shouted all the time	Teachers have favourites
Pupils were picked on by teachers	Pupils are picked on by teachers
Teachers did not listen to pupils	Teachers are rude to pupils
Teachers had favourites	Teachers shout all the time
Pupils were unfairly blamed	Teachers do not listen to pupils
Good work wasn't noticed	Teachers are too soft
Teachers were rude to pupils	Good work isn't noticed
Teachers had bad moods	Pupils are unfairly blamed
Teachers gave too many detentions	Teachers have bad moods
Teachers were too soft	
Pupils didn't like teacher	
	Pupil vulnerability to peer influence and adverse family circumstances
Pupil vulnerability	
Other pupils wanted pupil to be in gang	Other pupils tell pupil to misbehave
Other pupils told pupil to misbehave	Other pupils want pupil to be in gang
Pupil was unable to see mum/dad	Families do not have enough money to eat or buy clothes
Pupils were worried about other things	
Pupils liked misbehaving	Other pupils want to copy work
Other pupils wanted to copy work	Other pupils stir up trouble
Pupils needed more help in class	Pupil is unable to see mum/dad
Classwork was too difficult	Parents let pupils get away with too much
Other pupils stirred up trouble	
	Pupils like misbehaving
	There are fights and arguments at home
....	....
	Differentiation of classroom demands and expectations
Strictness of classroom regime	
Too much classwork was given	Too much homework is given
Too much homework was given	Teachers are too strict
Teachers were too strict	Too much classwork is given
Adverse family circumstances	Classwork is too difficult
There were fights and arguments at home	Pupil needs more help in class
Alcohol/drug abuse by family members	Pupil doesn't like the teacher
Parents let pupils get away with too much	Pupil is worried about other things
Families did not have enough money to eat or buy clothes	

Factors above the dotted line across the table were rated as statistically more influential as causes than those below.

after a brief examination of other areas where the perspectives of teachers, students and parents can be seen to clash and correspond in an unpredictable fashion.

Teachers', students' and parents' identification of effective rewards and sanctions

A small series of British studies, which have come to be known as 'reward preference' studies, have repeatedly found that students, in both primary schools (Harrop and Williams 1992; Merrett and Tang 1994) and secondary schools (Sharpe *et al.* 1987; Houghton *et al.* 1988), select 'information sent home to their parents reporting on their achievements and their transgressions' as likely to be the most potent from a selection of various rewards and sanctions.

However, studies exploring teachers' views about effective rewards and sanctions (e.g. Caffyn 1989) and about the frequency with which various approaches are used (Harrop and Williams 1992) have provided evidence of a lack of concordance between teachers and pupils. These studies have shown that positive information home is not considered by teachers to be a particularly potent reward or to be used frequently, although a complaint home is relatively common. The beliefs of pupils and teachers therefore also conflict over the potential efficacy of parental involvement in strategies to improve school-based behaviour.

In terms of the possible concordance between parents and students over rewards and sanctions, Miller *et al.* (1998) carried out a survey of primary school students and their parents. They found both groups to be in clear agreement over the potency of positive information being sent home, but there was considerable disagreement between parents and pupils over the likely relative efficacy of school-generated punishments.

These results are clearly of immediate relevance to those engaged in developing school behaviour policies, where this research suggests that, among other measures, information home, especially for positive aspects of conduct and not just academic achievement, should be a prime component. Again, the implications of these studies are examined in the final section of the chapter.

Teachers' and students' judgements as to who should take responsibility for intervening over difficult classroom behaviour

So far, this chapter has examined the correspondence, and lack of it, between teachers', students' and parents' perspectives on what is seen as difficult behaviour and who is judged to be displaying it, the major causes of this behaviour and the likely efficacy of positive information being sent home as part of an intervention strategy. The final area of research now to be briefly examined is that of teachers' and students' views about who is most able to bring about an improvement in behaviour that is judged unmanageable or disruptive in classrooms.

In Chapter 7 a vignette study was introduced in which students were asked whom they felt was most able to bring about a positive change in the behaviour of John, a hypothetical student (Miller and Black 2001). In addition to the 206 primary school students who participated in the study, 30 teachers from seven different schools completed the same sets of questionnaires in response to the same vignette presentation. Adding the results from these teachers to the data contained in Table 7.1 allows a direct comparison to be made between students and teachers' views, as in Table 8.5.

Table 8.5   A contingency table to show the number and percentages of pupils and teachers choosing each agent as the person most able to help improve the behaviour

	Pupils' choice		Teachers' choice	
	No.	%	No.	%
Parents	79	38.5	8	26.7
John himself	57	27.8	2	6.7
Teacher	24	11.7	13	43.3
Someone else	23	11.2	7	23.3
Other pupils	22	10.7	0	0.0

Source: from Miller and Black (2001).

Although some caution must be exercised in drawing firm conclusions from a questionnaire survey sample of only 30 teachers, nevertheless, especially given the other research examined in this chapter, some interesting differences appear to emerge. The strongest of these are the students' much greater belief that John himself is able to bring about an improvement and their far less developed faith in teachers being able to achieve this.

Acknowledging differing starting points while also avoiding blame: the fine line

Before we consider the practical implications of the research studies described in this chapter, it may be helpful to summarize some of the major areas of concordance and clash that have been uncovered:

- teachers and parents do not, in the majority of cases, identify the same students as having difficulties and problems;
- parents and students agree that 'teacher unfairness' is a major cause of difficult behaviour in schools, but teachers do not;
- teachers and parents, and perhaps students, agree that adverse home circumstances are a major cause of difficult behaviour;
- pupils and parents view positive information being sent home as a particularly potent reward for acceptable behaviour in schools, but teachers do not;
- teachers think that they are the party most able to bring about improvement in a student's classroom behaviour, but students do not.
- students think parents are the party most able to bring about such improvement, but teachers do not.

The pattern of clash and concordance between various of the views of these three important parties is clearly a complex one. And given this, is it any wonder that attempts to produce agreement over joint strategies, with or without the involvement of external consultants, are often characterized by extreme sensitivities and the sense of 'walking on eggshells'?

The implications of these findings are likely to be extremely important. At the outset, it seems essential to acknowledge that conflicting and coinciding views exist and that these should be acknowledged as legitimate starting points for different parties. In particular, there is a need to recognize that attributions are always one particular way of making sense of phenomena and born of our natural human desire to understand the causes of phenomena. There is a very fine line, and a crucial one, to be drawn between acknowledging this and seeming absorbed with a desire to apportion blame. This may be an area in which the contribution of skilled external mediation can be successfully utilized, as in the Successful Strategies study.

In order to achieve outcomes similar to those in that study, a number of prerequisites are likely to be required:

- Teachers will need to be aware of the attributions that they make for the causes of difficult behaviour.
- Once acknowledged, a way must be found to 'put to one side' these attributions.
- Teachers will also need to be aware of the attributions being made by pupils and parents, whether or not these are actually voiced.
- Similarly, ways must also be found to allow all parties to step to one side of these attributions, in the quest for an acceptable strategy. Engaging directly with beliefs about blame and responsibility, debating, challenging or seeking to establish the one ultimate truth are all likely to be extremely counter-productive, whereas

acting as if they do not exist can sometimes feel like dishonesty or a failure of nerve.

The barriers to setting up interventions such as these can be considerable and may appear insurmountable. To ask a lone teacher to navigate successfully and lead others through this web of attributions is a tall order, especially on occasions when feelings are running high. Support from within schools, both that obtainable through the formal and hierarchical channels and that reached through the more informal avenues within the psychosocial system, as well as that available from outside agencies, will need to be based on a recognition that the issue of 'difficult behaviour' often gives rise to intense and unpalatable feelings. Rather than denying these, or labelling them as 'unprofessional', the climate within a school will need to permit their safe expression.

It is towards the sensitive area of staff culture, and the ways in which it may help to be a support to individual teachers and to the development of school policy, that Part 4 of this book now turns.

PART 4
Grasping the Nettle: Coherent Psychosocial Interventions

9 Intervening within staff cultures

Previous chapters have highlighted informal but powerful psychosocial processes within schools that are bound up with difficult behaviour, influencing how this is defined, understood and responded to. In particular, staff culture has been shown to operate in such a way as sometimes to suppress news of promising interventions carried out in classrooms. This chapter examines research and practical interventions that have attempted to support teachers in the demanding work they are required to carry out around student behaviour. Different approaches to working with groups of teachers are examined and shown to impact variously upon the formal and the less public aspects of schools. Then a detailed account is given of approaches from organizational psychology that can successfully address both the explicit policy and procedures of a school, while at the same time taking account of, and harnessing, the power of staff culture towards the same end. Unlike in earlier chapters, the work reported here moves beyond a concern with practical behaviour management strategies, training and policy developments, to engage crucially and productively with the strong but less public emotions, belief systems and social relationships reported by much of the research in this book.

Introduction

The psychosocial model of the school depicted in Figure 2.3 derives from much of the research reported in this book. On the left-hand side of this diagram can be found the processes most directly impinging on individual teachers:

- leadership, policy and procedure;
- staff organizational grouping;
- staff culture;
- reference group.

As indicted in Figure 2.4, the first two of these tend to be formal and public, whereas the third and fourth are characterized by being less easily accessible to scrutiny.

This chapter describes examples of practice that have attempted to work with these less tangible aspects of schools in an attempt to bring about real change and dignified outcomes for all parties bound up with the issue of behaviour in school. In the light of what has already been said in preceding chapters, it is highly likely that attempting to address these relatively elusive processes will require high degrees of trust, awareness and sensitivity.

All the developments described in the chapter, which have usually been initiated by external personnel, involve group work with teachers, but they differ from each other in a number of significant ways. For instance, some developments have been targeted at groups of teachers within the same establishment, whereas others have deliberately drawn participants from a number of schools. Many approaches have explicitly aimed to generate strategies for teachers to implement in their classrooms, either as general class management techniques or in respect of a specific student, while others have been concerned with the development of more general policies and procedures. The majority have concentrated on strategies of one form or other, sometimes with an implicit or explicit acknowledgement that psychosocial processes within schools – emotions, beliefs, allegiances and informal support systems – will also be engaged and affected by the interventions. A few, however, have been directly and explicitly concerned with these psychosocial aspects. There is also variation in the extent to which approaches are purely pragmatic in nature or claim some particular theoretical rationale and adherence. Finally, some reported interventions are by nature one time only occurrences, whereas others either anticipate further external support or attempt to build in the mechanisms whereby the school staff maintain some form of changed practice within the school.

Within this chapter, these themes weave in and out of the various initiatives examined according to the approximate chronology of their being reported.

Working with groups of teachers

In the British context, the publication of the Elton Report (DES 1989) is usually taken as a watershed, after which far greater concerted attention was paid to issues of behaviour in schools. Among its many recommendations the Report endorsed what was then a nascent trend towards various forms of peer support work among teachers.

With origins firmly within a psychodynamic approach towards educational issues, Osborne (1983) provided very early and sensitive accounts of work with groups of teachers in which, through the discussion of real life cases, it was possible to acknowledge and legitimize the teachers' feelings surrounding particularly contentious interactions with pupils and/or their parents. Although these groups worked towards the generation of strategies, the organizer was explicitly concerned with teachers' emotional responses. Chapter 5 has demonstrated the power of such emotions to undermine teachers' attempts to manage challenging behaviour and it is not difficult to imagine that, if unacknowledged or treated as 'unprofessional' and then set to one side, these could sabotage the confident and assured implementation of any strategy.

A particularly influential contributor to early work with groups of teachers was Rogers (1990), who adopted a more extensively 'educational' approach, building in exchanges of ideas about teaching approaches and curriculum planning alongside the provision of opportunities for reflection on practice, problem-solving and the development of classroom management approaches. To reduce further the sense of isolation and stress experienced by teachers, Rogers sought to extend peer support among teachers by encouraging them to participate in mutual observation in classrooms.

Chisholm (1994) also reported on a specially funded scheme that involved the training of facilitators in 75 schools. This programme attempted to clarify what 'peer support' actually entailed, illuminate the role played by facilitators in school projects, present techniques for organizing groups and make available appropriate materials to aid the promotion of projects. There were no preconceptions about how the school projects would develop and a subsequent review of outcomes revealed considerable variety and originality. In some schools, the peer support projects had led to policy development, sometimes as an intentional and at other times as an unintentional outcome. Other consequences for some schools involved peer support projects helping to implement already existing policies. Most projects also had a direct classroom research component, commonly involving a focus on classroom climate and the minimization of disruption.

An earlier account of the training of teachers as facilitators of school-based peer support groups was provided by Stringer et al. (1992). This influential paper described and reflected upon the setting up of around 30 different groups over a four-year period, the majority of the groups comprising the whole staff or self-selecting groups of staff from individual schools. In addition, and drawing on membership from a range of schools, a group for headteachers only met for three years, with other sets of workshops being run for teachers from nursery schools, infant reception years and middle schools. The team responsible for this initiative was able to cement the effectiveness of their programme of group workshops by referring to a strong and diverse research, theory and practice base within the consultation literature, a range of previous professional activity, family therapy and educational legislation and policy.

These groups, like many others discussed in this section, adhered to a set structure as a deliberate strategy for providing 'safety and support'. The facilitators always worked in mixed gender pairs and alternated roles between facilitating group discussions and leading the concluding 'process discussion' about how the group had worked together.

Discussions of problem-solving approaches can sometimes become tainted with a sense of procedural inflexibility, especially when notions of set structures are introduced. However, an important distinction exists between structures that provide a safe environment for potentially sensitive and contentious discussions and approaches that smother genuine expression and interaction under the weight of rigid protocols:

> Spontaneity is emphasised (we discourage such things as rotas for presenting a concern, or someone sharing a concern because their headteacher thought they should). We do not give marks for the dramatic nature of a concern, rather we constantly remind groups that much can be gained from using the time and support to work on something which may prevent a niggling difficulty becoming a huge problem.
>
> (Stringer *et al*. 1992: 91)

The programme of facilitator training was evaluated by means of questionnaires completed by 61 staff from 'a nursery, primary, special and high school, three comprehensive schools and two support services'. In response to these, Stringer *et al*. (1992: 94) comment that

> Teachers valued such things as being able to discuss problems without interruptions, in an atmosphere of trust and concern, and where 'status was left at the door'. They valued the sense of community the groups developed, the reduction in feelings of isolation and the 'support for staff under stress; support in practical and psychological ways'.

Creese *et al*. (1997) carried out a feasibility study for the then DfEE on the setting up of 'teacher support teams' as a means of providing peer support for teachers experiencing teaching difficulties in relation to special educational needs. In their particular model, it was intended that individual teachers would voluntarily request support, in the form of collaboratively seeking better understanding of a problem and designing an intervention, from a team that usually consisted of the SENCO, a senior teacher and another class teacher. When investigating how such teams developed, Creese *et al*. found that they tended to function in a much broader way than originally envisaged, in some schools acting as a support for teachers' problem-solving that went far beyond the original SEN remit.

Watkins and Wagner (2000) have worked with groups of staff at both primary and secondary level to improve the behaviour of students in schools. Typically, the pattern of intervention involves the use of their checklist, the Diagnostic Behaviour Questionnaire, which all staff complete in respect of a particular student. A first meeting with staff in secondary schools consists of discussion of the information collected on the questionnaire, as well as the feelings of staff and the various strategies they have already attempted. Watkins and Wagner report that positive changes in the student's behaviour are often reported a month or so after a jointly agreed strategy is implemented and that any such changes are then usually maintained over the following year. Referring to two prominent themes to be found within this book – the potential effects of attributions for behaviour and the nature of recursive causation in complex systems – these two authors comment:

> Although it may be tempting to hypothesise an explanation for such change, the reality is that we do not and will not have sufficient evidence. Perhaps small but significant changes from some teachers led [the student] to behave differently overall. Perhaps those teachers who said they did not want to join the strategy nevertheless had a different approach . . . occasioned by hearing different views on him. Such change reminds us of the multiple interconnectedness of effects in such a situation.
>
> (Watkins and Wagner 2000: 107)

Monsen and Graham (2002) have provided an account of an approach devised in New Zealand – the Staff Sharing Scheme – which parallels some of these other interventions, as well as introducing original and distinctive features. Used within a school, and led by an external consultant, this scheme also puts forward a problem-analysis framework and explicitly includes attempts to enable staff 'to gain emotional distance and a shared language' (Monsen and Graham 2002: 138) in order to explore problem situations causing concern. Drawing on some of the sources discussed in Chapters 5 and 6, and using techniques deriving from counselling and therapeutic approaches, the Staff Sharing Scheme attempts to address the sensitive issue of the difference between 'espoused theories' and 'theories in action' in regard to managing behaviour within the school:

> At this stage, it is important to assist staff in taking a 'snapshot' of what they currently observe and experience, rather than what they think might be happening. For example, in many of the schools visited in the original project, it was reported by senior management that 'staff worked in teams and shared problems'. Yet when this assumption was tested out, very often the headteacher managed staff

as individuals and staff reported feeling deskilled, defensive and isolated.

(Monsen and Graham 2002: 142)

Clearly, such an approach can only be used with great tact and diplomacy. Monsen and Graham (2002: 146) rightly pay attention to the fostering of trust and were able to report that, in evaluating the efficacy of the scheme,

> one of the most robust findings was that individual teachers positively changed the way they perceived their students, themselves and their colleagues. School staff reported that they felt 'more in control', 'discussions are more focused and businesslike', 'things don't seem so impossible' and 'there is hope'.

Bozic and Carter (2002) have investigated in more detail the response of teachers to certain aspects of the types of workshops run by Stringer *et al.* (1992). In particular, they followed up, by means of questionnaire, 25 teachers in first, middle, high and special schools who had participated in similar workshops. In addition to finding that 84 per cent 'agreed' or 'strongly agreed' with the statement 'Participation has been a good use of my time', they elicited from the teachers a more precise view of the perceived definite benefits, as shown in Table 9.1.

A major influence behind most of the British developments described in this chapter has been Gerda Hanko (1985, 1999), whose work as an educational consultant specializing in the emotional and social factors in learning and failure to learn has been informed by a rich seam of psychodynamic and educational insights. Over the years, Hanko has provided a series of detailed

Table 9.1 The effects of peer-support groups upon participating teachers

	Percentage of teachers who agreed or strongly agreed (N = 25)
Made me think more deeply about individual children	92
Made me aware of teaching strategies that I could try	80
Being in a group has led me to try new things in the classroom	64
Feel more confident about working with children with SEN	56
Other staff have asked me about what happens in the group	56
Feel less stressed by things that happen at school	52

Source: from Bozic and Carter (2002).

case descriptions of group consultations with teachers over concerns presented by pupils with a range of emotional needs and behavioural difficulties. These are often characterized by an acknowledgement that the emotional distress of children and young people is usually intimately bound up with that of parents, and that these can also trigger and resonate with the feelings of teachers.

Because being a consultant is not the same as being a therapist, Hanko's case descriptions are characterized by *general discussions* of the types of hidden and powerful emotional consequences of working with certain students and their parents, even though it is likely that these may resemble the reactions of some of the individual members of peer support groups when working together to understand certain problems. It is this deeply respectful and insightful style of facilitation, reflected in the various case studies, that has almost certainly led to the successes achieved by these consultation groups and their wider adoption by those working with teachers facing particularly challenging circumstances.

Working with groups of teachers: effects on the psychosocial system

Returning to the psychosocial model of the school, it is readily apparent that these examples of working with groups of teachers illustrate the interaction between a number of the subsystems on the left-hand side of Figure 2.3.

For instance, a strong resemblance between the 'reference groups' that Nias found teachers valued so highly (Chapter 6) and Stringer *et al.*'s (1992) accounts of their consultation groups may be seen. Nias identified one function of a reference group as being the creation of norms that are used by the individual as an anchoring point to help to indicate which events to pay attention to, and what degrees of saliency to ascribe to each. Additionally, these self-created groups provided an emotional support and a sense of being among 'like-minded friends'. A very similar set of experiences must surely have been in evidence in consultation groups where 'status was left at the door', a sense of community developed, there was a reduction in feelings of isolation and staff under stress felt supported (Stringer *et al.* 1992). The work described by Osborne (1983) and Hanko (1999), with its strongly psychodynamic orientation, also resonates clearly with the notion of the reference group.

In the work reported by Chisholm (1994) and Creese *et al.* (1997), many peer support groups continue after the initial involvement of external facilitators. This is an example of new 'staff organizational groupings' – the ongoing peer support arrangements – coming into existence, presumably with the blessing and encouragement of those responsible for leadership and policy development within the school.

There is also likely to be a complex and influential relationship between these groups and staff culture. Watkins and Wagner (2000), for instance, speculated that meetings in which strategies for individual students were discussed may have led to changed perceptions and behaviour on the part of staff, who nevertheless did not wish to join in the explicit delivery of a new approach to the student.

In terms of implications for the leadership of the school and for the development of policy and procedure, accounts of these groups present a range of perspectives. Chisholm (1994) reported that some of the teacher support groups in his project went on to help to develop policy, both intentionally and unintentionally, and some to help implement already existing policies. Monsen and Graham (2002), on the other hand, describing an approach that is far more prescribed by the external facilitators, referred directly to attempts to work with a recognition of the gap that is likely to exist in all organizations between 'espoused theory' and 'theory-in-action' (Argyris and Schon 1978). Stringer *et al.* (1992: 91), yet again, started from a clear recognition of the separate function of their consultation groups:

> We are careful to avoid the group raising school policy issues, which are not the business of a consultation group, and which might promote perceptions of the group as being threatening to non-members – in particular non-members from senior management.

The relationships between reference groups, staff culture and formal leadership and policy development are clearly arenas of potentially extreme delicacy. And, as much of this book has sought to demonstrate, there are sensitivities here that can easily become highlighted and exacerbated by the difficult behaviour of some students within a school. It is a challenge of a high order for schools to engage safely and productively with these delicate but powerful psychosocial processes in a wider social climate that seeks so crudely to label schools as 'good' or 'bad', 'failing', 'improving' or 'successful'.

But engage they must, not only because the issue of challenging behaviour refuses to go away but also because, if the complicated terrain of these psychosocial processes can be navigated, successful outcomes can be attained. In addition to the lessons to be learned from the range of teacher support groups described so far, there are also important principles embedded in areas of organizational psychology. This chapter now turns to, and considers in some depth, two illustrative projects from this domain.

Intervening with the 'organizational health' of schools

A particularly promising and pertinent line of study has been developed within organizational psychology around the notion of 'organizational healthiness'. One of the originators of the model of the school as a psycho-social system presented in Figure 2.3, Gerv Leyden, also carried out a study into the relationship between the general well-being of individual teachers and various of the more subjective, 'cultural' aspects of the schools in which they worked (Cox *et al.* 1993).

This study drew on the earlier research of Cox and Kuk (1991), who discovered that teachers' perceptions of their schools as organizations fell into three distinct categories: the task, the problem-solving and the development environments. These three 'environments' are subjective perceptions obtained from staff by means of the Organizational Health Questionnaire developed by these authors. One purpose of this study was to investigate whether concentrating on 'soft' rather than 'hard' aspects of the school system could lead to positive changes in aspects of staff culture and school policy and procedures:

> Organisational change traditionally addresses the objective dimension, in the expectation that if the structures, procedures, job analyses and specifications are rationally developed, then uncertainty will be reduced and the change accepted by all who have to implement or operate them. The crucial *subjective* dimension – the collective sense or understanding shared by the members of that organisation about the changes – is seldom tackled directly. Yet whether or how the changes are implemented depends to a large extent on the perceptions and attitudes held by those working in the organisation.
>
> (Cox *et al.* 1993: 19)

Another purpose of the study was to examine whether an intervention aimed at improving the teachers' perceptions of these three environments within their schools would also result in an increased sense of their own individual well-being.

The research was carried out in nine junior and primary schools and, as a first step, staff were asked to complete the Organizational Health Questionnaire and the General Well-being Questionnaire, the latter providing a respectable measure of such factors as tension, anxiety and tiredness. Following this, two schools were selected for a series of four workshop interventions, while the others served as comparison schools for research purposes. The workshops took place over a summer term and the same questionnaire measures were then repeated for all nine schools at the end of this term.

The content of the first three workshops focused upon task, problem-solving and development dimensions of the school. The first session briefly introduced the technical aspects of the Organizational Health model and provided feedback information from the initial audit that had been collected in that school. Following this, the staff worked on selected aspects from these three dimensions in small groups and presented the results of this work to colleagues for discussion. The final workshop summarized the outcomes from the previous three sessions, which then led to staff being invited to choose one aspect and devise follow-up action strategies as the basis for subsequent implementation.

The results from this study present a fascinating picture. In the comparison schools, questionnaire results yielded the unsurprising result that the teachers reported feeling more 'worn out' over the summer term period. However, in the intervention school where high attendance at the workshops had taken place, the teachers had reversed this seemingly inevitable trend and reported feeling significantly less 'worn out' at the end of the summer term than at the beginning.

Although this research did not specifically focus upon behaviour in schools, it will not be hard to imagine its potential contribution. Tired, stressed or anxious teachers are unlikely to be best prepared for managing challenging student behaviour. However, interventions that are able to address more subjective and hidden aspects of the school – and previous chapters have demonstrated the complex relationship between student behaviour and staff culture – have considerable potential. Put simply, teachers who feel confident, supported and in tune with the organization in which they work must be far more able to access the energy, flexibility and determination required to respond successfully to their most demanding students.

This study has also justified the adoption of an organizational psychology perspective. While some might insist that schools are unique as organizations, thus making attempts to borrow techniques from other, highly dissimilar settings either naive or inappropriate, great care should be taken not to discard potentially useful perspectives and interventions. It is a central theme of this book that the behaviour of students in schools cannot be completely understood or effectively addressed without an appreciation of such processes as circular causation and the objective and subjective aspects of organizations. Where these psychosocial factors have been studied to effect in other organizations, there may well be lessons for education professionals, especially in those areas – and responding to difficult behaviour is surely one – in which traditional approaches have failed to bring about desired levels of change. The remainder of this chapter examines another way of working with organizations with a very positive track record: soft systems methodology.

Soft systems methodology

Soft systems methodology (SSM) was developed by Checkland (1981) and has been used in Britain and elsewhere across a very wide range of organizational contexts, including business, industry, military, health and educational settings. This novel and impressive procedure for facilitating organizational change was introduced to educational settings by Frederickson (1990b), who collected accounts of SSM being used with schools to help with, among other initiatives, the development of behaviour policies in secondary schools, a system self-review within a secondary school, an approach to classroom layout and case-focused consultation at primary level.

Checkland and Scholes (1990) developed this approach by attempting to solve 'messy', complex and intransigent problems across such a range of contexts and, in doing so, were able to learn and report on a rich and detailed set of insights about the working of all manner of organizations. It is not possible here to give anything like a full description of SSM, but an example of its use in a school context is presented in order to outline an effective use of the approach, and to make links with this book's model of the school as a psychosocial system.

Using SSM in a secondary school to revise policy towards exclusion

The author, along with other educational psychologist colleagues, was invited by the headteacher of a secondary school to work with staff on an organizational response after an external inspection commented on the high level of exclusion of students from the school for disciplinary reasons. During initial discussions with the headteacher, the use of SSM was suggested as a possible starting point and a one-day workshop was arranged for the dozen or so 'pastoral managers', including the headteacher.

SSM is a seven-stage process and, in working through these, a brief rationale and wider commentary is given alongside the more practical and specific details.

Step 1. The problem situation unstructured: using rich questions

At this preliminary stage, the participants are encouraged to engage in a wide description of areas of concern. In order to provide a starting point, the 35 teachers within the school had been circulated with a brief questionnaire prior to the day, and the results from two of the questionnaires, as in Tables 9.2 and 9.3, were presented.

During the initial discussion phase, prompted in this instance by the data, the facilitator attempted to make sure that everyone made an early contribution. Opportunities were also taken to model ways in which views, including dissenting ones, could be respectfully presented and valued as providing the potential for eventual ways forward. In leading this discussion, the facilitator used what Checkland had referred to as 'rich questions', which are designed to help to 'surface' some of the hidden and informal cultural processes that will almost certainly exist among the various staff members.

So, questions of an interactional and comparative nature – such as 'who agrees with that?', 'who least agrees with that?' and 'when X does that, how do

Table 9.2 Replies to the question 'What are the main behaviour problems you encounter on a day-to-day basis in school?'

Reply	No.
Talking inappropriately in class	26
Loudness lining up outside of class	8
Pupils shouting	8
Manners/politeness	5
Handing in homework late	4
Aggressive attitudes	4
Pupils bringing in problems from outside	4
Running/moving around school	3
Cheek/defiance	2
Inability to sit still	2
Pupil breaking physical contact rule	2

Table 9.3 What does our school do well in managing behaviour?

Reply	No.
Ground rules clear	16
Supportive system for staff	16
On-call system	10
Incidents followed through	6
Swiftness/consistency of approval	6
Starting well with Year 7	5
Parental involvement	5
Setting clear/high expectations	5
Good classroom management	1
Positive policies	1
Time spent on counselling pupils	1
Interesting lessons	1
Threat of exclusions	1

you respond?' – constitute part of the facilitator's repertoire. Instead of debating any of the emerging issues, the facilitator continued with rich questions, with the intention that the full complexity of the school's public and hidden beliefs and actions pertaining to 'difficult behaviour' and 'exclusion' were brought out into the open. During this step, the facilitator's status as a person external to the school staff is important, in that it allows the expression of thoughts, opinions and emotions that will sometimes carry histories within the organization.

Other types of rich questions concerned with such features as establishing perspective ('Tell us what would happen during a typical . . . '), highlighting differences ('Can you think of another way to . . . ?'), hypothesizing ('What would X say if . . . ?'), reflecting ('So what you're saying is . . . ') and reiterating ('Can I sum up what has been said?') are also employed. This can be quite a lengthy process and, it should be emphasized again, this step is not attempting to solve problems, establish priorities or 'right old wrongs'. It is attempting to lay out the issue of 'difficult behaviour' and 'exclusion from school' in all its messy complexity, which will probably include the school's stated policies and procedures, hidden and subjective thoughts and feelings, and the potential gaps between espoused theories and theories in action.

This is territory into which the unwary are usually cautioned not to stray. Free ranging and unfocused discussions such as these often run the risk of 'getting out of hand', 'opening old sores' and not being able 'to see the wood for trees'. One of the strengths of SSM is that it is able to build productively from among all this ill-disciplined information. In deliberately eliciting the complexity, SSM harnesses rather than clashes with the staff culture. On the other hand, such discord can unfortunately often be the unsatisfactory result, taking either argumentative or quietly resentful forms, *if* new policy is handed down from senior management as a *fait accompli*, perhaps after some cursory 'consultation'. Often an even less generous reception can await suggestions about managing behaviour made by external personnel unaware of the full history and politics of previous initiatives within the school.

Step 2. The problem situation represented: the rich picture

The second step in the SSM process aims to capture as much as possible of the previous discussion in a visual form. Participants are divided into small groups, three groups of four being created in this example. The groups are asked to draw, in rudimentary and cartoon form, all the major issues that emerged during the first step, as well as any others that come to mind. A set of conventions can be provided with which to depict, for example, groups and sub-groups, relationships, thoughts, ideas, worries and discontent.

This stage can elicit a number of responses. Sometimes it is difficult to start, some people wishing to carry on using words rather than graphic images. Others set to enthusiastically and, at times, animated emotions burst from small groups as a way is found to represent pictorially something contentious or risky ('the way things are') that cannot be put safely or diplomatically into words. As with the rich questioning, this step aims to represent the full complexity of the current situation so that, first, everyone present hears it. It then also serves as an easy visual record upon which decisions can be based concerning priorities for taking things forward. Finally, after subsequent steps that use a formal and logical approach to 'hard systems' development, these rich pictures can be used to make comparisons between the existing complexity and jointly agreed ideal systems, and thus yield sensitively targeted and shared action plans.

One of the three rich pictures drawn in the school, which serves as an example here, is shown in Figure 9.1.

A characteristic of fluent users of SSM is that they will be observed throughout the work drawing pictures and diagrams as well as

Figure 9.1 One of the three rich pictures drawn in the school

taking notes and writing prose. The reason for this is that human affairs reveal a rich moving pageant of relationships, and pictures are a better means for recording relationships and connections than is linear prose.

(Checkland and Scholes 1990: 45)

After the three rich pictures had been produced they were displayed, and members talked through their contents with the whole group. The facilitator then asked for help in listing all the issues depicted in the pictures. Table 9.4 shows the full list produced by this school.

Once all the issues represented in the rich pictures have been identified and written down, it is necessary to make a decision about which area to tackle during the remainder of session. In this case, the discussions highlighted a number of pressing issues and a voting procedure revealed that the pastoral managers thought that their priorities should be to develop:

- a 'system' for improving the quality of classroom practice;
- a 'system' for empowering teachers to deal with problems immediately without recourse to 'on call' arrangements or senior staff.

Because the first of these was regarded as more likely to subsume the second, it was the one chosen for further development on the day.

Table 9.4 Issues related to behaviour management and exclusion as depicted in the three rich pictures drawn by pastoral managers

- Behaviour on the field
- Misbehaviour out of sight of teachers
- Pupils aware of 'on call' system
- Blocked information, in both directions, between curriculum and pastoral managers
- Over-dependency of class teachers on 'on call' system
- Curriculum coordinators not as prominent as they should be
- Class teachers 'passing the buck' upwards too quickly
- Effectiveness of teaching, learning and praise
- Teacher role outside of classrooms
- Expansion of school roll because of being oversubscribed
- Legislation and external (LEA) policies
- Varied staff expectations
- Policy on observation in class
- Training
- How to use data intelligently

Step 3. Writing 'root definitions'

After considering in depth the complexity of this picture of how the school is operating in terms of behaviour management and exclusion, steps 3 and 4 change the tone and focus and enter into a much more formal, detailed and logical set of procedures. It is not possible in this account to do full justice to the careful and creative thought developed by Checkland and others here, but the example, I hope, illustrates the general nature of these procedures.

The next task is for the facilitator to work with the group on developing what Checkland termed a 'root definition' of the 'ideal system' that will subsequently be 'modelled', in this case, a 'system' for improving the quality of classroom practice. This root definition has to contain certain features, such as the identification of what it is trying to achieve (expressed as transforming something into something else), the 'actors' who will carry out the implementation, the 'customers' who will be its beneficiaries and the owner (or person who could prevent the system from being put into operation).

The group of pastoral managers produced the following root definition for the system to improve the quality of classroom practice:

> A headteacher-owned system operated by senior and middle managers to transform teachers who felt threatened by the expectation on them into teachers who are confident that they can do what is expected of them. The system will operate in a climate of fairness and equality of opportunity and a belief that the school is a community of learners in which all can improve their performance, and also in the context of conditions of service and procedures agreed with the teacher associations.

At first sight, such definitions can easily appear overly wordy and removed from the cut and thrust of the everyday life of the organization. But the above definition was not easily arrived at, and in the discussions that preceded it, this group of managers safely explored real issues about the boundaries between their various individual and collective responsibilities. Staff morale was also sensitively considered within its wider context. Within the definition, it may be possible to discern echoes of discussions that would not have been possible had not steps 1 and 2 already prepared the ground, in terms of the tone and rich account of the interconnections (and recursive causality) within the school as a psychosocial system. Because time and care were taken over this step, a considerable degree of energy and commitment was generated for the joint planning of a model for how ideally the quality of classroom practice could be developed within the school.

Step 4. Building conceptual models
This step is again technical and formal in its style and Checkland provides detailed guidance on how it should be facilitated. In essence, the group is building a logical and detailed model of all the procedures that will need to be in place for the root definition to become a reality. Again, the debate and discussions as this model is developed enhance the sense of joint ownership and purpose, with a consequent commitment to see practical action subsequently ensue. At this stage the focus is totally upon what is logically necessary within the conceptual model; comparison with the realities represented in the rich pictures comes next. The conceptual model produced with the pastoral managers is shown in Figure 9.2

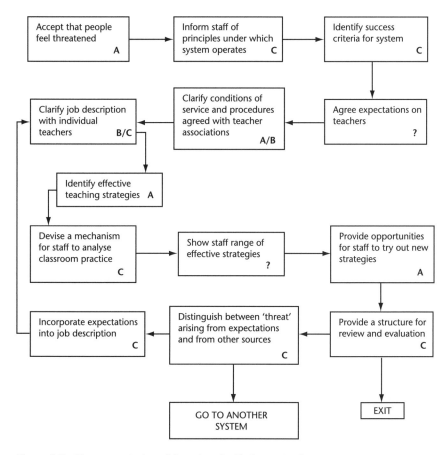

Figure 9.2 The conceptual model produced with the pastoral managers

Step 5. Comparing the ideal conceptual model with the current situation

> No matter how the [conceptual] models are used for a comparison
> with the real world, the aim is not to 'improve the models' – as man-
> agement science enthusiasts sometimes tend to think – it is to find an
> accommodation between different interests in the situation, an
> accommodation which can be argued to constitute an improvement
> of the initial problem situation.
>
> (Checkland and Scholes 1990: 44)

The purpose of this comparison, between the conceptual model as in Figure 9.2
and the rich pictures, is to focus discussion upon how much of what ideally
needs to happen is already successfully in existence within the school and
which aspects need to be developed or enhanced. To do this each box, or 'sub-
system', within Figure 9.2 was examined and, following discussion, allocated
to one of three categories (subsequently marked as A, B or C in Figure 9.2):

- procedures that are already in place and functioning (A);
- procedures that are in place but not functioning (B);
- procedures that are not in place (C).

Step 6. Debate on desirable and feasible changes

As a result of the previous step, areas for necessary action become clearly identified. The extent to which these are feasible, and the most desirable sequence
for any implementation, is then a matter for debate. In the present example,
the managers had agreed that, in order to put their jointly agreed new model
into practice, attention would have to be directed to those aspects of the model
currently designated by a 'B' and a 'C'.

Step 7. Taking further action to improve the situation

At the end of the day, it was agreed that the group of school staff present would
consider ways in which to take forward the development points that had been
identified. It was also agreed that more discussion would take place with the
educational psychologists, and this led to a further SSM workshop being carried out with senior staff responsible for subject specialisms. Obviously,
further reflection might suggest that the particular issue extracted from the
rich pictures and pursued through root definitions and conceptual modelling
was not, in retrospect, the most useful or pressing. If so, it would be perfectly
possible to select another issue and subject this to SSM analysis and planning.

Some time later, the considerable development work subsequently carried
out by the school staff was acknowledged when a further external inspection
commented positively upon the new arrangements in place for managing the
behaviour of students within the school.

SSM: effects on the psychosocial system

This example of SSM in action illustrates one of its major distinctive features, its equal focus upon both the cultural and the policy 'streams' within an organization: 'it is obvious that the logic-driven stream and the cultural stream will interact, each informing the other' (Checkland and Scholes 1990: 30). This approach was born from the observation that a focus solely on logically precise sets of policies and procedures – 'off the shelf' whole-school behaviour policies come to mind here – had repeatedly failed to result in meaningful organizational change.

The conceptual model developed above, however, clearly demonstrates that attention to formal detail within the organization is very much a part of the approach. But SSM also simultaneously addresses staff culture in its complexity rather that attempting to put it to one side in order to proceed with policy development: 'Overall, the aim is to take seriously the subjectivity which is the crucial characteristic of human affairs and to treat this subjectivity, if not exactly scientifically, at least in a way characterised by intellectual rigour' (Checkland and Scholes 1990: 30).

The final chapter returns to one of the central themes of this book, the contentious and unclear relationships between teachers and parents that surround student behaviour in school. In particular, it examines ways in which knowledge of the various psychosocial processes examined so far may help to surmount the barriers to effective working to the full benefit of all concerned.

10 Across the great divide? Intervening with teachers and parents

This final chapter returns to the subject of teachers and parents working together in instances when students are judged to be difficult to manage within schools. Earlier chapters have revealed that these partnerships can achieve very positive outcomes and that there are often enormous barriers to setting up such interventions. This chapter returns to the Successful Strategies study and examines in detail, by returning to some of the book's theoretical concerns, how and why effective partnerships come about, before drawing conclusions for practice. The chapter then considers a study of teachers' views about the most effective forms of support that may be offered by external consultants, before concluding with a brief look at examples of interventions that have simultaneously targeted a number of subsystems within the coherent psychosocial model of the school.

Introduction

The relationship between teachers, parents and the behaviour of students in schools and classrooms is a central theme of this book. Chapter 1 discussed the increase in legislation and policy guidance concerning this relationship and Chapter 8 has considered research findings demonstrating the many differences (and commonalities) to be found between the perspectives of teachers, parents and students. Chapter 4 has outlined the promising evidence base demonstrating the effectiveness of home–school strategies, results we would be very foolish to ignore in the ever increasing clamour for strategies known to be effective. But the Successful Strategies study and other practitioner accounts discussed in Chapters 4 and 5 have also shown that getting to the point where teachers and parents can begin to plan together in a spirit of genuine cooperation often seems a massive challenge. The main reason why this book asserts that it is not predominantly concerned with tips and techniques, but is dedicated to encouraging a deeper understanding of psychosocial processes, is because *what to do* if teachers and parents are able to work together is not really the main issue. *How to get there*, to the position where this cooperation can take place, on the other hand, very much is.

One of the distinctive features of the Successful Strategies study discussed in Chapters 4 and 5 is the widely perceived change for the better that occurs in the relationship between school and home. The extent to which this is deliberately engineered by the consultant EP or comes about more as a consequence of successfully carrying out practical tasks together is also discussed at some length in these chapters. Given ongoing concerns about the divide between teachers and parents over the issue of behaviour, this final chapter returns again to data from the Successful Strategies study in order to understand more fully how these positive changes might be brought about. In keeping with the psychosocial orientation of the book, the data are considered from two theoretical perspectives – attributions and system boundary issues.

Attributing the causes for successful teacher–parent interventions

Table 8.1 listed all the causes for the original behaviour difficulties suggested by the teachers in the Successful Strategies study. To complement this, the interviews also asked these same teachers why they thought the positive improvements had occurred, to identify all the mechanisms they thought had contributed to the successful outcomes. Table 10.1 presents all the causes to be found within the interview transcripts, again grouped as pertaining to pupils, parents and teachers.

As with Table 8.1, the first level of analysis to be applied to Table 10.1 concerns the lengths of the various lists. Again this is a highly elaborated list, 36 items in total, demonstrating that within the discourse of these teachers there is a range of possible explanatory mechanisms for improved behaviour. In Table 10.1 the relative lengths of the teacher and parent lists are quite striking. In essence, the teachers in the study have been able to hypothesize 20 different ways in which they have been implicated in creating this improvement, but only three ways in which the actions of the parents may have contributed to these positive outcomes.

Comparing Tables 8.1 and 10.1, the differing length of the two parent lists makes an immediate impression. Eiser's (1978) argument that the degree of differentiation within a set of attributions gives a strong indication of that set's relative importance can help interpret this finding. In essence, these two lists are saying that the teachers in this study have a range of ways for thinking and talking about how parents can be a cause of difficult behaviour in schools and classrooms, but have considered far less their potential contributions to the success.

The concept of controllability in respect of causes was considered in Chapter 8 and is also highly pertinent here. A range of studies (Weiner 1980; Dix *et al.*

Table 10.1 Teachers' attributions for the success of the strategy

Attributions made to pupils	Attributions made to parents	Attributions made to teachers
Knowledge of general social norms (6)	General management of child (3)	Positive attention to pupil (13)
Maturity (5)	Encouragement of child (2)	Interest level of work set (8)
Knowledge of specific school rules (5)	Feeling supported by teachers (2)	Work expectations/steps set (5)
Feeling valued/self-esteem (5)		Incentives/tangible rewards (5)
Respect for teacher (5)		Understanding pupil's personality (3)
Temperament/personality (5)		Teacher feeling valued (3)
Developing self-control (2)		Consistent approach (3)
Awareness of being monitored (2)		Individualized attention to pupil (2)
Acceptance of school rules (1)		Record keeping (2)
Knowledge of sanctions (1)		Understanding pupil's motivation (2)
Awareness of effect on teacher (1)		Gaining affection/sympathy for pupil (2)
Intelligence (1)		Maintaining awareness of pupil (2)
Awareness of behaviour/reward link (1)		Having information about home (2)
		Specific management techniques (1)
		Reduction of teacher's anxiety (1)
		Making an exception of pupil (1)
		Pressure from within school (1)
		Didactic teaching (1)
		Prioritizing problems (1)
		Ignoring aspects of pupil's behaviour (1)

1989; Johnston *et al.* 1992) has shown that the dimension of 'controllability' is closely related to adults' judgements about appropriate reactions towards children's behaviour, about the degree of sympathy and willingness to help that they may feel. More recently, Poulou and Norwich (2002) have constructed an elaborate model of the relationship between teachers' causal attributions, emotional and cognitive responses and actions towards pupils with emotional and behavioural difficulties. Consequently, once again, the items in Table 8.1 were examined by a team of judges and all those deemed to be within the control of the 'actor' (pupil, parent, teacher) to which they were attributed were extracted.

The next step was to undertake a case-by-case analysis and note whether each teacher made high controllability attributions to parents, pupils or teachers for either the origins or the solutions. Table 10.2 shows the number of teachers who made 'high controllability' attributions to parents, pupils and themselves for both origins and solutions. This table shows the teachers in the Successful Strategies study to have made very different attributions towards themselves, the students and their parents. Bearing in mind what has been argued about the importance of the perception of controllability, the teachers in this study were clearly more likely to see the *blame for the original difficult behaviour* as lying first with the parents, then with themselves and then with the pupils. In contrast, despite witnessing the input of parents in 18 cases and attesting to an increased level of 'support from home' in 16 cases, only four of the 24 teachers cited parent factors as actually contributing to the solution. So, in contrast to the attributed origins for the problems, these teachers were far more likely to apportion the *credit for the success* to the efforts of themselves, then, to a much lesser extent, to the pupils and finally the parents.

Another way to think about these results is by means of a simple but very useful model proposed by Fiske and Taylor (1984). In this, judgements about the responsibility for effecting a solution to a problem are set alongside judgements about responsibility for original causes, as in Figure 10.1. Thus, for example, an agent (e.g. teacher, student, parent) may be perceived as having the responsibility for finding a solution to a particular problem whether they were responsible for causing it in the first place (moral model) or not

Table 10.2 The number of teachers making *high* controllability attributions to the three agents in respect of the origins of and improvements in pupils' behaviour

	Parent	Pupil	Teacher
Origin	17	9	12
Solution	4	6	21
Origin: solution ratio	4.25	1.5	0.6

Responsibility for solution?

		Yes	No
Responsibility for cause?	**Yes**	Moral model	Enlightenment model
	No	Compensatory model	Medical model

Figure 10.1 Fiske and Taylor's model of combinations of attributions for the cause and solution of problems

(compensatory model). Similarly, differing responsibilities for effecting a solution may also be attributed whether or not an agent is deemed responsible for the original cause of the problem.

The interview transcripts reveal examples of all four models and these are variously attributed to teachers, pupils and parents. Examples of some of these are given to provide a flavour of the accounts, and illustrate these differing attributional patterns.

Medical model attributed to pupil

> Having my own daughter, who is two, I could draw so many parallels between their behaviour. It was incredible because you see he was six and she was two. But he was acting in a very toddlerish way . . . It was as if I'd got a big two-year-old in the room all the time.

> Well, something worked . . . I think he matured obviously as he went on a little bit. (Interview 17)

Compensatory model attributed to teacher

> It's nearly always the problem is in the home and your hands are tied a little bit.

> I think it was purely and simply because of the total pressure and rules that I kept him under. (Interview 2)

Enlightenment model attributed to parent

> The more you learn about his home background the more you realize how negative it is, and has been.

> She [mother] needed help in that area of being consistent because she was so extreme. The first sign of anything and he was up to bed for the rest of the evening. It's no wonder he climbed out and wrecked his bedroom because this was tea-time. (Interview 1)

Moral model attributed to teacher

> There weren't enough records being kept, and there wasn't enough incentive for him to improve.

> I think it was [me] being positive [that led to the improvement] and I think it was the incentive of the rewards. I think it was the attention as well – him having a chance to speak to me. (Interview 21)

Returning to the 24 interview transcripts, it was possible to identify which patterns of responsibility were applied to parents, pupils and the teachers themselves, and Table 10.3 shows the number of teachers making these different forms of attribution. By statistically comparing frequencies, a compensatory model attributed to the teachers themselves is found in more than twice as many cases as would be expected. In other words, 37 per cent of this group of teachers adopted a compensatory model, not seeing themselves as having had any involvement in the origin of the problem but still seeing it as their responsibility to effect a solution (and as having achieved one). Half of the sample also adopted a moral model – almost twice the frequency that would be expected – by which they saw themselves as having taken action that had contributed to the problem and assumed a responsibility for enacting (and reaching) a solution.

An enlightenment model was applied to parents far more readily than a moral model. More than half the teachers (58 per cent, again more than twice the expected frequency), although seeing the parents as having contributed to the origin of the problem, did not see the improvement that was achieved as being due to the efforts of the parents. The moral model, which credited parents with a contribution to the solution as well as the origin, consisted of a much lower 12 per cent.

Another model again characterizes the majority of attributions made to the pupils. A medical model in which pupils were seen to have no control over factors responsible for the problem and not to have taken an intentional role in the successful strategy accounted for 54 per cent of the cases, almost twice the expected frequency.

This analysis hints at the important differences that may take place at the level of implicit, and probably unconscious, assumptions made by teachers

Table 10.3 The numbers of teachers attributing different models of responsibility to each agent

	Medical (resp. orig. x; resp. soln x)	Compensatory (resp. orig. x; resp. soln √)	Enlightenment (resp. orig. √; resp. soln x)	Moral (resp. orig. √; resp. soln √)
Parent	6	1	14	3
Pupil	13	3	5	4
Teacher	3	9	0	12

about the relative culpability of various parties, and about the extent to which each might be expected, and able, to contribute towards a successful strategy. Fortunately, it is not necessary to make these complicated patterns explicit, as success can be achieved without the conscious awareness or application of such knowledge. But a sensitivity to such processes will help to illuminate the psychological territory across which successful strategies may have to travel.

Mechanisms leading to the resolution of boundary tensions in the Successful Strategies study

Another perspective that helps to explain the mechanisms underlying successful interventions derives from systems theory. Chapter 5 presented findings to show that uncertainties for teachers about the respective responsibilities of home and school (boundary location) and about the 'predictability of the environment' added to the tensions between home and school. The process of actually carrying out a plan within which both parents and teachers perform certain designated or negotiated actions was usually accompanied by the informal trading of information, especially in the form of the teacher gaining additional information about the pupil's behaviour at home or about particular domestic arrangements. This latter phenomenon was attested to in 16 of the 24 cases and could occur by three routes.

First, the strategy required regular contact between teacher and parent and this information was an incidental by-product of these meetings:

> His mum came in on Fridays to check to see how he'd got on . . . I think he gets a better deal at home if he was good at school. (Interview 16)

> [Mum] would now come and talk to me about all sorts of things . . . the marriage was a bit dicey . . . [she] goes out to work full-time. (Interview 15)

> It's helpful for me to talk to [EP] and mum . . . because you can get more of an insight . . . I mean I know a bit more about his background now so I can see the reasons why he acts like he does. (Interview 12)

Second, meetings were arranged for which part of the explicit agenda was the sharing of this information:

> We have frequent meetings and . . . there's no holds barred, we just say how we feel . . . We had no idea of the depth of the problems he was shouldering for a boy of his age. (Interview 6)

More rarely, the EP acted as a go-between, relaying this information to school:

> He [EP] is the liaison between home and school. He puts me in the picture officially . . . he obviously explains the problems . . . he's heard or discussed with mum. (Interview 9)

Participation in a joint plan and the acquisition of this additional information contributed to the resolution of boundary tensions in one of three different ways.

The first was an *increase in shared meanings*:

> He would go home and talk about things at school whereas before he never mentioned school . . . And the next day he would come in with books and things . . . Ivan's mum . . . also said she thought it should go a step further. (Interview 11)

> The positive things were going home but we were also getting the positive things back. (Interview 22)

Second was a *reduction in the unpredictability of the environment*:

> [The meetings] help you realize what the home situation is. His mum's come in and she's been very upset because she's having a lot of trouble with the older girl. (Interview 4)

> So we're getting back up from them [parents] . . . they seemed quite concerned and, from talking to them, they did discipline him at home, they weren't happy with what he was doing. (Interview 8)

> Now I'm quite pleased with that, the contact, the fact that she can come in and tell me not just the nice things, the not so nice things. (Interview 15)

> I don't think it was his home background because he's got older and younger brothers and sisters and they were fine. So, I don't think it was parenting skills really. (Interview 21)

Third was a *clarification of the boundary location*:

> It was important that I could report back because his mum then could be positive and praise him at home . . . All the time you're getting that feedback from home, so that definitely helps to improve his behaviour during class as well. (Interview 12)

> When somebody else was supervising it they probably would see that it would be quite obvious who had let the side down if they [the parents] didn't pull their weight, if the school were following their side of the programme. (Interview 20)

These quotes flesh out notions of the resolution of boundary tension and make an intuitive appeal. Whatever patterns of attribution for may or may not be operating, the resolution of boundary tensions certainly seems to be a welcome and liberating outcome for these teachers.

Psychodynamic perspectives on teacher–parent interventions

Finally, in terms of casting understanding on the teacher–parent working relationship from various theoretical perspectives, Hanko (1999) makes a number of careful observations from a psychodynamic orientation. So, for instance, referring to one possible mechanism underlying the strained relationships that can exist between parent, teacher and student, she offers this explanation:

> Teachers will also know nothing of the damaged childhood that causes some parents to induce their children to re-enact their own early battles with teachers and the unjust world that they seem to represent: they cannot make allowances for what they do not know, but they can learn to suspect some such reason for parental hostility.
> (Hanko 1999: 79)

Again, attention to unconscious motives and feelings throws a new light on the relationships that have occupied many chapters of this book:

> Wherever it was relevant in a specific case discussion, teachers were able to consider what can take place 'between the words' when parents and teachers meet, what facts, feelings and fantasies may ease or disturb a meeting and what fears, anxieties or expectations may disturb or distort the intended communication.
> (Hanko 1999: 78)

> Teachers in the groups found it helpful to examine in general terms (i.e. without individual exposure) how easy it is to judge parents without full understanding, to see teacher–parent relationships in one-way terms of experts giving advice to laymen and to fear that lay people will find them wanting and reject or attack their authority.
> (Hanko 1999: 79)

It is not hard to envisage processes such as these operating at the same time as patterns of attributions shift and the home–school boundary falls into a more comfortable alignment. Like some complex psychological mechanism quietly at work at many levels, these simultaneous processes may be seen to form an underlying structure to successfully mediated consultations between teachers and parents.

How effective do teachers think mediated meetings with parents will be?

The difficulty of setting up and initiating joint teacher and parent strategies has been examined from a number of perspectives through this book. This section now turns to a study of teachers' views about the likely relative effectiveness of such joint interventions compared to other approaches discussed earlier and located in different segments of the psychosocial model in Figure 2.3.

As part of a larger study (Miller and Colston 2003) within the Nottingham Project, 12 different potential interventions were outlined to 70 teachers from eight primary schools in the north of England. The results described here derive from the section of the study in which the teachers were asked to indicate which intervention they thought would provide the most effective help in the case of a pupil displaying uncooperative and anti-social behaviour. The behaviour itself was outlined in a vignette that was very closely modelled on that used to study students' views in Chapter 7. The possible interventions were described in a set format and then the teachers were asked to rate which they deemed would be the most effective contribution from an educational psychologist, by filling in a chart as in Figure 10.2.

The percentage of the 70 teachers choosing each intervention as the most effective use of the educational psychologist's time is shown in Table 10.4. Table 10.5 shows these same results but collected together in terms of the level of focus of the intervention within the psychosocial model (each level comprising two possible interventions).

Obviously, Figure 10.2 gives only a very limited account of interventions but in the study these had already been presented earlier in a standard and fuller form. The item concerning the use of the drug Ritalin was included because of the increasing frequency with which this is prescribed following a diagnosis of attention deficit disorder. In the study it was explained that this was not an intervention in which a psychologist would be directly involved, but in this hypothetical example the school might ask the psychologist for help in contacting parents so that they in turn might seek a medical diagnosis and prescription.

Tables 10.4 and 10.5 demonstrate a strong preference among these teachers for interventions that focus upon the peer group – specifically social

The educational psychologist only has three hours of school time remaining. Listed below are the interventions with possible time allocations. Please list your top three choices (one highest) in the end column.

Intervention	Time allocation	Rating
Ritalin	Half-hour consultation with parents, half-hour monitoring, 2 hours left over	
Solution-focused intervention (pupil)	Three 1-hour sessions	
Teacher trained in behaviour programme	1 hour training, 1 hour monitoring, 1 hour left over	
Solution-focused intervention (teacher)	Three 1-hour sessions	
Parenting skills workshops	Half-hour consulting with parent (LEA time), 2.5 hours left over	
Solution-focused intervention (parent)	Three 1-hour sessions	
Circle of Friends	1 hour introduction, 1 hour monitoring, 1 hour left over	
Social skills groups	Six half-hour sessions	
INSET on behaviour management	Three 1-hour sessions	
Soft systems methodology	Three 1-hour sessions *May* need another session	
Home–school book	Half-hour setting up, two half-hours monitoring, 1.5 hours left over	
Regular parent–teacher meetings	1 hour setting up, two half-hours monitoring, 1 hour left over	

Figure 10.2 The chart used to determine which interventions teachers judged would best utilize a fixed amount of time available from an educational psychologist (from Miller and Colston 2003)

Table 10.4 A table to show interventions seen by teachers as the most effective of use of an educational psychologist's time

Intervention	Percentage of teachers placing intervention in their top three preferences (N = 70)
Social skills group	44
Circles of Friends	44
Parenting skills	39
Regular teacher–parent meetings	31
INSET for whole staff	29
Teacher training in individual programme	26
Solution-focused consultation with pupil	24
Home school record	21
Soft sytems methodology	14
Solution-focused consultation with teacher	11
Solution-focused consultation with parent	11
Ritalin	4

Table 10.5 A table to show the focus of interventions seen by teachers as the most effective use of an educational psychologist's time

Focus of intervention	Percentage of teachers placing one or both interventions in their top three preferences (N = 70)
Peers	89
Teacher–parent partnership	53
Parent	50
Whole school staff	43
Teacher	37
Pupil	29

skills groups and the Circles of Friends intervention. Especially pertinent to the subject matter of this chapter is the finding that the items that direct attention to the relationship between the teacher and parent feature at the next level of prominence. Whereas a home–school book may provide a shared record, the intervention involving actual meetings in which some external mediation can take place are judged to be particularly effective.

Despite the strong focus often placed upon the difficult student as an individual in need of 'cure', pupil-focused interventions, and particularly the prescription of drug treatment, are seen as the least desirable of the options on offer. These findings accord with the arguments and recommendations advanced within this chapter and augur well for the reception that coherent psychosocial interventions might receive in schools.

Intervening across the psychosocial framework

Finally, this chapter draws attention to a selection of interventions that appear to take a broad focus and deliberately target a number of the subsystems within the coherent framework of Figure 2.3. For example, in the late 1990s the Educational Psychology Service and the Social Services Department in Portsmouth put into operation a joint initiative to support schools and families in preventing and reducing the exclusion of pupils from junior schools and up to Year 8 in secondary schools. This programme involved interventions in classrooms deriving from the literature reviewed in early chapters on behavioural approaches. In addition, support at home focused on various aspects subsumed within family culture. Mindful of the tensions and intense emotions that are found to exist between school and home in such circumstances, the project built upon attainments within the school pro-gramme to influence positively the developing relationship between teachers and parents.

Bettle *et al.* (2002) provide another example of intervening across a num-ber of the subsystems within the coherent framework. This action research project provided support to a middle school placed in special measures follow-ing an external inspection, and involved educational psychologists employing a range of detailed measures to sample staff and pupil cultures as a precursor to feeding back information to help to influence the development of policy and practice in managing behaviour within the school.

In addition to the Circles of Friends technique, Forrest *et al.* (1996) developed and pioneered the use of other action planning techniques. The rationale for these approaches, particularly MAP (making action plans) and PATH (planning alternative tomorrows with hope), lies within the drive for a mainstream education system that includes all pupils, whatever their level of special needs or disability. One central aim of these planning techniques is to engage with the fundamental hopes and fears of the young people involved and their parents, thus energizing commitment to an extent seldom encountered within more formal contexts. Of direct relevance to the idea of intervening across a range of subsystems is the unique way in which MAP and PATH physically bring into the planning process pupils with special needs, their teachers, family members and, often, a Circle of Friends or classmates of the 'target' pupil.

In the light of the subject matter of this and preceding chapters, a poten-tially rich area of exploration may lie with applying soft systems methodology within schools to the crucial topic of teacher–parent relations in instances when student behaviour is proving particularly challenging.

In general, it is a central contention of this chapter that the more interventions can engage with a combination and conjunction of interests within the formal and informal school staff, family and peer subsystems, and break down the barriers between these subsystems, the more likely are interventions to have significant and lasting effects for pupils, teachers and parents.

Conclusion

I hope the research and practice examples presented in this book will be of assistance both to staff within mainstream schools and to other professionals, policy-makers and parents, who are external to the boundaries of schools. Although the focus has been very much on difficult student behaviour, many wider lessons will be lost if they are seen as pertinent only to this aspect of life in schools. The discussions in preceding chapters also apply directly to concerns about the emotional well-being and mental health of students, teachers' job satisfaction, home–school relationships, 'joined-up' multi-agency working, school development and improvement, and the wider issue of social exclusion.

This book's perspective – the psychosocial – has concerned itself with the thoughts and feelings of students, parents and teachers. It has examined the consequences of being members of class groups, working as a staff team and sharing a range of responsibilities across the sometimes ill defined boundary between home and school. It has delved into the effects of formal policies on hidden cultures, and vice versa, and illustrated the tensions inherent in a life lived between the two. The security and perspective provided by friends and reference groups has also been brought to the fore. The shadow of these phenomena reaches far beyond a concern just with 'difficult behaviour'.

There is a danger that the psychosocial may become marginalized by reductionist approaches that stake a claim for the genetic pre-determinants of difficult behaviour or by psychometric instruments capable of measuring with precision the exact proportion of the population that would be expected to display more or less of some behavioural trait. These developments often present a seductive appeal to media and public understanding alike.

Yet it is within the realm of the psychosocial that abused, unfulfilled or friendless children and young people disrupt their personal environments. It's here that feelings of helplessness provoke some teachers into considering an early exit from their careers, some parents fear blame and censure and respond with a defensive belligerence, and leaders and policy-makers come up against unspoken resistance. Genuine efforts can founder on beliefs that others are unwilling to cooperate or shoulder their responsibilities, not because of neuro-logical or biochemical influences. Multi-agency conferences may pass the parcel of blame because of conflicting or unclear policies or roles, not as a result of personalities that lie stranded, but too many standard deviations from some statistical mean.

It is also from within the psychosocial, this book has argued, that positive strategies can arise, strategies that provide a strong alternative to demoraliza-tion, defeatism and exclusion.

Media, political and professional rhetoric gravitate almost inevitably towards the sensational and the pessimistic. Morale in schools can then be further undermined by the relentless bombardment of criticism and bad news. The major practical lesson to emerge from the research presented in Part 2 of this book is that teachers and other education professionals are able to bring about positive changes in the behaviour of some of their most difficult pupils. *This point needs to be made emphatically.* Much of the book, however, counters the simplistic assumption that teachers can therefore be left to manage alone and unaided. Parts 3 and 4 have detailed the subtle and potentially delicate psychosocial processes within a school, and between home and school, which may need to be addressed before these positive outcomes can be achieved.

These are serious challenges for headteachers, SENCOs and all teachers, as well as external professionals. Some interventions require specialist skills and knowledge, while others depend on a facilitator who is external to certain recursive processes within the organization. The need for a strong collabor-ation between school personnel and external support agencies, with a clear differentiation of their roles, would thus seem to be self-evident. However, external agencies will confuse rather than assist if they lack awareness of the power and centrality that the psychosocial can assume in such circumstances.

A solid research and practice base for work with and in schools will be all the more necessary if the war of attribution over pupil behaviour continues to escalate. The crude and simplistic blaming of teachers, students or parents, alternating as the merry-go-round of fashion grinds on, must be countered, if only because professional optimism and clear-headedness cannot be allowed to drain away into a pit of demoralization. Equally, over-zealous pursuit of medical model attributions as evidenced by the increasing diagnosis of atten-tion deficit disorder and other 'syndromes' may also leave professionals, par-ents and students themselves feeling that they have little effective personal agency.

While crusades against undesirable pupil behaviour sit easily within the public lexicon, notions of the psychosocial require more thought and reflec-tion. Examples of successful consultations exist and their underlying mechan-isms have been clarified. With the potential for all parties – teachers, students and parents – to benefit, with successful outcomes realizable, the time must surely have arrived for a reappraisal of approaches to difficult behaviour in schools. We do now have the opportunity to draw on a growing body of research into successful practice.

References

Aponte, H. J. (1976) The family–school interview: an eco-structural approach, *Family Process*, 15: 303–11.

Argyris, C. and Schon, D. (1978) *Organizational Learning*. Reading, MA: Addison-Wesley.

Atkeson, B. M. and Forehand, R. (1979) Home-based reinforcement programs designed to modify classroom behaviour: a review and methodological evaluation, *Psychological Bulletin*, 86(6): 1298–308.

Ball, S. J. (1987) *The Micro-politics of the School*. London: Methuen.

Barth, R. (1979) Home-based reinforcement of school behaviour: a review and analysis, *Review of Educational Research*, 49(3): 436–58.

Berger, P. and Luckman, I. (1966) *The Social Construction of Reality*. London: Penguin.

Bettle, S., Frederickson, N. and Sharpe, S. (2002) Supporting a school in special measures: implications for the potential contribution of educational psychology, *Educational Psychology in Practice*, 17(1): 53–68.

Bozic, N. and Carter, A. (2002) Consultation groups: participants' views, *Educational Psychology in Practice*, 18(3): 189–203.

Bridges, D. (1987) 'It's the ones who never turn up that you really want to see'. The 'problem' of the non-attending parent, in J. Bastiani (ed.) *Parents and Teachers 1*. Slough: NFER.

Burden, R. L. (1978) Schools' systems analysis: a project-centred approach, in B. Gillham (ed.) *Reconstructing Educational Psychology*. London: Croom Helm.

Burland, P. M. and Burland, J. R. (1979) . . . and teacher came too!, *Behavioural Psychotherapy*, 7(1): 7–11.

Burland, R. (1979) Social skills as the basis for coping strategies in school, in *Proceedings of the 1979 DECP Annual Course*, British Psychological Society.

Caffyn, R. E. (1989) Attitudes of British secondary school teachers and pupils to rewards and punishments, *Educational Research*, 31(3): 210–20.

Campion, J. (1984) Psychological services for children: using family therapy in the setting of a school psychological service, *Journal of Family Therapy*, 6: 47–62.

Cannell, C.F. and Kahn, R.L. (1968) Interviewing, in G. Lindzey and E. Aronson (eds) *The Handbook of Social Psychology* (2nd edn). Reading, MA: Adison-Wesley.

Canter, L. and Canter, M. (1992) *Lee Canter's Assertive Discipline: Positive Behaviour Management for Today's Classroom*. Santa Monica, CA: Canter and Associates.

Caplan, G. (1970) *An Approach to Community Mental Health*. London: Tavistock (cited in Conoley and Conoley 1990).

Checkland, P. B. (1981) *Systems Thinking, Systems Practice*. London: Wiley.

Checkland, P. (1994) Systems theory and management thinking, *American Behavioral Scientist*, 38(1): 75–91.

Checkland, P. and Scholes, J. (1990) *Soft Systems Methodology in Action*. Chichester: Wiley.

Chisholm, B. (1994) Promoting peer support among teachers, in P. Gray, A. Miller and J. Noakes (eds) *Challenging Behaviour in Schools*. London: Routledge.

Chisholm, B., Kearney, D., Knight, G., Little, H., Morris, S. and Tweddle, D. (1986) *Preventative Approaches to Disruption*. Basingstoke: Macmillan Education.

Clarke, D. D. with Crossland, J. (1985) *Action Systems. An Introduction to the Analysis of Complex Behaviour*. London: Methuen.

Conoley, J. C. and Conoley, C. W. (1990) Staff consultative work in schools, in N. Jones and N. Frederickson (eds) *Refocusing Educational Psychology*. Basingstoke: Falmer.

Cooper, P. and Upton, C. (1990) An eco-systemic approach to emotional and behavioural difficulties in school, *Educational Psychology*, 10(4): 301–21.

Cooper, P. and Upton, G. (1991) Controlling the urge to control: an eco-systemic approach to problem behaviour in schools, *Support for Learning*, 6(1): 22–6.

Coulby, D. and Harper, I. (1985) *Preventing Classroom Disruption. Policy, Practice and Evaluation in Urban Schools*. London: Croom Helm.

Cowie, H. (1998) Perspectives of teachers and pupils on the experiences of peer support against bullying, *Educational Research and Evaluation*, 4(1): 108–25.

Cowie, H. and Wallace, P. (2000) *Peer Support in Action: From Bystanding to Standing By*. London: Sage.

Cox, T. and Kuk, G. (1991) Healthiness of schools as organisations: teacher stress and health, Paper presented at the International Congress on Stress, Anxiety and Emotional Disorders, University of Minho, Braga, Portugal.

Cox, T., Leyden, G., Kuk, G. and Cheyne, A. (1993) Teacher well-being and the health of schools as organizations: an intervention study, Unpublished manuscript, Centre for Organizational Health and Development, University of Nottingham.

Creese, A., Daniels, H. and Norwich, B. (1997) *Teacher Support Teams in Primary and Secondary Schools*. London: David Fulton.

Croll, P. and Moses, D. (1985) *One in Five. The Assessment and Incidence of Special Educational Needs*. London: Routledge and Kegan Paul.

Dalin, P. (1993) *Changing the School Culture*. London: Cassell.

Dallos, R. (1991) *Family Belief Systems, Therapy and Change*. Milton Keynes: Open University Press.

Day, C., Pope, M. and Denicolo, P. (eds) (1990) *Insight into Teachers' Thinking and Practice*. Basingstoke: Falmer.

Deal, I. and Kennedy, A. (1982) *Corporate Culture*. Reading, MA: Addison-Wesley.

Department for Education (1993) *Code of Practice on the Identification and Assessment of Special Educational Needs*. London: HMSO.

Department for Education (1994a) *Pupil Behaviour and Discipline*. Circular 8/94. London: DfE.

Department for Education (1994b) *The Education of Children with Emotional and Behavioural Difficulties*. Circular 9/94. London: DfE.

Department for Education (1994c) *The Education of Sick Children*. Circular 12/94. London: DfE.

Department for Education and Employment (1998a) *School Standards and Framework Act*. London: DfEE.

Department for Education and Employment (1998b) *Circular 1/98: LEA Behaviour Support Plans*. London: DfEE.

Department for Education and Employment (1999) *Circular 10/99: Social Inclusion: Pupil Support*. London: DfEE.

Department for Education and Employment (2000a) *Home–School Agreements. Guidance for Schools*. London: DfEE.

Department of Education and Science (1978) *Special Educational Needs: Report of the Committee of Enquiry into the Education of Handicapped Children and Young People* (The Warnock Report). London: HMSO.

Department of Education and Science (1989) *Discipline in Schools* (The Elton Report). London: HMSO.

Department of Education and Science (1990) *Statistics for Schools*. London: HMSO.

Department for Education and Skills (2001) *Code of Practice on the Identification and Assessment of Children with Special Educational Needs*. London: DfES.

Department for Education and Skills (2003) *Promoting Children's Mental Health within Early Years and School*. London: DfES (http://www.dfes.gov.uk/mental-health/mhealth.shtml).

De Shazer, S. (1982) *Patterns of Brief Family Therapy: An Ecosystemic Approach*. New York: Guilford Press.

Dix, I. (1993) Attributing dispositions to children: an interactional analysis of attribution in socialization, *Personality and Social Psychology Bulletin*, 19(5): 633–43.

Dix, I. and Grusec, J. E. (1985) Parent attribution processes in the socialization of children, in I. Sigel (ed.) *Parental Belief Systems: Their Psychological Consequences for Children* (cited in Dix 1993).

Dix, I., Ruble, D. N. and Zambarano, R. I. (1989) Mothers' implicit theories of discipline: child effects, parent effects, and the attribution process, *Child Development*, 60: 1373–91 (cited in Dix 1993).

Dowling, E. and Osborne, E. (eds) (1985) *The Family and the School: A Joint Systems Approach to Problems with Children*. London: Routledge and Kegan Paul.

Dowling, E. and Osborne, E. (1994) *The Family and the School. A Joint Systems Approach to Problems with Children*, 2nd edn. London: Routledge.

Dowling, E. and Taylor, D. (1989) The clinic goes to school: lessons learned, *Maladjustment and Therapeutic Education*, 7(1): 24–8.

Eiser, R. J. (1978) Interpersonal attributions, in H. Tajfel and C. Fraser (eds) *Introducing Social Psychology*. Harmondsworth: Penguin.

Ferguson, E., Miller, A., Lambert, N. and Beadell, R. (2004) A longitudinal study of students' causal attributions for difficult behaviour in schools in relation to academic attainment (forthcoming).

Fine, M. J. and Holt, P. (1983) Intervening with school problems: a family systems perspective, *Psychology in the Schools*, 20(1): 59–66.

Fiske, S. I. and Taylor, S. E. (1984) *Social Cognition*. New York: Random House.

Forehand, R., Sturgis, E. I., McMahon, R. J., Aguar, D., Green, K., Wells, K. C. and Beriner, J. (1979) Parent behavioural training to modify child noncompliance. Treatment generalization across time and from home to school, *Behaviour Modification*, 3(1): 3–25.

Forrest, M., Pearpoint, J. and O'Brien, J. (1996) 'MAPS': Educators, parents, young people, and their friends planning together, *Educational Psychology in Practice*, 11(4): 41–8.

Frederickson, N. (1990a) Systems approaches in educational psychology, *Journal of Applied Systems Analysis*, 17: 3–20.

Frederickson, N. (ed.) (1990b) *Soft Systems Methodology. Practical Applications in Work with Schools*. London: University College London.

Frederickson, N. and Turner, J. (2003) Utilizing the classroom peer group to address children's social needs. An evaluation of the 'Circle of Friends' intervention approach, *Journal of Special Education* (forthcoming).

Fry, L. (1980) Behaviour modifications at Lea Green School, *Newsletter of the Association for Behaviour Modification with Children*, 4(1): 2–19.

Galvin, P., Mercer, S. and Costa, P. (1990) *Building a Better Behaved School*. Harlow: Longman.

Galvin, P. and Costa, P. (1994) Building better behaved schools: effective support at the whole school level, in P. Gray, A. Miller and J. Noakes (eds) *Challenging Behaviour in Schools*. London: Routledge.

Gersch, I. S. and Nolan, A. (1994) Exclusions: what do the children think?, *Educational Psychology in Practice*, 10(1): 35–45.

Gillham, W. (1981) *Problem Behaviour in Secondary Schools*. London: Croom Helm.

Glaser, B. (1978) *Theoretical Sensitivity*. Mill Valley, CA: Sociology Press (cited in Strauss 1987).

Glaser, B. and Strauss, A. L. (1967) *The Discovery of Grounded Theory*. Chicago: Aldine.

Glatter, R. (ed.) (1989) *Educational Institutions and Their Environments: Managing the Boundaries*. Milton Keynes: Open University Press.

Grace, N. C., Kelley, M. L. and McCain, A. P. (1993) Attribution processes in mother–adolescent conflict, *Journal of Abnormal Child Psychology*, 21(2): 199–211.

Gray, P. (ed.) (2002) *Working with Emotions. Responding to the Challenge of Difficult Pupil Behaviour in Schools*. London: Routledge.

Gray, P., Miller, A. and Noakes, J. (eds) (1994) *Challenging Behaviour in Schools. Teacher Support, Practical Techniques and Policy Development*. London: Routledge.

Gray, P. and Noakes, J. (1992) Multidisciplinary work, in D. A. Lane and A. Miller (eds) *Child and Adolescent Therapy: A Handbook*. Milton Keynes: Open University Press.

Gupta, R., Stringer, B. and Meakin, A. (1990) A study of the effectiveness of home-based reinforcement in a secondary school, *Educational Psychology in Practice*, 5(4): 197–200.

Gurney, P. (1987) The use of operant techniques to raise self-esteem in maladjusted children, *British Journal of Educational Psychology*, 57: 87–94.

Hammersley, M. (1984) Staffroom news, in A. Hargreaves and P. Woods (eds) *Classrooms and Staffrooms*. Milton Keynes: Open University Press.

Hammersley, M. and Atkinson, P (1983) *Ethnography: Principles in Practice*. London: Routledge.

Hammill, P. and Boyd, B. (2001) Rhetoric or reality? Inter-agency provision for young people with challenging behaviour, *Emotional and Behaviour Difficulties*, 6(3): 139–49.

Hanko, C. (1985) *Special Needs in Ordinary Classrooms: Supporting Teachers*, 2nd edn. Oxford: Blackwell.

Hanko, G. (1999) *Increasing Competence through Collaborative Problem Solving: Using Insight into Social and Emotional Factors in Children's Learning*. London: David Fulton.

Hargreaves, D. H. (1967) *Social Relations in a Secondary School*. London: Routledge and Kegan Paul.

Hargreaves, D. H. (1975) *Interpersonal Relations and Education*, rev. edn. London: Routledge and Kegan Paul.

Hargreaves, A. and Woods, P. (eds) (1984) *Classrooms and Staffrooms. The Sociology of Teachers and Teaching*. Milton Keynes: Open University Press.

Harrop, L. A. (1978a) Behaviour modification in the ordinary school setting, *Journal of the Association of Educational Psychologists*, 4(7): 3–14.

Harrop, L. A. (1978b) Another gain for the modifers? *Special Education – Forward Trends*, 5(4): 15–17.

Harrop, L. A. and McNamara, E. (1979) The behavioural workshop for classroom problems. A re-appraisal, *British Journal of In-Service Education*, 1(1): 47–50.

Harrop, L. A. and Williams, I. (1992) Rewards and punishments in the primary school: pupils' perceptions and teachers' usage, *Educational Psychology in Practice*, 7(4): 211–15.

Henning-Stout, M. and Conoley, J. C. (1988) Influencing district change, in J. L. Graden, J. E. Zins and M. J. Curtis (eds) *Alternative Educational Delivery Systems: Enhancing Instructional Options for All Students*. Washington, DC: National Association of School Psychologists (cited in Conoley and Conoley 1990).

Henwood, K. L. and Pidgeon, N. F (1993) Qualitative research and psychological theorizing, in M. Hammersley (ed.) *Social Research, Philosophy, Politics and Practice*. London: Sage.

Hickey, K. A., Imber, S. C. and Ruggiero, E. A. (1977) Modifying independent work habits of elementary students through parent–teacher involvement and co-operation, Paper presented at Council for Exceptional Children, 55th annual International Convention, Atlanta, GA, April (cited in Barth 1979).

Hood, S. (1999) Home–school agreements: a true partnership?, *School Leadership and Management*, 19(4): 427–40.

Houghton, S., Merrett, F. and Wheldall, K. (1988) The attitudes of British secondary school pupils to praise, rewards, punishments and reprimands, *New Zealand Journal of Educational Psychology*, 23, 203–14.

Hoy, W. K. and Miskel, C. C. (1989) Schools and their external environments, in R. Clatter (ed.) *Educational Institutions and Their Environments*. Milton Keynes: Open University Press.

Hutchinson, S. A. (1988) Education and grounded theory, in R. R. Sherman and R. B. Webb (eds) *Qualitative Research in Education: Focus and Methods*. Lewes: Falmer.

Johnston, C., Patenaude, R. L. and Inman, C. A. (1992) Attributions for hyperactive and aggressive child behaviours, *Social Cognition*, 10(3): 255–70.

Jones, N. and Frederickson, N. (eds) (1990) *Refocussing Educational Psychology*. Basingstoke: Falmer.

Kauffman, J. M. and Smucker, K. (1995) The legacies of placement: a brief history of placement options and issues with commentary on their evolution, in J. M. Kauffman, J. W. Lloyd, D. P. Hallahan and T. A. Astuto (eds) *Issues in Educational Placement. Students with Emotional and Behavioural Disorders*. Hillsdale, NJ: Lawrence Erlbaum Associates.

Kolvin, I., Garside, R. C., Nicol, A. R., Macmillan, A.,Wolstenholme, F. and Leitch, I. M. (1981) *Help Starts Here. The Maladjusted Child in the Ordinary School*. London: Tavistock Publications.

Lane, D. A. (1990) *The Impossible Child*. Stoke-on-Trent: Trentham Books.

Lane, D. A. (1994) Supporting effective responses to challenging behaviour: from theory to practice, in P. Gray, A. Miller and J. Noakes (eds) *Challenging Behaviour in Schools*. London: Routledge.

Leach, D. J. and Byrne, M. K. (1986) Some 'spill-over' effects of a home-based reinforcement programme in a secondary school, *Educational Psychology*, 6(3): 265–76.

Leach, D. J. and Ralph, A. (1986) Home-based reinforcement: a case study, *Behaviour Change*, 3(1): 58–62.

Leyden, G. (1996) 'Cheap labour' or neglected resource? The role of the peer group and efficient, effective support for children with special needs, *Educational Psychology in Practice*, 11(4): 49–55.

Lieberman, A. (ed.) (1990) *Schools as Collaborative Cultures: Creating the Future Now*. Basingstoke: Falmer.

Lieberman, A. and Miller, L. (1990) The social realities of teaching, in A. Lieberman (ed.) *Schools as Collaborative Cultures*. Basingstoke: Falmer.

Little, J. W (1990) Teachers as colleagues, in A. Lieberman (ed.) *Schools as Collaborative Cultures*. Basingstoke: Falmer.

Long, M. (1988) Goodbye behaviour units, hello support services, *Educational Psychology in Practice*, 4(1): 17–23.

Long, R. (2002) The 'E' in EBD, in P. Gray (ed.) *Working with Emotions. Responding to the Challenge of Difficult Pupil Behaviour in Schools*. London: Routledge Falmer.

Lortie, D. (1975) *Schoolteacher. A Sociological Study*. Chicago: Chicago University Press.

McBrien, J. and Weightman, J. B. (1980) The effect of room management procedures on the engagement of profoundly retarded children, *British Journal of Mental Subnormality*, 26: 38–46.

MacDonald, W., Gallimore, R. and MacDonald, C. (1970) Contingency counselling by school personnel: an economical model of intervention, *Journal of Applied Behaviour Analysis*, 3: 175–82 (cited in Barth 1979).

McGee, R., Silva, P. A. and Williams, S. (1983) Parents' and teachers' perceptions of behaviour problems in seven-year-old children, *The Exceptional Child*, 30(2): 151–61.

McMahon, R. J. and Davies, C. R. (1980) A behavioural training program and its side effects on classroom behavior, *B C Journal of Special Education*, 4(2): 165–74.

McNamara, E. (1977) Results and impressions of using behaviour modification in a psychological service, *British Association for Behavioural Psychotherapy Bulletin*, 5(3): 55–62.

McNamara, E. and Harrop, L. A. (1979) Behaviour modification in secondary schools – a cautionary tale, *Occasional Papers of the DECP*, 3(2): 38–40.

McNamara, E. and Harrop, L. A. (1981) Behaviour modification in the secondary school: a rejoinder to Wheldall and Austin, *Occasional Papers of the DECP*, 5(2): 60–3.

McNamara, N. (2002) Motivational interviewing and cognitive intervention, in P. Gray (ed.) *Working with Emotions. Responding to the Challenge of Difficult Pupil Behaviour in Schools*. London: Routledge Falmer.

Madsen, C. H., Becker, W. C. and Thomas, D. R. (1968) Rules, praise and ignoring: elements of elementary classroom control, *Journal of Applied Behavioural Analysis*, 1(2): 139–50.

Mental Health Foundation (1999) *Bright Futures. Promoting Children and Young People's Mental Health*. London: Mental Health Foundation.

Merrett, F. and Blundell, D. (1982) Self-recording as a means of improving behaviour in the secondary school, *Educational Psychology*, 2: 147–57.

Merrett, F. and Tang, W. M. (1994) The attitudes of British primary school pupils to praise, rewards, punishments and reprimands, *British Journal of Educational Psychology*, 64: 91–103.

Merrett, P. and Wheldall, K. (1978) Playing the game: a behavioural approach to classroom management in the junior school, *Educational Review*, 30(1): 41–50.

Merrett, P. and Wheldall, K. (1987) Natural rates of teacher approval and disapproval in British primary school classrooms, *British Journal of Educational Psychology*, 57: 95–103.

Miller, A. (1980) Systems theory applied to the work of the educational psychologist, *Association of Educational Psychologists Journal*, 5(3): 11–15.

Miller, A. (1994a) Staff culture, boundary maintenance and successful behavioural interventions in primary schools, *Research Papers in Education*, 9(1): 31–51.

Miller, A. (1994b) Parents and difficult behaviour: always the problem or part of the solution?, in P. Gray, A. Miller and J. Noakes (eds) *Challenging Behaviour in Schools*. London: Routledge.

Miller, A. (1995a) Building grounded theory within educational psychology practice, *Educational and Child Psychology*, 12(2): 5–14.

Miller, A. (1995b) Teachers' attributions of causality, control and responsibility in respect of difficult pupil behaviour and its successful management, *Educational Psychology*, 15: 457–71.

Miller, A. (1996) *Pupil Behaviour and Teacher Culture*. London: Cassell.

Miller, A. (1999) Squaring the triangle: pupil behaviour, teachers and parents – and psychology, *Educational Psychology in Practice*, 15(2): 75–80.

Miller, A. (2003) Educational psychology and difficult pupil behaviour: qualitative, quantitative or mixed methods?, in Z. Todd *et al.* (eds) *Mixing Methods in Psychology. The integration of qualitative and quantitative methods in theory and practice.* London: Routledge.

Miller, A. and Black, L. (2001) Does support for home–school behaviour plans exist within teacher and pupil cultures?, *Educational Psychology in Practice*, 17(3): 245–62.

Miller, A. and Colston, G. (2004) Intervening with student behaviour: which levels within the school's psychosocial framework do teachers prefer? (forthcoming).

Miller, A., Ferguson, E. and Byrne, I. (2000) Pupils' causal attributions for difficult classroom behaviour, *British Journal of Educational Psychology*, 70: 85–96.

Miller, A., Ferguson, E. and Moore, E. (2002) Parents' and pupils' causal attributions for difficult classroom behaviour, *British Journal of Educational Psychology*, 72: 27–40.

Miller, A., Ferguson, E. and Simpson, R. (1998) The perceived effectiveness of rewards and sanctions in primary schools – adding in the parental perspective, *Educational Psychology*, 18: 55–64.

Miller, A. and Leyden, G. (1999) A coherent framework for the application of psychology in schools, *British Educational Research Journal*, 25(3): 389–400.

Miller, A. and Todd, Z. (2002) Educational psychology and difficult behaviour in schools. Conceptual and methodological challenges for an evidence-based profession, *Educational and Child Psychology*, 17(3): 82–95.

Miller, E. J. (ed.) (1976) *Task and Organization*. Chichester: Wiley.

Molnar, A. and Lindquist, B. (1989) *Changing Problem Behaviour in Schools*. San Francisco: Jossey-Bass.

Monsen, J. and Graham, B. (2002) Developing teacher-support groups to deal with challenging child behaviour, in P. Gray (ed.) *Working with Emotions. Responding to the Challenge of Difficult Pupil Behaviour in Schools*. London: Routledge Falmer.

Morgan, G. (1997) *Images of Organisations*, 2nd edn. London: Sage.

Mortimore, P., Sammons, P., Stoll, L., Lewis, D. and Ecob, R. (1988) *School Matters*. Wells: Open Books.

Moseley, J. (2001) *Circle Time*. London: Positive Press.

Newton, C., Taylor, G. and Wilson, D. (1996) Circles of friends: an inclusive approach to meeting emotional and behavioural needs, *Educational Psychology in Practice*, 11(4): 41–9.

Nias, J. (1985) Reference groups in primary teaching, in S. J. Ball and I. E. Goodson (eds) *Teachers' Lives and Careers*. Lewes: Falmer.

O'Dell, S. (1974) Training parents in behaviour modification. A review, *Psychological Bulletin*, 81: 418–33.

Osborne, E. (1983) The teacher's relationship with the pupils' families, in I. Salzbergber-Wittenberg, G. Henry and E. Osborne (eds) *The Emotional Experience of Learning and Teaching*. London: Routledge.

Palazzoli, S. M., Cecchin, G., Prata, G. and Boscolo, L. (1978) *Paradox and Counter Paradox: A New Model of the Family in Schizophrenic Transaction*. London: Jason Aronson.

Parsons, C. (1999) *Education, Exclusion and Citizenship*. London: Routledge.

Poulou, M. and Norwich, B. (2002) Cognitive, emotional and behavioural responses to students with emotional and behavioural difficulties: a model of decision-making. *British Educational Research Journal*, 28(1): 111–38.

Power, I. and Bartholomew, K. (1985) Getting uncaught in the middle: a case study in family–school system consultation, *School Psychology Review*, 14(2): 222–9.

Power, M. J., Benn, R. I. and Morris, J. N. (1967) Delinquent schools?, *New Society*, 19 October.

Power, M. J., Benn, R. I. and Morris, J. N. (1972) Neighbourhood, school and juveniles before the court, *British Journal of Criminology*, April, 111–32.

Presland, J. (1978) Teachers' reactions to behaviour modification workshops, *Occasional Papers of the DECP*, 2(1): 13–19.

Presland, J. (1981) Modifying behaviour long-term and sideways, *Association of Educational Psychologists Journal*, 5(6): 27–30.

Rennie, E. N. F. (1980) Good behaviour games with a whole class, *Remedial Education*, 15: 187–90.

Reynolds, D. (1992) School effectiveness and school improvement: an updated review of the British literature, in D. Reynolds and P. Cuttance (eds) *School Effectiveness: Research, Policy and Practice*. London: Cassell.

Rhodes, J. (1993) The use of solution-focused brief therapy in school, *Educational Psychology in Practice*, 9(1): 27–34.

Riccio, C. A. and Hughes, J. N. (2001) Established and emerging models of psychological services in school settings, in J. N. Hughes, A. M. La Greca and J. C.

Conoley (eds) *Handbook of Psychological Services for Children and Adolescents*. New York: Oxford University Press.

Rice, A. K. (1976) Individual, group and inter-group processes, in Miller, E. J. (ed.) *Task and Organization*. Chichester: Wiley.

Rogers, W. (1990) *You Know the Fair Rule*. Harlow: Longman.

Rutter, M., Tizard, J. and Whitmore, K. (1970) *Education, Health and Behaviour*. London: Longman.

Rutter, M., Maughan, B., Mortimore, P. and Ouston, J. (1979) *Fifteen Thousand Hours*. Wells: Open Books.

Salmivalli, C. (1999) Participant role approach to school bullying: implications for intervention, *Journal of Adolescence*, 22, 453–9.

Schein, E. H. (1988) *Process Consultation, Volume 1*, 2nd edn. Reading, MA: Addison-Wesley.

Sharp, R. and Green, A. (1975) *Education and Social Control. A Study in Progressive Primary Education*. London: Routledge and Kegan Paul.

Sharp, S. (1996) The role of peers in tackling bullying in schools, *Educational Psychology in Practice*, 11(4): 17–22.

Sharpe, P., Wheldall, K. and Merrett, F. (1987) The attitudes of British secondary school pupils to praise and reward, *Educational Studies*, 13: 293–302.

Sheridan, S. M. and Kratochwill, I. R. (1992) Behavioural parent–teacher consultation: conceptual and reseach considerations, *Journal of School Psychology*, 30: 117–39.

Smith, P. K. (1999) England and Wales, in P. K. Smith, Y. Morita, J. Junger-Tas, D. Olweus, R. Catalano and P. Slee (eds) *The Nature of School Bullying: A Cross-national Perspective*. London: Routledge.

Strauss, A. L. (1987) *Qualitative Analysis for Social Scientists*. Cambridge: Cambridge University Press.

Strauss, A. and Corbin, J. (1999) *Basics of Qualitative Research: Techniques and Procedures for Developing Grounded Theory*. London: Sage.

Stringer, P., Stow, L., Hibbert, K., Powell, J. and Louw, E. (1992) Establishing staff consultation groups in schools, *Educational Psychology in Practice*, 8(2): 87–96.

Taylor, D. (1982) Family consultation in a school setting, *Journal of Adolescence*, 5: 367–77.

Thomas, G. (1992) *Effective Classroom Teamwork: Support or Intrusion?* London: Routledge.

Tizard, B., Blatchford, P., Burke, J., Farquar, C. and Plewis, I. (1988) *Young Children at School in the Inner City*. Hove: Lawrence Erlbaum Associates.

Topping, K. J. (1983) *Educational Systems for Disruptive Adolescents*. Beckenham: Croom Helm.

Tsoi, M. M. and Yule, W. (1976) The effects of group reinforcement in classroom behaviour modification, *Educational Studies*, 2: 129–40.

Tucker, B. S. and Dyson, E. (1976) The family and the school: utilizing human resources to promote learning, *Family Process*, 15: 125–41.

Wagner, A. C. (1987) 'Knots' in teachers' thinking, in J. Calderhead (ed.) *Exploring Teachers' Thinking*. London: Cassell.

Wagner, P. (2000) Consultation: developing a comprehensive approach to service delivery, *Educational Psychology in Practice*, 16(1): 9–18.

Ward, J. (1971) Modification of deviant classroom behaviour, *British Journal of Educational Psychology*, 41: 304–13.

Ward, J. (1976) Behaviour modification in education: an overview and model for programme implementation, *Bulletin of the British Psychological Society*, 29: 257–68.

Watkins, C. and Wagner, P. (2000) *Improving School Behaviour*. London: Paul Chapman Publishing.

Weiner, B. (1980) A cognitive–attribution–emotion–action model of motivated behaviour: an analysis of judgements of help-giving, *Journal of Personality and Social Psychology*, 39: 186–200.

West, J. F. and Idol, L. (1987) School consultation (Part 1): an interdisciplinary perspective on theory, models, and research, *Journal of Learning Disabilities*, 20(7): 388–408.

Wheldall, K. (1981) 'A' before 'C' or the use of behavioural ecology in the classrooms, in P. Gurney (ed.) *Behaviour Modification in Education. Perspectives 5*. Exeter: University of Exeter.

Wheldall, K. (ed.) (1987) *The Behaviourist in the Classroom*. London: Allen and Unwin.

Wheldall, K. and Austin, R. (1981) Successful behaviour modification in the secondary school: a reply to McNamara and Harrop, *Occasional Papers of the DECP*, 4(3): 3–8.

Wheldall, K. and Merrett, F. (1985) *The Behavioural Approach to Teaching Package*. Birmingham: Positive Products.

Wheldall, K. and Merrett, F. (1988) Which classroom behaviours do primary school teachers say they find most troublesome?, *Educational Review*, 40(1): 13–27.

Winnet, R. A. and Winkler, R. C. (1972) Current behaviour modification in the classroom: be still, be quiet, be docile, *Journal of Applied Behaviour Analysis*, 8: 259–62.

Woods, P. (1984) The meaning of staffroom humour, in A. Hargreaves and P. Woods (eds) *Classrooms and Staffrooms*. Milton Keynes: Open University Press.

Index

BEHAVIOUR IN SCHOOLS
THEORY AND PRACTICE FOR TEACHERS
Louise Porter

Behaviour management in the classroom and playground is one of the most challenging aspects of teaching. Behaviour in Schools offers a comprehensive overview of the major theories of behaviour management in primary and secondary schools, illustrated with detailed case studies.

The theories covered range from teacher-dominated methods to more democratic approaches. They include assertive discipline, applied behaviour analysis, the new cognitive behavioural approaches, neo-Adlerian theory, humanism, Glasser's control theory and systems theory. Porter outlines how teachers can develop a personal approach to classroom management based on a solid understanding of theory. The emphasis is on proactive approaches to discipline which allow teachers to achieve their educational and social goals for their students and themselves. Porter also shows how to enhance students' motivation and help students become confident and independent learners.

Behaviour in Schools is a textbook for education students and a reference for experienced teachers who want to improve their ability to cope with disruptive behaviour.

Contents
Part one: The theories – Introduction – The limit-setting approaches – Applied behaviour analysis – Cognitive-behaviourism – Neo-Adlerian theory – Humanism – Choice theory – Systems theory – Critique of the theories – Part two: Motivating students – Safeguarding students – Meeting students' need for autonomy – Fostering competence – Meeting students' social needs – Part three: Beyond the classroom – Collaborating with parents – Formulating a discipline policy – References – Index

344pp   0 335 20668 9 (Paperback)

TOWARDS BULLY-FREE SCHOOLS
INTERVENTIONS IN ACTION
Derek Glover, Netta Cartright with Denis Gleeson

This book considers the progress made towards changing pupil attitudes to bullying in twenty-five secondary schools. It begins with a consideration of the present situation and looks at the way in which policies have been developed to make school life more enjoyable for all pupils. It recognizes that families and the community at large are also involved and considers how schools can integrate their anti-bullying work with social activities, and the subject curriculum. It shows a way forward for those schools and parents who are seeking to bring about change.

Three questions are addressed:

- How can schools change attitudes so that there is a decline in all forms of bullying behaviour?
- What difference does action against bullying make to pupil life and the quality of teaching and learning?
- Is action leading to a longer term improvement in the school society?

The book is directed at those responsible for policy development in schools and colleges. It relies heavily upon case study material and so is more lively than many educational books. It will attract school governors and parents who are interested in the subject and will also be of value to those in teacher education.

Contents
Preface – Summary of schools – Tables – Feelings of security – Me – coming to terms with self-image – Getting on with others – School culture – School policies – Reaching the parents – The community – Changing attitudes – They did it this way – Taking stock – Bibliography – Index.

192pp   0 335 19929 1 (Paperback)   0 335 19930 5 (Hardback)